Parting Ways

Parting Ways

NEW RITUALS AND
CELEBRATIONS OF
LIFE'S PASSING

DENISE CARSON

UNIVERSITY OF CALIFORNIA PRESS
Berkeley Los Angeles London

University of California Press, one of the most distinguished university presses in the United States, enriches lives around the world by advancing scholarship in the humanities, social sciences, and natural sciences. Its activities are supported by the UC Press Foundation and by philanthropic contributions from individuals and institutions. For more information, visit www.ucpress.edu.

University of California Press
Berkeley and Los Angeles, California

University of California Press, Ltd.
London, England

Library of Congress Cataloging-in-Publication Data

Carson, Denise.
  Parting ways : new rituals and celebrations of life's passing / Denise Carson.
    p. cm.
  Includes bibliographical references.
  ISBN 978-0-520-25108-3 (cloth)
  ISBN 978-0-520-26873-9 (pbk.)
  1. Death—Psychological aspects.   2. Mourning customs.
3. Funeral rites and ceremonies.   I. Title.
BF789.D4C32 2011 155.9'37—dc22   2010040360

Manufactured in the United States of America
20 19 18 17 16 15 14 13 12 11
10 9 8 7 6 5 4 3 2 1

The paper used in this publication meets the minimum requirements of ANSI/NISO Z39.48-1992 (R 1997) (Permanence of Paper).

To my parents, Linda and Richard Carson
Your love and spirit of adventure live on

Contents

Acknowledgments

This book would not have been possible without my mother, Linda Carson, asking me to interview her, trusting me to write her story, her unfailing honesty in examining her life, her devotion as a mother to the last breath, and her leaving her hard-earned reserves as an inheritance that enabled me to take the time to heal and write this book.

My deepest gratitude goes to Professor Sam Freedman for giving me the map to navigate the journey that became this book. I'm forever indebted to you for bestowing your wisdom of narrative nonfiction, and challenging me to stretch beyond my personal experience. Your confidence in me became mine.

With the same honor and gratitude, I thank Marty Geltman, Barbara Kernan, Juanita Marquez-Kelly, Carol Ann Wikstrom, John Marting, Jim Wells, Tommy Odom, Alex Cameron, Jack Chernobieff, and Marilyn Noonan for your inspiring journeys through life's final frontier. You all will live on in my memories and the pages of this book. I'm eternally grateful to your families, the Geltmans, the Poppers, the Martings,

Ron Wikstrom, Jill Cross, Beverly and Ashley Wells, Sondra Cedillo, Manya Treguboff, Ian Duncan, Ed Noonan, and the St. Gregory of Nyssa congregation.

A special thank you to Zella Geltman for opening your arms, your home, and your life to me. Linda Marquez, David Lavine, and Rosaria Cabrera, you've enlightened me and taught me about the miracles of death. Elizabeth Vega, you're a kindred spirit and I appreciate your trusting me to turn the interview around on you. Mary Dexter, your legacy of lessons will live on to teach many students. Donna Miller, thank you for letting me shadow you for two years and teaching me the ins and outs of hospice. Robert Ostmann, thank you for inviting me into your classroom.

Barbara Kernan, Eric Putt, and Jerrigrace Lyons, you all helped me walk to the threshold to discover that the lines between life and death blur. Megory Anderson, thank you for teaching me about the sacred in end-of-life rituals. Rebecca Love, much gratitude for our reflective conversations, the tapes, and a faire to remember. Orin and Bernardo, you are stars and thanks for sharing the celebration of your lives with me. Lynn Isenberg and Jack Susser helped me to touch the untouchable, my own mortality. Jay Gianukos, thank you for giving me the vision to find the truth about my parents' lives.

Thank you to Dr. Agustin Garcia for your honesty and inviting me to scour your doctor notes in my mother's medical file. You are a model for doctors. Professor Tony Bell, I have a full-circle thank you for introducing me to death and dying sociology and helping me fine-tune my manuscript.

Dr. Robert Butler, I appreciate your leading me to define the significance of taking on the role of listener in what I thought was a collection of interviews to preserve my mother's life story, but turned out I tapped into her life review. Thank you for an illuminating interview Markella Rutherford, Dr. Harvey Max Chochinov, Dr. Diane Meier, Dr. Susan Block, David Rothman, Robert Burt, Sharon Kaufman, Rev. Paul Ratzlaff, John Melloh, James Hitchcock, Dr. Holly Prigerson, Gary Laderman, Justin Holcomb, Joe Sehee, Kurt Soffe, John Hogan, Sharon Mace, and Rabbi Regina Sanders-Phillips.

To the 2005 Columbia University Graduate School of Journalism book class, my first critics, thank you for helping me unearth the seeds that became this book. Most especially, a thank you to Mara Altman for your thoughtful edits, steadfast support, and inspiration. And an extra special thank you to Cyrus Farivar, for keeping me focused on the end goal and abreast of all the latest news on end of life.

Thank you Buffy Daignault for reading and editing my manuscript just like my Mom would have done. Brenda Krissman, Tim Cuellar, and Matt San Andres, thank you for sharing your stories of my father that breathed life into my memories of him. Thank you to Robert Carson, Jolene Arambula, Jane Herges, Lisa Bramen, Sharon Dannels, Beverly Chambers, for continuing to keep me rooted and grounded. Thank you Gina Calderone for guiding me to a true healing. Denise Noble, you're my sister, thank you for your critical eyes and always willing ears.

Professor Jeff Brody, your unconditional support, guidance, and edits were all a compass for this book. You've believed in me since the day you read my first lede; I hope this book makes you proud. I'm truly grateful to Rebecca Allen for not only being my trusted editor but also giving me the public stage at the *Orange County Register* to write about people celebrating the end of life. Thank you to my editor, Naomi Schneider, for your patience and guidance. You saw my vision and helped me carve out the nuggets that became this book.

Thank you to my brother, Ryan Carson, for standing at my side in the past, present, and future. I hope this book will help keep the memory of our parents alive for you.

Prologue

I opened our front door to welcome a procession of family and friends to my mother's wake on a brilliant winter afternoon in February 2002. Her last wish was to die at home in San Dimas, our quiet suburban oasis near Los Angeles. The doctors predicted she had seven days or less to live following her choice to end intravenous feeding. That decision came as a surprise to me on the evening of our homecoming from a demoralizing stay in the hospital.

And so the countdown began on a Monday.

Tuesday, Day Two, hospice arrived.

It was Day Three when my mother, known to everyone else as Linda Carson, lay wide awake for her wake. She basked in the spotlight on a bed surrounded by not mourners, but revelers as the ambiance in our home turned from quiet pain to a quickening pulse of celebration. Friends regaled her with stories of old. Her laughter, rising in cadence, egged them on. I'd never felt so proud of her than at that moment. She radiated a picture of dignity and grace in motion.

Her spirit transcended the physical frailties brought on by the cancer. Her blue eyes shone through her pallid, porcelain face. She wore no wig, sponged no makeup or blush on her sharp cheekbones and slender nose. We'd just celebrated her fifty-fourth birthday, and I was a few months shy of my twenty-seventh, the same age as she was when giving birth to me. I sensed a distinct role reversal occur as she labored out of life. My nineteen-year-old brother, Ryan, with his spiky auburn hair and chest puffed out, stood like a guard at the head of her bed. I knew he too felt an instinctual need to watch over her.

No opening speeches, such as "We are gathered here today to honor the life of Linda Carson," commenced the wake. In the absence of cultural cues and modern-day deathbed customs, we devised our own. A rocking chair at her bedside became the designated speaker's chair. Customarily, ancient wakes took place in the living room, the home's inner sanctum, which was then called the parlor but renamed in the twentieth century to clear its reputation as the place reserved to honor and lay out the dead. In the early years of the twenty-first century, such a public ceremony marking this final passage at home was rare, but on the rise. Mom specifically requested no wake or open-casket funeral post-death at a funeral home. Instead, we invited everyone for the ceremonial farewell a bit early. We figured she could participate in the reunions, reminiscences, and festivities. Mom never missed a party.

Many of my father's friends commented on how much I looked just like my mother, but that's because they knew her when she was my age. Back then Mom rocked long fiery-red tresses that swept her hip-huggers on a twenty-five-inch waist.

"Luckily, I got her figure," I said, scooping blondish-brown tresses out of my face to wink at Mom. She and I both knew that more than just her physical qualities would live on in me.

"And the smile," Mom said.

I looked around our living room as the faces of our friends from church, my childhood neighborhood, my mother's friends from her Divorce Recovery Group and Parents Without Partners, relatives from my father's side of the family, and her colleagues I'd known since my first steps, came into focus. Each person symbolized a collection of shared memories with my mother, and all together they formed a moving mosaic of her thirty-six years lived in America. I must admit, although she carried herself with an air of British sophistication from a bygone era, she's a rebel survivor at her core. At eighteen years old, she emigrated alone from England with a one-way ticket to America. She left behind the old-world traditions to design the life she wished for in this country. Those instincts shunned our society's norm to die furtively behind the closed doors of an institution.

I stood amidst the collective reminiscences with no unanswered questions, but that hard-won calm didn't come without a struggle to map a new direction into life's final frontier that led to this extraordinary finale.

Introduction

My mother's living wake inspired an exploration to find other families involved in similar parting ways rituals. That day, we eclipsed her imminent death by bonding together to celebrate her life. The social gathering turned out to be preventive medicine for all the "survivors" left behind. Together we orchestrated the kind of deathbed experience that we Americans view as the ideal.

Eighty percent of Americans wish to die at home surrounded by family members, yet only 25 percent of the 2.4 million Americans who die every year do.[1] I realize a number of factors stamp out this possibility, but the most evident is that we don't know any other way than death in the medical realm. U.S. Census data indicate that approximately 75 percent of all deaths occur in persons aged 65 and older and further show that only 6 percent of all deaths are from unnatural causes.[2] Surprisingly, the majority of Americans die of natural causes in old age, and those 65 and older continue to be the fastest-growing section of the population making up 13 percent.[3]

Yet death remains an institutionalized event.

This book explores individuals reinventing the role of family and community in death care to wrest control back from the white coats in hospitals and the black suits in funeral homes at the turn of the twenty-first century. As a journalist, I report stories about everyday people to portray the lived reality of a larger cultural trend happening in society. America is experiencing an irrevocable upward trend of families breaking free of the uniform, depersonalized, alienated death ways of our modern society with a new set of personalized rituals closely related to practices of pre-modern society when death was omnipresent and Americans died in the familiar comfort of home and relied on intimate communal bonds.

In the last half of the twentieth century, gerontologist Robert Butler concluded in the book *Why Survive? Being Old in America,* "We're so preoccupied with defending ourselves from the reality of death that we ignore the fact that human beings are alive until they are actually dead."

Well, not anymore.

Experts and demographers predict an "end of life revolution" much like the sex revolution when baby boomers dispelled "the myths and half-truths" surrounding the taboo of sex in America.[4] When the baby boomers—the 75 million Americans born between 1946 and 1964—confront a new stage of life, societal shifts and cultural changes follow. Many of these individuals are approaching the last chapters of their parents' lives and consequently colliding with the institutions that have governed end of life for a century. The baby boomer bulge will continue padding the senior population year after year, growing to one in five U.S. residents by 2030.[5] Some of the baby boomers, like my mother and others in this book, are already trailblazing, and their passages are serving as cultural exemplars.

Since we often encounter discomfort in talking about death, I've taken on the task of aggregating a collection of family stories at this "pivotal, creative, and innovative period"[6] around confronting death and funerals to add to our collective wisdom. I've been graciously invited into the intimate lives and living rooms of people from the East to West coasts to report a rich, diverse, and changing landscape of individuals gathering to toast, roast, sing, bequeath a legacy of life stories, and pay reverence to a life in the midst of death.

These rituals close the gap between the social and biological death by transforming this once-sequestered stage of life into a social, spiritual, and self-growth journey. In contrast to traditional ritual, powerful because it's handed down through the generations, the power vested in these invented rituals is the authentic expression of the individual self and interpersonal relations that personalize a previously institutionalized occasion.

For example, the living funeral is a social gathering of family and friends to honor the dying person before death with illuminating eulogies, tributes, and lifetime achievement awards. The deathbed ceremonial farewell re-enchants a previously disenchanting stage of life. As the last breath nears, the individuals are now reassured their life will live on in the minds and hearts of their family and community. A new kind of end-of-life guide is recording life stories through interviews and assembling a legacy of memories in a life-story book to bequeath to the family. On that score, families are video recording an oral ethical will in a familial gathering set up for the dying person to pass on his or her values and life wisdom to the next generations.

The vigil, a post-death ritual of watching over the body in repose, is now transformed into a pre-death communal affair that creates a sacred space around the deathbed for familial prayers and songs to support the dying person laboring out of life. Death midwives and death doulas are recasting the deathbed scene like their birth midwife counterparts in the home-birthing movement of the 1970s. Midwives sought to return the communal and spiritual sides back to the personal experience of birthing, which they believed had become increasingly more medicalized as the woman became a patient in the modern-day institution.

Likewise, a death midwife empowers the family to reclaim the intimate final acts of ceremonially washing and preparing the body for a funeral in the home, thereby revising the tradition to call a funeral director to immediately usher the dead out of the living community for an institutionalized wake and funeral. This family-centered approach is often followed by a green burial, a new kind of internment connected to old world ways that forgoes embalming the body and instead simply wraps the body in a shroud or biodegradable pine box that is buried inconspicuously in a forest landscape without headstones.

We've seen some books that research and report on post-death rituals and many books on the various aspects of dying well, but there hasn't been a practical guide yet that carves out a holistic path anchored in rituals that celebrate life while marking the "whole" passage from dying to death to mourning. Most of the books on dying and death come from the voices of the professionals because they are, for the most part, society's guardians of this domain. This book is a synthesis of individual stories, voices of professionals, and my personal experiences around death to portray a living portrait of families and communities reshaping end of life. The book is organized into two parts: pre-death and dying rituals followed by post-death and mourning rituals. It's an easy-access resource to be read in pieces based on where an individual or family is on the end-of-life journey.

Since "most Americans are not afforded a dress rehearsal for their own dying and are often not present for long periods during the dying process of others,"[7] I've arranged the book to gradually immerse you deeper into the arcane realm of end of life with two related narratives.

The first narrative is a close-up lens on my familial experience living with dying and the driving forces and conditions that led us to create homespun rituals. My mother's journey into life's final frontier will provide a central road map and/or timeline on which to plot these new rituals. So at each new leg of our journey, I will pause to introduce a new ritual in the form of a chapter that widens the lens to explore the origins of the rite while demonstrating real-life application of this ritual practiced by a family and community. In the alternating chapters ahead, I will switch between the role of my mother's primary caretaker and journalist focused on how these rituals provide a "window" into the "cultural dynamics of how people make and remake their worlds" around death historically and at present.[8] I draw on interviews with sociologists, anthropologists, religious historians, doctors, nurses, clergy, and funeral directors to broaden and contextualize the scope.

I read in *The Hour of Our Death*, a vast study of death from the Middle Ages to the present day, about the need for established rituals at the end of life. Philippe Ariès, the author and social historian, writes, "The transition from the calm and monotonous world of everyday reality to the inner world of feelings is not made spontaneously or without help. The distance between the languages is too great. In order to establish communication it is necessary to have an accepted code of behavior, a ritual."[9]

We live in a culturally porous country where religious and cultural rituals are borrowed and personalized. I've unearthed the roots of these traditions and found that many of us, unwittingly or intentionally, are reaching back into our past to domesticate death in America. "Cultural lag" is a term used by social scientists to describe the phenomenon of societies falling behind in dealing with new social problems that result from technological advances.[10] Unfortunately, our social and personal responses failed to keep pace with the innovation of the twentieth century. The rapid influx of medical technology combined with urbanization moved death from the home to the institution. Hospitals, an outpost of science, have their own rituals for marking death. Sophisticated machines monitor biological functions such as heart rate and brain wave activity. Death has become calculable, predictable and efficient, but the scientists and machines squeeze out the human element like feelings and metaphysical questions about the nature of human life.[11] We are three, nearly four, generations removed from knowing how to be at the bedside of the dying. I'm not romanticizing the past, but should point it out as a frame of reference to explore the renaissance of family involvement in death care.

"For the most part families don't know what to do around the bedside because they've never seen anyone die before," said Dr. Diane Meier, director of both the Center to Advance Palliative Care and the Hertzberg Palliative Care Institute at Mount Sinai School of Medicine in New York City.[12] "Death is a stranger in our culture."

In preindustrialized societies, birth and death were essentially social affairs involving cultural rituals developed over centuries within the home and community.[13] Death was a public ceremony, and the bedchamber was a community space entered freely.[14] Dying alone is a fear that inflicts many people today, but back then was inconceivable. The presence of parents, children, friends, and neighbors was vital in the final moments.[15] The generational wisdom to hold, support, and guide these rites of passage disappeared when hospitals acquired the processes of dying and birthing from the family in the 1920s. Death became the enemy to be conquered in these curative institutions. This widely held belief manufactured absurd regimes silencing all talk of death in the hospitals and "protecting" families from the patient's final moments. The code of silence eventually spread out into society.[16]

The funeral industry flourished under these conditions as families called on the undertakers, now funeral directors, for swift body removal from the hospital for preparation and viewing in the funeral parlor, now funeral home. A familial affair for a millennium became a professional affair that disrupted the intimacy and emotions channeled through caring for our own dying and dead with our own hands in the familiar bosom of home.[17] Death, once as regular in daily and family life as the changing seasons, became invisible in the twentieth century.[18]

The modern hospice movement started in the 1970s as an alternative to, but also backlash against the mechanical and impersonal death in an institution. Hospice is an interdisciplinary medical team focused on holistic, low-tech, comfort care in the patient's home. The team guides the family and community on how to care for the needs of the dying patient at home. Today, hospice is a philosophy of care, not a place. America has seen an upward trend in the adoption of hospice at the turn of the twenty-first century from helping 158,000 Americans at the end of life in 1985 to 1.2 million in 2005 and rising to 1.5 million in 2009.[19] The most recent hospice studies report that 41 percent of all deaths in America happen in the comforts of hospice and more than 68 percent of hospice patients die in the place they call home. Today more than 5,000 hospices help people nationwide, up from one in 1974.[20]

America is emerging from the cultural lag of impersonally handling death. These new rituals have evolved from a constellation of cultural catalysts—the hospice and palliative care movement, religious pluralism, heightened individualism, the counterculture of the baby boom, the AIDS epidemic, and the revival of ancient rites. Funeral directors report a landmark shift in families taking control and individualizing the one-size-fits-all traditional service characterized by the body removal for an institutionalized wake and religious funeral.

The baby boomers rewrote the traditional vows of matrimony and moved weddings from the hallowed sanctuary of the church to the sacred gardens of their backyards or other grounds they deemed as holy. Interfaith marriages, divorce, and same-sex relationships became acceptable to the boomer cohort. They founded the New Age movement of spiritual awareness that strayed from institutionalized religion and popularized mega churches. The twelve steps, a recovery program for Alcoholics Anonymous, is now an acceptable model to guide personal growth journeys of all kinds in our society. Boomers initiated home offices, home schooling, and holistic wellness programs drawing on alternative Eastern medicine. The women's movement devoured medical paternalism and seeded the marginal homebirth movement of the 1970s that altered the birthing practices to shift away from institutionalized standards and move toward nurturing choices and the individual experience. At the other end of the life cycle, we are now seeing the convergence of these values and movements shattering the silence around this once taboo subject and making death visibly fashionable in America.

PART ONE **End-of-Life Celebrations and Pre-Death Rituals**

ONE Her Choice: Two Paths Leading to the Same Destination

In the waning last year of the twentieth century, I followed my mother through the double glass doors of Kenneth Norris Cancer Hospital on the University of Southern California campus. The wilting figures seated in the lobby assaulted my senses. We'd entered a departure terminal for death. I choked back my horror and threw my arm around her instead of turning to run for the exit. She made many solo journeys in her life, but this wouldn't be one of those.

"Thanks for coming with me, my love," she said. Mom appeared vigorous as she reverberated the lobby with the rhythmic click of her high heels, which added a few inches to her nimble five-foot-two physique in a business suit and blond bob.

My mother's gastrointestinal oncologist had summoned us late that afternoon. A nurse escorted us into a stark room. We sat in front of an

oak desk. The week before Mom had returned home from this office repeating her death sentence—three to four months left to live. They gave
no curative option after twelve arduous weeks of reconnaissance. The
USC team only offered to palliate the symptoms.

The doctor swept in and sat behind the desk. She opened Mom's flimsy
medical file and launched into a scripted spiel about an experimental
chemotherapy treatment that she thought could prolong my mother's
life. Skeptical, I interrupted the doctor's speech about mixing two kinds
of chemotherapies to test the toxicity levels in humans.

"This seems unsafe," I said.

"Denise, this may not help your mother, but her participation in the
study will help save the lives of others," she said.

I winced at her casual tone.

"My mother doesn't want to be your guinea pig," I quipped.

The doctor moved to corner of the desk and placed her hand on my
shoulder to gain pseudo-intimacy.

"With this experiment, we're killing two birds with one stone; it's a
chemo for gastrointestinal *and* ovarian cancer," she said. "It's exactly what
we need to treat your mother's cancer."

I burned with anger, but I couldn't stop the tears. My mother looked
at me. I wasn't the ideal pillar of support that I hoped to be for her.

"We need to think about it," Mom said. "My kids have already been
through this with their father. My goal is to have quality not quantity of
life."

EXTENDING LIFE OR PROLONGING DEATH
IN THE TWENTIETH CENTURY

I remembered the first time Mom had uttered that string of words. It was
the spring of 1987. I was just twelve years old. We walked side-by-side
toward the elevator on the ninth floor of UCLA Medical Center. My father,
Richard Carson, was a local by then on that floor. In the cancer unit, he
appeared out of place. At just thirty-seven years old with a marathon
runner's body and a full head of thick, shiny black hair, he looked so

invincible to me compared with other residents, who looked more like great-grandparents.

Mom had just visited his room. They had been divorced for five years, and he had remarried. Mom had little contact with my father during his illness, yet she felt it necessary to talk to him that evening when she came to pick me up from the hospital. I had been staying at a family residence, similar to a hotel, on the UCLA campus in Westwood for the weekend in order to visit Dad while he was undergoing aggressive daily radiation and chemotherapy.

She walked into the room to see a skeleton of the man she once called her husband. He'd lost a lot of weight since their marriage. His skin hung on his bones. He wore a white V-neck T-shirt and hospital pants. His bronze complexion was now tinged yellow, a sign of his failing liver. Shortly after his thirty-fifth birthday, they'd diagnosed him with colorectal cancer that spread to his liver.

"Have you had a will drawn up?" she asked.

"Yes," he said.

"Do you think you can write a letter to the kids, tell them about what your expectations of them are in the future, tell them about you?" she asked. "Especially for Ryan—he is still very young." Ryan, my younger brother, was four.

Dad didn't respond.

"Or even make a tape or video of yourself for them?" she added.

"Lin, I'm going to beat this," he said. His face twisted from the pain as he tried to sit up in his bed. They exchanged a few more words and then my Mom emerged and grabbed my hand. I looked up and saw tears in her eyes, but they disappeared before rolling down her face.

"Did you have fun, my love?" she asked.

"Yeah, Mom," I said.

"You know, if I ever get cancer, I wouldn't go through what your father is going through," she said. "I would let nature take its course. I would choose quality over quantity of life."

In his last days at UCLA Medical Center in 1987, my father became a young, human guinea pig willing to "green light" every experimental treatment. The "stabbing knives" in surgeries, the "bullets" of chemotherapies, the countless zaps of radiation—no matter how invasive or debilitating the side effects, the treatments lured my father into believing he was fighting for his life. They sucked him dry and left him with a porous body riddled with tumors.

Right before my naïve eyes, I watched him deteriorate. He'd routinely run three miles a day and competed in the Los Angeles Marathon. Just the year before, he launched his own business, Carson Medical Management, a medical billing company. He spent most of his career toiling as the director of a local hospital, St. Bernardine Medical Center, but he never tired. My dad was like the neighborhood doctor, our own Patch Adams. His silly jokes and goofy faces could turn around anyone's gloom. It was terrifying to see him slow down, become a patient, and fade from my daily life.

As his body broke down, the doctors replaced his internal organs with tubes and metal medical devices that transformed him into a half-man/half-machine. With each new treatment Brenda, his wife, asked his physician, "Is Richard going to make it?"

STRUCTURED SILENCE

In the late 1980s, when my father cycled in and out of the medical system, problems of over-aggressive care stemmed from the physicians' unwillingness to speak of dying and tell patients the truth about their prognosis, said Robert Burt, a professor at Yale University and author of *Death Is That Man Taking Names*. Physicians pressed all kinds of extremely invasive and incredibly painful treatments on patients with no realistic chance of success, he said.[1] As a consequence, people lost their autonomy and suffered miserable, intolerable pain in their last months of life.

Nicholas Christakis, a physician and sociologist, studied medical prognoses for twenty years and characterized the "structured silence" around death as part of the daily rhythm in medical practice in a book entitled *A Death Foretold: Prophecy and Prognosis in Medical Care*. Physicians tend to discuss a grim prognosis only when it's unavoidable, and more often than not they overestimate survival both to themselves and their patients.

Dr. Elisabeth Kübler-Ross, a physician and a pioneer in the death awareness movement that started in the 1960s, exposed the inflicted abuses on terminally ill patients living in hospitals in the book *On Death and Dying: What the Dying Have to Teach Doctors, Nurses, Clergy and Their Own Families*, published in 1969. She constructed the five stages of the death and dying model that provided an inner lens to view the dying experience as a psychological, not just a physical one. She taught us that with support and an inward journey of self-reflection, the dying person could reach "acceptance." She insisted on forgoing the "structured silence" in favor of honest dialogue between patient, physician, and family.

In 1972, Dr. Kübler-Ross testified at the first national hearings conducted by the U.S. Senate Special Committee on the subject of death with dignity. Two years later the U.S. Senate introduced the first hospice legislation. Hospice care adopted the model of "holistic care" to treat all encompassing physical, emotional, spiritual, and existential pain. Hospice/palliative care provides the family with an interdisciplinary team—a physician, a nurse, a social worker, a chaplain, and a volunteer aid—to support the patient at home. Though the U.S. Senate passed the Hospice Medicare benefit that stipulated patients could decline all life-prolonging treatments and have a six-months-or-less-to-live-prognosis in order to receive hospice in 1978, the "structured silence" impeded hospice from reaching patients and their families. So even in 1987, the year my father faced a terminal illness, hospice aided only 177,000 dying patients.[2]

Dr. Diane Meier, director of the Hertzberg Palliative Care Institute at Mount Sinai School of Medicine, clearly has witnessed "a sense of unreality and cognitive dissonance" veiling the deathbed.

"Patients and families are feeling like they can't trust their own eyes," Dr. Meier said.[3] "A patient can feel themselves getting sicker and sicker and the family sees that there is progressive decline, but none of the doctors are talking about it. The patient and family start to feel as if they are losing their minds. 'Is what we are seeing wrong? And if it is right, then why aren't the doctors saying anything about it?'"

A VEIL OF CONTRADICTION

Needless to say my father's doctor responded similarly on many occasions. "He's young, he's strong, and he's going to make it." If my father's doctor believed he would make it, why should we believe otherwise?

He *was* young and he *was* strong.

When I asked Brenda questions about my father's cancer, she said, "Everything is going to be okay, honey." All the information received from Brenda contradicted my own eyes. I searched for other ways to find out the truth. Bordering obsessive-compulsive behavior, purely out of survival, I sought out the real story to cope with a stifling fear. Ignorant bliss and denial didn't work for me.

On Saturdays at my dad's house in La Verne, Brenda often perched on the last barstool in the kitchen and talked for hours on the telephone to her mother and sister in Texas. She was oblivious to me sitting on the couch watching television. In stealth mode, I'd flick through the channels and reduce the volume when her voice lowered to a near whisper. I listened to her unfold the week's top stories. They were detailed, perilous, and not sugarcoated. I used the information I gathered to ask her pointed questions about the two more tumors growing in his liver, the CAT scan on his pelvic area, and the tumor growing in his lungs. While other kids in junior high chose to do their book report on gymnastics or NASCAR, I elected to explore this elusive enemy. I checked out a cancer book from the school library. I was inquisitive to the point of annoying. Often Brenda would hush me from asking questions.

"I don't want your father to hear," she'd say with tears streaming down her face. We all had to respect this code of silence.

BREAKING THE CODE OF SILENCE

Twelve years later, my mother and I sat in a research hospital on the USC campus, just across town from UCLA. I wanted to remind her that by signing the experimental chemotherapy papers, she chose "quantity," but I couldn't. The doctor gave her the sliver of hope she'd been waiting for. I wanted to tell her once you hop on the chemotherapy merry-go-round, it becomes addictive. They'll treat you till you die. An ominous shadow of the past eclipsed any glimmer of hope as I watched her sign the papers.

The following week, we walked into the Day Hospital, which struck me more as a laboratory. All these human specimen stations equipped with a recliner, television, and IV pole. As the poison entered by mother's veins, I was haunted by visions of Mom's face hovering over Dad's deteriorating body. Mom suggested I interview her during our downtime together. I defined eight hours in hospital for chemo as downtime.

The last time I conducted an interview with someone near death was in 1997 for my college newspaper. It was liberating speaking openly and publicly about death for the first time with a group of young men dying of AIDS in a Long Beach hospice. They fascinated me because they could articulate living with a terminal illness. Their rapidly aging faces, thrush-covered mouths, and emaciated bodies didn't put me off. Instead, I was strangely comfortable in their company. I'd never spoken to my father about fighting a terminal illness. As a journalist, I could vicariously ask these questions and reach a deeper understanding of the choices Dad made in his last days. My family and friends never talked about the imminence of his death. The denial bothered me most, his denial and the collective denial of death in America.

Still, it wasn't until my last year of college that I found a group of healthy individuals to discuss this social taboo. The course was called the Sociology of Death and Dying. I learned about grief and Elisabeth Kübler-Ross's stages of death and dying—denial, anger, depression, bargaining, and acceptance. I began to recognize my own invisible handicap, unexpressed grief from which, unfortunately, many Americans suffer. Grief, a primal response to death, has hardly the conducive environment for expression in our death-denying and grief-avoiding culture.

Philippe Ariès, the social historian, describes this forbidden death attitude as a strangling of sorrow and its public manifestation that consequently forced people to suffer alone and secretly aggravating the trauma stemming from the loss of an intimate family member or friend.[4] The forbidden death, a cultural construct designed by Americans, according to

Ariès, also informed us that children shouldn't be exposed to death and that parents shouldn't cry or show emotion in front of the children.

I unknowingly rebelled against this destructive silence in my first interview and subsequent interviews in the chemo lab with my mother. I asked how she defined death. She gave me some heavenly metaphors about the soul passing on to another time and place. When I asked her how she defined quality of life, she said, "I can now look at life as a gift. If I can talk to people, I can smile at people, I can interact with others, then life can be good."

We discussed her diagnosis, proximity to death, and decision to enter chemotherapy. Then I decided to ask some open-ended questions to get her to reflect on her life.

"Okay, let's take a look at your life from day one to now. Are there any memories that stand out in your mind that you want to reflect on?" I asked.

"My divorce," she said.

"Why is that?"

"As soon as you asked that question, I remembered him telling me," she said.

"That's the most significant moment in your life?" I asked, trying to disguise my bruised ego. Her answer stung. It felt as if she bit me hard on the face. I thought she might say, "The moment I first laid eyes on you after you were born."

Her reminiscence spiraled downward into a grim discussion about working seventy hours a week at First Interstate Bank in downtown Los Angeles for two and half decades. She confessed to becoming a workaholic and then recounted, in excruciating detail, the demise of her banking career when she was taken hostage at gunpoint for forty-five minutes during a bank raid. Then, nine months later, she was caught in another hostage crisis with a gang of gunmen. She wondered if these searing moments triggered her body to turn against itself. Cancer essentially was her own malignant cells attacking the healthy cell tissue.

That interview certainly set the precedent. We shed the mother and daughter roles. When the tape recorder was on, I was the reporter and she was my source. She chose not to shield me from her true thoughts like most parents, or at least mothers, might. Likewise, I chose not to pussyfoot around her. I wasn't deterred—quite the contrary, her candor intrigued me.

I asked her to take some time off work between chemotherapy regimens and return to England to visit our family while she was still relatively healthy. She refused. My fear of losing her evoked an urge to build a reservoir of memories that I could tap into during her inevitable absence. The oncologist said she'd be on chemotherapy for the rest of her life, but for some reason she translated that to mean her life was indefinite, citing that some people live on chemotherapy for eight years. My mother was a calculated realist, yet that rational person seemed to vanish in the fight for survival. Her hair and long eyelashes fell out followed by her eyebrows, and her taste buds for her favorite "meat and potato burrito" dried up. The nausea steadily increased as the toxicity levels rose in her body.

One Thursday afternoon, during our weekly interviews at the chemo lab, I asked, "How do you go on?" She quietly sang me the mantra she sang every morning when she woke up: "I pick myself up, dust myself off, and start all over again." Mom carried barf bags on her 100-mile-round-trip to her investment company in West Los Angeles to work four ten-hour days.

The four-bedroom, two-story house that my stepfather, Gil Lisko, and Mom rattled around in proved to be too small for both the cancer and me. His entrance into our family home marked my exit in 1994. They sold the house and split up. My mother and I returned to the townhouse where she'd lived before they married and he moved to an apartment nearby. He still remained in her life, just no longer in her bed. We were both adjusting to the vicissitudes.

My mother soldiered through six months of grueling chemotherapy. The cancer began to retreat. We hit a stalemate in our fervent sport of arguing about how to embrace what I believed to be borrowed time and she believed to be limitless time. She wanted to act like life was normal, so I cast off the martyr, stopped living like an old maid, moved out, and seeded my career in Los Angeles.

I could handle the chaotic confrontation with cancer, but the humdrum of pretending it was invisible plunged me into a panic. I started writing for a feature section at the *Los Angeles Times* in the Santa Monica bureau. In the buzz and spin of toiling away on deadlines and reporting on the subcultures and personalities of Hollywood, I'd managed to escape the claws of cancer. But as a curious reporter I retraced my footsteps at UCLA Medical Center where my father had spent the majority of his borrowed time. I made rounds visiting patients with a hospital chaplain guiding first-year medical students on how to carve out a personal and sacred space to listen and talk in a high-tech, sterile environment. In general, medical students visited with patients in their third year. I was reporting on a newly installed "bedside manner 101" class at the UCLA Medical School.

I watched these young medical students hold the hand of a frail man weeping about leaving his family behind. I wondered if doctors today might benefit from a refresher course on bedside manner guided by the chaplain. The doctor-patient communication had become more like a business transaction than an authentic human interaction. The chaplain taught the students not to look at their watches or the clock on the wall and to be present with the patient. At the end of their class, they orchestrated a memorial service for the cadavers from anatomy class. They gave eulogies, wrote remembrance cards about what they learned most from this person's body donation, and lit white votive candles atop an altar. The story received quite a bit of reader response. The class was part of a larger effort by the UCLA Medical School to restore the human element in medicine.

I learned that UCLA Medical Center, my father's second home in 1987, was part of the landmark study SUPPORT, the Study to Understand Prognoses and Preferences for Outcomes and Risks of Treatment, launched by the Robert Wood Foundation in 1989 to address the growing national concern with the relentless ferocity of modern medicine and technology in dying. In Phase I of the study, physician researchers interviewed 9,105 patients diagnosed with life-threatening diseases at five hospitals across America. Dr. Joanne Lynn and Dr. William Knaus reported shortcomings in physician-patient communication and poor decision making. Ninety percent of patients reported pain and frequency in aggressive treatment. Phase II, the intervention of the study, rolled out in 1992 to 1994. Researchers sought to provide physicians with some tools to improve end-of-life care such as computer printouts of estimates on survival chances up to six months in advance; a nurse whose job was to talk to patients about end-of-life issues while opening a clear line of communication between patient, physician, and family; and a detailed end-life-plan of wishes written by the patient and family for the doctor. They hoped to enhance understandings of life trajectory, bolster attention to pain control, and cultivate advanced planning, but they failed to incite significant change. Sadly, in the end, SUPPORT concluded, "In order to improve the experience of seriously ill and dying patients, greater individual and societal commitment and more forceful measures may be needed."

A REFLECTION ON DYING IN THE TWENTIETH CENTURY

My father's brutal dying days epitomized the problems that the SUPPORT study revealed. The unnecessary treatments continued until my father's body caved. The tumors collided with his nerves and sent shockwaves of pain through his body. His was the kind of dying that made you feel selfish for wanting him to live. Brenda, his young brunette wife, stripped his bed sheets and T-shirts, drenched from the torrents of sweat, multiple times a day. Every four hours she switched between methadone and morphine injections yet still he writhed. The physicians chose to toggle between the two, around the clock, for fear of my father getting addicted or his body becoming resistant to the opiates. They couldn't control his pain, so he couldn't see anyone in his last days. The bedroom door at the top of our stairs was always shut. Death was hidden from the eyes of the children in our house, like the scenes in an R-rated film or pornography. Concealing his dying only made it scarier and uglier. Death is natural. Hiding death is unnatural.

School was out. In the summer of 1987, I sat on my lacy bedspread and stared at the floral wallpapered walls instead of sunbathing and swimming in our backyard pool. Just the summer before, our house brimmed with our neighbors and all of my father's cousins. Our home was like

Club Med, where the cocktails, barbecue steaks, and seafood buffets—spread by Dad, who loved to cook—flowed from noon until dark. He was the nexus of all activity. We were an inseparable pair—I was always at his side. At night the tables cleared and the flashing lights illuminated the darkness. My Dad danced in his slick Italian tailored suit with gleaming gold cuff links. Dancing with him or just watching him was equally entertaining. He looked just like John Travolta in *Saturday Night Fever*.

Death, the unwanted houseguest, intruded on those dreamy summer days. With it came stillness, whimpers from every bedroom. Groans of pain reverberated the walls and a stale smell of decay hung in the air. As a family we didn't acknowledge our houseguest. So it crept into our bedrooms and it was most active at night. I saw very little of Dad in the final months of his life. I felt banished, denied of his affection too early.

He sent me away in late July 1987. On a clear Saturday morning, he called me up to his bedroom before I departed for Kauai. I tapped on his bedroom door.

"Come in, babe," he said.

"Hi, Dad," I said. I climbed up onto his bed carefully because every movement sent shudders through his body. The slightest bump was equal to a punch from a two-ton gorilla. He wore oxygen tubes in his nose that he lifted up off his face. His once-healthy olive complexion looked yellowish now from liver failure. I could see that every surface inch of his skin felt like a deep open wound.

Tears dripped out of my eyes.

"Dad," I said.

"Denise, don't cry," he said.

"Maybe I shouldn't go, Dad."

He reached for a book titled *Kauai*. His shaking fingers pointed out some of the places he thought I should visit: Waimea Canyon, the Fern Grotto, and Hanalei Bay on the North Shore where I would be staying. I looked at these full-page *National Geographic*–quality photographs of lush pristine rain forests and dreamlike waterfalls. He planned to send me off to paradise. I turned my eyes up to my father. He was fading. Death seized him and just a drop of his magnetic soul inhabited the diseased body.

"You go and have the best time of your life for me," he said.

"Could I take a picture with my new camera before I go?"

He agreed and tried to smile. I clicked the photograph then realized it was on "normal." I wanted a "telephoto," so I switched the setting atop the camera.

"One more," I said.

He used the last bit of strength dwelling in the depths of his body and summoned a macho look. He crossed his arms and posed like a tough Superman.

"Okay," I said, then snapped another photograph. "Thanks, Dad."

I crawled back on to his bed and threw my arms around his neck, which was covered in sweat. His T-shirt was damp and his skin was clammy.

"I love you, Dad," I cried.

"I love you too, babe."

Those were our last words.

THE SEARCH FOR AN ALTERNATE ENDING

In the millennium summer heat, our family congregated on the football field of San Dimas High School where Ryan, my brother, accepted his diploma. I snapped photos of Mom in her wig with Ryan in his cap and gown. For a split second, I understood why she kept pushing on through the toxic treatments. It gave her precious time. Seeing Ryan at graduation was a gift, a reward for enduring the relentless nausea. It was one of those milestone moments that I marked her reaching after the terminal diagnosis. Mom often would joke she didn't expect to see him graduate even if she survived.

Fall came and went, then just before Christmas, my boyfriend, Simon Foster, handed me a box while we sat in the warmth of his boat cabin on a foggy night in Marina del Rey, just four miles from the newsroom.

"I got this so that you could record your mother and keep your memories forever, even after she's gone," he said.

I opened the box and took out a video camera and set it on the table. My eyes traced his heaps of chestnut brown hair framing his fair-skin face blushing a bit. Simon was in the film industry and his father was an animation director at Warner Bros. Since his youth, he knew the magic and permanence of film. I was already interviewing Mom with a voice recorder. He suggested I use both.

This was the one tool I wish I had owned to record my father's voice telling me "I love you" and his actions I missed most, like him hugging me, dancing with me, laughing, and pulling his funny faces.

On Christmas, I turned the video camera on Mom as she unwrapped her gift from Simon and then looked into the camera.

"Ooh la la," she said as she fingered the white silk pajamas in the red Victoria Secret box. She slung them around her arms and waist and then sashayed across the living room.

"See, now I can hang out and look like a movie star," she said smiling into the video camera lens. "You know that's what movie stars used to wear instead of sweats, they'd wear silk PJs."

The New Year brought news of a remission from my mother's doctor, Agustin Garcia. He was thirty-seven years old and stood about five-foot-seven with curly, dark brown hair. He spent 20 percent of his time teaching, 50 percent researching, and 30 percent visiting with patients. Dr. Garcia developed the experimental chemotherapy that shrank the tumors in Mom's body. He opened her medical file, which was now two inches thick. We only had minutes to rejoice because he framed the remission with a surgery recommendation.

Since her diagnosis was inoperable cancer, none of the surgeons at USC felt she was a candidate for surgery. Dr. Garcia thought she had a chance of a clean bill of health if she opted for surgery. His words felt slippery as he handed over a referral to a surgeon outside USC. The surgery failed to live up to its promise of living cancer-free. In fact, Mom began to spiral downward in the aftermath. The tumors blocked her intestines, causing her to lose one of life's greatest gifts—eating. She began taking in nutrition via intravenous feeding in June 2001.

My mother went out on disability from work. In July her best friend, Beverly Chambers, moved into the guest bedroom in our house. She was like my aunt. She had a background in nursing. They'd known each other for three decades. Beverly always said that when the time came, she'd quit her job in Nevada and move to California. Her arrival marked the beginning of the end. The stays in the hospital began to outnumber the days spent at home.

On the morning of September 11, I raced down the halls of the third floor of Norris Hospital to find my mother reclining in a bed all alone watching the replays on CNN of the airplanes hitting the towers. The flames devouring the Twin Towers and people jumping off the building into the plumes of smoke reflected in her eyes. She was entranced when I walked in. It felt like we'd entered the End of Days. A sinister malaise suffocated me.

I called Dr. Garcia to discuss a hospice referral. He explained the intravenous feeding was life-sustaining treatment and that she would have to terminate it in order to enter hospice care. Still unclear as to what he was saying, I asked, "Why?"

"TPN is considered life support," he said.

"Don't you think you should tell her that?" I said, as a quiet fury consumed me.

Life support no longer looks like the ventilator machine keeping your family member in a coma alive in the intensive care unit. Neither of us realized it at the time but the seven IV bags delivered every Monday, stacked in our refrigerator and marked with expiration dates for use, were life support. My nightly routine of puncturing the IV bag with an intravenous line, injecting vitamins and the anti-nausea medication Reglan into it and then connecting it to an automated IV dispense machine about the size of a Palm Pilot was part of the life support. The IV bag, the line, and the machine strapped into a backpack transformed the TPN into a mobile life support machine. At seven o'clock each night, I connected my mother to an intravenous line through a pic line on her right upper arm. At seven o'clock each morning, I freed her from it.

I had no idea how my mother would take this information, but I knew that it needed to come from him, not me.

A MODERN PORTRAIT OF DEATH

The last time I saw my father was the morning of my departure for Kauai, an island paradise. I hopped into a Super Shuttle rumbling in the driveway of my childhood home that I'd lived in since I was three years old. It was the last morning I woke up in that house. The next day my Dad woke up for the last time in our house too. He turned to Brenda.

"It's time to go," he said, tossing back the sheets to expose his legs. It looked like something alien had invaded his body, like crawling algae. His legs were blackish-green from his toes to his thighs and the loss of circulation, gangrene, moved rapidly toward his torso. Brenda called an ambulance. The EMTs entered our house, strapped him to a stretcher and carried him out. They loaded him into the back.

Upon arriving at the hospital he was connected to a respirator. A web of tubes like tentacles connected his body to a morphine bag dangling from an IV pole; a catheter bag hung at the foot of his bed and machines monitoring his vital signs. As his lungs collapsed he gasped for air. Eventually they removed the respirator. Brenda whispered permission saying, "Go ahead and let go, we'll be alright." He fought to keep his eyes open and his last glances of life were those of a stark, sterile hospital chamber reverberating with machines whirring and hissing. Alienated in a cold, prefabricated room surrounded by strangers—the doctors, nurses, and anonymous attendants—was no place for a revered father. In the end darkness filled the space and whispers echoed around him. People who loved him all of his life, his children and intimate family members were absent as he slipped into a coma and died on Wednesday, July 22, 1987.

A short time later, his doctor telephoned Brenda at her office in San Bernardino to offer his condolences. The doctor praised her courage and strength to stay at Richard's side till the very end. She listened but had one question for the doctor.

"Why didn't you tell us Richard was dying? I could've prepared the family. You kept telling us he was strong and he would survive it," she said.

"Oh, Brenda," he said. "I'm sorry to admit that sometimes doctors think they are God. I thought I could save his life."

He paused. Brenda said nothing.

"I was in my own denial," he said.

My father died of cancer but his harrowing journey was a casualty of an even greater societal disease. He fought to his last breath, which left us, his family, to drag his pulverized body off the battlefield. It was a violent, inhumane departure. His death mirrored thousands of Americans dying in hospital in the mid-to-late years of the twentieth century. The "never say die" attitudes of physicians and aggressive medical intervention came under intense scrutiny on the cusp of his death.[5] At that time, many Americans feared losing their autonomy and worried that dying would be prolonged, mechanical, and impersonal.[6]

I spoke to Sharon Kaufman, a medical anthropologist at University of California at San Francisco, about the changes between my father's death and my mother's end of life journey. My parents represented cultural markers for the shifts in end-of-life care. She helped me to understand that 1987 marked the end of an era.[7] My father's death was before the widespread use and understanding of hospice and before consumer desire to be more involved with and name death.

The 1990s ushered in a surge of the death awareness movement as physicians and researchers received the SUPPORT reports. The right-to-die movement swelled, euthanasia cases hit the Supreme Court, and Americans awoke to a twisted reality that medical technology gave them a new lease on life by increasing life spans nearly two-fold in the twentieth century—but it extended the adversities of dying. The question became, prolonging lives at what cost? The cost was not necessarily in dollars (yet that was a factor), but really the mutilation of the sanctity of human life. In 1993, Dr. Death, a.k.a. Jack Kevorkian, drew massive media attention with sensational antics in aiding helpless terminally ill patients hasten their death by using a carbon monoxide mask.

The heroic interventions of medicine leading to futile outcomes and patients suffering protracted illnesses like cancer and AIDS blew open the doors of the medical institutions. The hospice movement burgeoned and indeed shored up the movement's efforts in pain management during this state of crisis.

In response to SUPPORT in 1994, George Soros, a billionaire philanthropist, launched the Open Society Institute's Project on Death in America

(PDIA), which awarded $45 million in grant rewards over nine years to individuals and organizations working to humanize the dying experience and transform the culture surrounding death and bereavement in America. His inspiration came when comparing the polar opposite experiences of the death of his father—which he denied, and thereby letting his father "die alone"—with the death of his mother, which he and his family "participated" in.

Dr. Robert Butler, board member of PDIA, renowned gerontologist, and founding director of the National Institutes of Health's National Institute on Aging, said of the mission, "Our job was to transform the personal experience of dying. Can you imagine such bluster?"[8] He made me chuckle because I believed their mission was sound but know that family members must join the professionals to personalize and humanize the dying experience. Family members must participate and communicate at the deathbed, not leave death and dying solely in the hands of professionals.

The Project on Death in America tried to disband the absurd regimes silencing talk of death in medicine while also fostering a less panicked view of death in society. Although the hospice movement made great strides, more than 50 percent of Americans continued to die in hospitals. The doctors heading PDIA recognized the need for a bridge, a middle ground for doctors to give hospice care to those dying in hospital. Palliative care is the hospice care model now available to patients without the stipulation of six months or less to live.

"The culture on death in America was one of 'death is optional.' With enough research, enough NIH dollars, and enough new devices, no one will ever have to die," Dr. Meier, renowned pioneer in palliative care and Project on Death in America scholar, said.[9] "That is still the culture of death in America. Palliative care emerged as the one way to address the suffering of patients and families caught up in that system."

These unique palliative care physicians, like Dr. Meier, aren't afraid to name death and help patients prepare for it. They diagnose and treat pain that erupts when patients worry about their family members' well-being, financial burdens, personal regrets, and anticipation about where the death will occur. The growth of palliative care practice within hospitals ushered in a wider acceptance of hospice within the traditional medical field. Experts say a good death gives the person dying a generous amount of time to foster a quest for personal growth. My father had no time for this quest. The changes in palliative care, choices in dying, and the growing power of the individual over the institution dramatically altered the milieu for me as a caregiver, and for my mother as a patient, at the dawn of the twenty-first century.

AN HONEST PROGNOSIS

On Thursday, October 1, 2001, nearly two years after my mother began chemotherapy, I sped up the hospital driveway and parked my car in front of the double glass doors of USC Norris Cancer Hospital. For days I'd been anticipating how the events of this meeting might unfold after the private phone call with Dr. Garcia. A valet opened my door and then my mother's door.

"We need a wheelchair," I said to the valet.

I walked around my car. My mother was idle. The wheelchair arrived and I helped lift her in. We rolled through the automatic double glass doors, the hospital lobby, and into the blood lab. After the phlebotomist pricked my mother in the lab, I rolled her out into the hospital corridor.

"I think, I need to lie down," she said.

"Okay, we'll go into the Day Hospital," I suggested. She was recovering from a recent surgery that implanted a suction pump in her stomach to vacuum her intestines. She suffered from second-degree burns inflicted by stomach acid leaking out of an incision atop her belly, so it hurt to sit upright. As we entered the Day Hospital, a.k.a. the chemo lab, all the nurses greeted my mother by first name. I requested a hospital bed and a nurse escorted us into an empty ward. My eyes caught a small figure approaching.

Dr. Garcia approached us and stood at the foot of my mother's hospital bed. I'd already played out this meeting and the aftermath in my mind a hundred times since my "hospice" telephone conversation with him.

"Hi, Dr. Garcia," I said.

"Hello, hi," he stuttered. His brown eyes blinked rapidly. His smirk was gone. He paced up and down the side of the bed while asking Mom general questions about her new stomach pump, pain, and nausea. He hesitated for a moment. We all sat there in silence. Then he delivered the news. The blood tests revealed that her red blood cell count was severely low. This meant she wasn't fit for chemotherapy.

"And the cancer is still growing," he said. "The chemotherapy is not working anymore."

He stumbled over his words.

"I can recommend hospice," he said. "But you would have to quit TPN because it's life-prolonging and hospice doesn't permit it."

"You would die of dehydration in a week," he said. "It would be fairly peaceful—you'll slip into a coma after a few days."

I watched my mother frown at the doctor. She was trying to understand the message he blurted out. Until now, he had always been the ringleader coaching her through the next treatments and cheering her on. Dr. Garcia stopped to observe her reactions. He rocked back and forth on his left foot and then his right while clenching her three-inch-thick medical file. He went on to deliver his second option to discontinue chemotherapy and just treat the symptoms. His third option was to try two more rounds of the slow-acting chemotherapy, called Doxil. My mom finally responded.

"Well, I see them more as steps," she said lowering the timbre in her voice, giving off an air of steadfast strength. "So I want to try two more rounds of chemotherapy."

"Alright, we'll give it shot," Dr. Garcia said with a sigh. He then went on to explain she would have to get a blood transfusion if she wanted more chemotherapy. She agreed.

On the ride home she mentioned that hospice came out of the clear blue sky. I realized that a physician is really the only person with enough authority to speak realistically about "hospice" even when the signs are clearly evident.

I tentatively asked Mom if she wanted to begin interviewing again to chronicle her life story. I felt like we'd lost touch. We were obviously seeing the same situation through two distinctly different pairs of lenses. She agreed.

The discussion with Dr. Garcia stirred Mom to begin her own quiet investigation of her church's formal position on making a purposeful decision to give up treatment and die of dehydration. She probed advisors at Glenkirk Presbyterian Church in Glendora. Tom Naylor, her minister, already visited a couple of times a week to counsel my mother and read passages out of the Bible with her since she could no longer go to church on Sundays. She contacted him to discuss her concerns about coming off TPN. He promised to get her an official position from the church, but he initially said, "It's not committing suicide. Looking at it from the flipside, it may be delaying God's will for you," Tom said. "It may be prolonging the life that God was ready to take over."

There was so much to consider. It was dizzying. I wondered, how does one finally arrive at the moment when she can honestly say, "My work here is done"?

When we arrived home from Dr. Garcia's office, I entered Mom's bedroom with a comfort offering. Raspberry iced tea was a small pleasure she relished since she'd been banished to IV feeding. She'd only started drinking tea in the last few weeks after the insertion of the stomach pump that functioned as an external intestine. Her bedroom now looked like a quasi-hospital room, with a mechanical bed in place of her queen-size bed.

With a sigh of relief I sank into the bedside rocking chair facing her balcony window. I suppose the fear of my mother suffering an excruciating death like my father disintegrated when Dr. Garcia said, "It would be fairly peaceful." I really respected him for his courage to talk truth to my mother and me. The time that rolled out before us no longer felt like warfare but a time of peace.

"Mmm, I love tea," she beamed. Each sip lit up her pale face.

"So today the doctor gave us three options," I said.

"I'm excited. It's like a new adventure," she said with a smile reflecting tranquility that now swept over me. She paused.

"It really gives me peace of mind to know I can just request to be taken off TPN and it would take about a week and I would pass away. It's a relief. I have control over my life," she said.

The recent news gave my mother comfort and direction in confronting the path ahead. Whilst peering over a stack of travel guides, she'd often say, "The exciting part of the trip is planning it." She was the self-designated trip organizer of our family vacations. I marveled at her strength and wisdom in navigating this new frontier set before us. She had the information and power to choose the time, place, and guest list, if she wished, for her final journey.

TWO

Living Funeral:
Celebrating the End of Life

In the opening years of the twenty-first century, my search for families participating in rituals that celebrate the end of life landed me at a natural starting point in West Orange, New Jersey. Marty and Zella Geltman, a couple in their sixties, captivated me with a new kind of exit strategy that centered on inviting their family and community to cast a shining spotlight onto life in the shadow of death.

On the big day, Marty inspected the tuxedo hanging in his bedroom closet that Zella pulled out and laid on the bed. The occasion called for a regal appearance. He choreographed it in his mind. The venue. Who would sing his praises. The jokes they'd tell. The songs. The poems. The eulogy. Who would and wouldn't be seated in the audience.

The suit buttons glinted turquoise in the June morning sun that streamed through the bedroom window. Nearly a decade had passed since Marty danced in his bow tie and tails at his retirement party in the summer of 1992. He watched his wife, Zella, lift the tuxedo off the rack and spread it out on the king-size bed. A five-disc CD player set to shuffle rotated a collection of jazz and classical songs in their bedroom on the second floor of a condominium on the periphery of a nature preserve.

They both reveled in the memories attached to the suit. Marty shunned formal attire, but bought the tux to play a prank on his colleagues. The school principal insisted, year after year, on summoning Marty to her office and scolded him for wearing moccasins and no socks to class. "You need to set an example for your students," she'd say. Marty resisted conforming to institutional standards. He never shed his playful nature, reflected in his mutton-chop sideburns and casual threads, until the evening of his retirement celebration honoring thirty-four years devoted to teaching children at Gaudineer Elementary School in Springfield, New Jersey. He waltzed in with the grandeur of a distinguished gentleman, standing six feet, three inches in a tuxedo complemented by his bronzed baldhead, white-as-snow trimmed sideburns, piercing eyes, and a grin. He stunned his guests and succeeded in pulling off the first practical joke at his own roast on June 23, 1992. Zella remembered swinging with Marty in that tux after their wedding two months later on the dance floor of their favorite Big Band joint surrounded by friends and family at the reception. Marty prepared to dust off the suit for one last spin.

His buddy had suggested a week before that Marty should wear the infamous tux to his own memorial service. What else would a man wear as the guest of honor to the grandest celebration of his life? This differed from any milestone birthday, anniversary, rite of passage or retirement because this unparalleled event marked the sum total, a life mission accomplished celebration. If cancer threatened to cheat him of a long life with Zella, then he aimed to get one up on death. Why not indulge in the festivities now? Why wait for it to be over?

Zella pulled the tuxedo shirt off the hanger, held it for Marty to slip into, then buttoned it up. She opened an ornate shiny box on the oak dresser and lifted out the same multicolored bow tie. Marty slipped into the jacket adorned with satin lapels and Zella fastened his bow tie. The suit infused him with an air of confidence. As she turned the wheelchair around to roll Marty out of the bedroom, their eyes met in the reflection of the dresser mirror. Tears slid down her tanned cheeks. Her misty brown eyes and brilliant smile emanated an unfathomable love. To show solidarity, she wore a black T-shirt silk-screened with a picture of a tuxedo top and black pants. She remembered when Marty would stand tall, turning from side to side checking out his profile in the dresser mirror before bounding out the front door.

Zella backed his wheelchair into the bathroom and aligned it with a large chrome bar on the bathroom wall. He retained strength in his right arm and leg. Even after months of physical therapy, his left side was still paralyzed, a side effect of his malignant brain tumor. He reached out and clutched the bar, pushed himself out of the chair and stood up straight. He towered over Zella, a short, yet stately five feet, two inches. The crinkled coat and shirt cascaded down past his waist. Zella tucked in the shirt and straightened out his coat. She'd gracefully accepted the challenge to care for him without any nursing assistance. She had earned her caregiver merit raising five children into adulthood. Marty would often say, "I have to trust a mother of five" when relying on Zella.

"Ready?" she asked, primping Marty like it was his first day of school.

"I'm ready, baby," he responded.

Marty sat back down, and Zella kneeled to push on his white sneakers. She rolled him into the living room.

Zella walked out the front door, down the front porch steps, into the muggy air. She drove their green Saturn up to the porch and went back in to get her husband. She pushed Marty out the front door, helped him into the electronic chairlift, flipped on the switch, and accompanied him down the steps. At the bottom, she became his left side and helped him into the car. Throughout their relationship, he had always pointed out that they weren't joined at the hip—but that had changed.

"Hey, lefty," he said to Zella, who is left-handed, "now we're really joined at the hip."

Zella transferred him into the front seat and quickly settled into the driver's seat.

She revved the engine, then turned to Marty.

"It's showtime," Marty said with a smile.

THE PATH TO ACCEPTANCE

Six months earlier, in January 2001, the brain cancer announced itself. Marty and Zella escaped the bitter New Jersey winter and danced barefoot on the silver moonlit shore of Siesta Key, Florida. Music pulsed from the drum circle of musicians pounding on bongos and jamming on guitars. It was the weekend of Zella's sixty-second birthday. She beamed up at Marty as he twirled and dipped her on the wet sand. The waves crashed at their feet. Their six-week vacation in Florida had become a birthday tradition. This one was extra special because they were also celebrating Marty's clean bill of health. After a year of battling lymphoma cancer, he was in remission.

Both were in their sixties, but still gyrated their hips like teenagers to the music thumping on the beach. Marty began to feel seasick, like his equilibrium was off. He tried to hide the symptoms from Zella because he didn't want to spoil the fun. Marty hoped it would subside, but instead it became increasingly worse. The following weekend, he told Zella as they stood in the kitchen of their friend's Florida condo.

"I'm just not feeling right, Z," he said. Zella suggested they return home immediately to the physicians familiar with his cancer history. Marty dreaded returning to Jersey. He relished these trips. Marty often flirted with the idea of moving to the sunny state for winter escapes, but Zella was not fully retired like him. She still taught English at Montclair State University in New Jersey.

"Do we have to go home?" Marty asked in a vulnerable little boy's voice. "I wanna stay and play."

"Yes, M. We have to go," Zella cajoled in a concerned loving tone. "The doctors at home will take care of you better than the ones here."

"But I don't wanna go home," Marty cried. The couple often bantered, even in a possible crisis. Marty and Zella considered each other playmates. Their endearing nicknames, M and Z, inevitably surfaced in these mild exchanges. Marty eventually conceded. They packed the car and began the road trip home. On January 20, as they crossed the Washington, D.C., beltway, Zella turned on the radio and tuned in to a live broadcast of George W. Bush being sworn in as the forty-third president of the United States followed by his address.

"Do we have to listen to this?" Marty said. Zella insisted.

Marty hated bad news. He had even created his own all-good news radio show called *Good News with the Geltmans*, on EIES, Electronic Information Educational Service for the blind, in New Jersey. He vigilantly read many news publications every day, but cut out only the articles he judged as good news to read on his radio show. Volunteering virtually became a full-time job, a second career, for Marty. Outside of their weekly radio show broadcasts, the Geltmans assisted medical students by role-playing to enhance patient management skills at the University of Medicine and Dentistry of New Jersey. Similarly, they served in a troupe of volunteer actors called the Mental Health Players using role-playing and interactive audience participation to enhance the lives of community members dealing with challenging problems, such as difficult relationships. He and Zella were also active members of the Morristown Unitarian Fellowship, which was where they had first met on April Fool's Day eleven years prior.

If this wasn't enough, Marty also was an active volunteer at the Jewish Community Center and the patient advocate at the Daughters of Israel Nursing Home in West Orange. A vibrant model for retirees, he encouraged many of his friends to join him. His community service didn't go unnoticed. Locals stopped him on the street to ask if he was the mayor. When he said, "No," they'd often say, "Well, you should be." His former students chased him down at the mall or the grocery store to say hello and update "Mr. Geltman" on their achievements and lives beyond grade school. His social and civic activities had dipped when the lymphoma hit, so he was eager to get back in the swing of things. He worried that this obscure queasiness would land him back in the hospital.

Upon their return, Marty underwent many tests, but the physicians failed to link a diagnosis to his symptoms. Three weeks later, on an icy day in February, he and Zella welcomed visitors at the newcomers table in the atrium of the Morristown Unitarian Fellowship. For a few minutes Marty lost all control of his speech. He opened his mouth and the words failed to emerge. The lapse in speech alerted Marty's medical team to trace his random symptoms to possible brain failure. They performed a CAT scan and detected a glioblastoma, a malignant tumor, which would eventually impede his speech patterns and motor functions. The prognosis was a year to live at best without any treatment. Surgery to remove the mass could slow the deterioration of his mental capabilities but the odds for prolonging his death sentence were slim.

Zella and Marty sought out a neurosurgeon at Memorial Sloan Kettering in New York City. The consultation was on Monday, March 6. The weatherman forecasted a blizzard the weekend before, so Zella booked a hotel in the city to avoid getting snowed in and not being able to get out of Jersey for their appointment. On Sunday afternoon, they took in a movie and dined at the London Grill. Marty indulged in his favorite entrée, Surf and Turf. As they strolled the streets of New York, his arm around her shoulder and her arm around his waist, Marty stopped and turned to Zella.

"I'm complete, Z," he said. "These have been the best eleven years of my life."

The blizzard never arrived, but that weekend would be forever frozen in Zella's memory. That Sunday afternoon fortified their commitment to ride this rollercoaster whatever the outcome. The following day at Memorial Sloan Kettering, they set a date for brain surgery.

In the weeks leading up to the surgery, Marty prepared for the worse—he could enter a vegetative state, he could die. He called Reverend Paul Ratzlaff from the Fellowship. Marty and Zella had attended enough funerals to know that Paul delivered the life story and then invited members to the microphone to share memories. Marty chose to have his interview now to give Paul the highlights for a stellar eulogy. He reviewed his life and talked with Paul about his preparation for death. Marty studied Buddhism and was particularly comforted by the philosophy that his soul would live on and return to Earth.

Every morning he meditated. In the afternoons he cloistered himself in his office at home to update his documents and research end-of-life options and crematories. Marty also prepared his living will to name Zella as his healthcare proxy to make decisions for him in the event he became totally incapacitated. His living will stated clearly that he did not want his life to be artificially extended. Before the surgery, Marty reviewed the document with Zella, then left it on his desk for easy reference and direction.

On a cold day in March, Marty rolled into the surgery prep room for the brain operation at Memorial Sloan Kettering Hospital. Zella paced the waiting room floor. Finally, five hours later, Marty entered the recovery room. The doctors eagerly awaited his awakening. They didn't know which functions would still be intact and which ones would require rehabilitation. As Marty awoke from an unconscious state, he heard Zella talking to the doctors at the foot of his bed. He blinked his eyes and focused on four white coats standing in a circle around him.

"Whoops, there are too many white coats in here for me," he said. And everyone in the room laughed with relief. At least he still had his wit, Zella thought. The doctors asked him a battery of questions.

"What year is it?" one asked.

"Two thousand one," Marty said.

"Who's the president?" another questioned

"Do I have to answer that?" Marty quipped.

The following afternoon Marty was holding court in the waiting room of Sloan Kettering with a group of friends and close family members when his son Steve stepped out of the elevator. A younger, stockier version of Marty, Steve had his father's boyish looks and a full head of curly brown hair. He scoped the room and then called out.

"I'm looking for the man with the smallest brain." Marty raised his right hand and tilted back his head in laughter.

"That's me," Marty said.

Steve and his brother, David, had been estranged from their father for years after Marty and their mother divorced. Steve chose to reconcile with his father when he became a father himself because he wanted his daughters to have their grandfather.

Although Steve was working in Florida at the time, he committed to spending weekends with his father after the surgery. They forged a deeper relationship during these visits.

Marty was eventually transferred to the Morristown Memorial Rehabilitation Center in New Jersey. He had speech therapy classes in the mornings followed by physical therapy. The brain tumor had damaged some message systems, but not others. One Saturday afternoon, Steve walked in on Marty in the middle of occupational therapy. Marty was stacking blocks.

"What's next? Jacks?" Steve joked.

Marty laughed so hard, he nearly fell out of his wheelchair. Though there were moments of laughter, like this one, Marty felt like he was slipping into the abyss of institutional living. It became difficult for him to read, which felt like torture to a lifelong intellectual and teacher.

He was in rehab for two months. He even celebrated his sixty-fifth birthday in the hospital room, on April 28. He dressed up like a clown and wore a silly duck hat to surprise his granddaughters, nieces, and nephews. The costume deterred them from noticing his own deteriorated condition, but he couldn't hide the tears of his family members shocked by his condition. His left side was paralyzed. Honking his red nose, Marty explained to the children that not all tears meant sadness.

"Some people cry tears of happiness," he said, imparting wisdom on the children. Marty found it difficult to mask his stuttering speech.

Everyone realized that the surgery had been unsuccessful. Worse, Marty was stuck in the hospital, and he yearned to return home with Zella.

"I DON'T WANT TO BE A PATIENT ANYMORE"

He and Zella suffered long periods of silent tears together in the confines of that hospital room. A few days after his birthday, Marty began to talk to Zella about some end-of-life issues and his memorial service. He'd never recovered function of his left side. He felt there was just no reason to go on.

"I don't want to be a patient anymore, Z," he said to Zella as she sat on a cold vinyl chair next to his hospital bed. This was no life for them. As she stared into his weary eyes and pasty face, she thought about how horrible it would be to sit alone at his memorial service. She couldn't bear to think about it. Zella had lost her parents very early in life. She was only eleven years old when her mother died and just thirty-five when her father died. Both were sudden deaths, and she had always harbored feelings of wishing she'd spent more time with them and more fully expressed her appreciation of and feelings for them. The thought of losing Marty was overwhelming. Tears streamed down her face and then it dawned on her.

"Wait," she said. "Marty, I don't want to be at your memorial service months from now without you, hearing all those wonderful stories. Why don't we have a celebration, like Susan Schneider did?"

"Yeah," Marty said, perking up. "That's an excellent idea."

"I'll check out the book at the Fellowship and find a date when the meeting room will be available," Zella said.

LIVING FUNERAL LINEAGE

Back in 1993, Zella and Marty had participated in a Celebration of Life for Susan Schneider at their Fellowship. She was dying of breast cancer. Like Marty, Susan practiced massage, yoga, Buddhism, meditation, and alternative healing therapies. Although she was only forty-nine when the cancer seized her body, she decided against conventional treatment. Instead, she set out on a farewell tour, a road trip with her dog across the country, in a camper to visit friends and family. The trip culminated with a gathering of her closest friends and family members in the Fellowship.

Susan set up a circle of chairs and two rocking chairs in the middle of the octagon-shaped sanctuary. She sat on one rocking chair and reserved the other rocking chair beside her for people who wanted to speak at the intimate ceremony. About twenty-five people attended and delivered warm stories. There were tears of joy and sorrow coupled with laughter and hugs. Marty spoke at Susan's celebration. He and Zella were profoundly affected by the opportunity to reminisce with Susan in her final days. Everyone in the circle had the time and stage to say those sometimes difficult sentimental last words. Susan drank in every "I love you" and "You taught me to . . ." and all of the "I remember when . . ." memories. She died six days later and chose not to have any of the traditional funeral services.

Zella remembered Susan's life celebration each time she attended a funeral at the Fellowship. She always wished the departed ones had been honored while alive, like Susan, so they could hear the amazing tributes given at the open-microphone ceremony. These services steer away from the cookie-cutter funerals Zella attended in her youth, when most clergy delivered impersonal eulogies. Back then she had never wished the person being honored could hear what the clergy was saying, those often-canned eulogies sprinkled with clichés like "She was so full of life." In contrast, the open mic tributes of today are personal and intimate.

Rev. Paul Ratzlaff, the minister at the Morristown Unitarian Fellowship points out that these celebrations reflect the narcissism of his generation, the baby boomers.

He added, "It's useful for a person to have others participate in a celebration, and it helps us take stock of our own lives and learn who are the people we touched." The Morristown Unitarian's memorial services focus on the individual's life and accomplishments rather than a prescribed religious procedure. It believes in an interdenominational fellowship, in which members are encouraged to make their own individual value-system and adapt new rituals.

Gary Laderman, author of *Rest in Peace: A Cultural History of Death and the Funeral Home in Twentieth-Century America,* suggested the living funeral is more about the cult of personality than some kind of social structure or institutionalized rituals of the church.[1] The living funeral is a gathering to honor the life of the dying person before his or her death, in a social setting that invites all involved to express their love for, reflect on their memories of, and eulogize about the dying person. It is a reflection of a ritual anchored in individualism. In the words of sociologist David Moller, author of *Confronting Death: Values, Institutions, and Human Mortality,* "In both metaphoric and real way, individualism has become a modern type of religion."[2] He adds, "The modern rituals of the cult of individualism unite people in a common setting whereby individuals participate in reciprocal process of self-expression. A sense of well-being is generated by this process in that an opportunity is created to promote, represent, and assert one's self. And these rituals obviously reaffirm the legitimacy of the idea of individualism as a central value of the broader society."[3]

Although the living funeral may have grown out of this American value of individualism, in many ways the tributes are closely connected to and borrow from old Irish Catholic wake customs of celebrating the life of the departed. For centuries, Irish Catholics have gathered around the dead to tell funny stories, toast his or her life, and weep together. They light candles, drink Guinness, and indulge in feasts. They light a pipe full of tobacco and pass it around until plumes of smoke fill the room around the deceased. Seán Ó Súilleabháin suggests in *Irish Wake Amusements* that there are 134 games of lamentation dating back to Celtic rituals performed at the death of a warrior. Some common ones adapted into the Irish Catholic wake include storytelling, verbal sparring and fighting, and singing and dancing to the tunes of the bagpipe. Nina Witoszek and Pat Sheeran pointed out in *Talking to the Dead: A Study of Irish Funerary Traditions* that "the wake served as a social rehabilitation in which useless praise was expended on those who were denied a good word in life." The wake even had "the power to transmute, to bring the dead person out of anonymity, disgrace even, and transform him into a local legend."

Author Mark Twain portrays this transformation into a local legend when writing about his protagonist Tom, a naughty little boy who stages his death and eavesdrops on his own funeral in the classic *The Adventures of Tom Sawyer*. From a room in the back of the church, Tom hears glowing eulogies that talk about his winning ways, and he "confessed in his heart that it was the proudest moment of his whole life."

Celebrating with the dead, or in this case the soon-to-be-dead, is inherently an Irish custom, so it's not surprising that the first recorded living funeral celebrated the life of an Irish Catholic priest, Bob Ogle, on July 8, 1986. He invited eighty of his friends and family to St. Paul's Church in Ottawa. The fifty-seven-year-old Ogle held a living funeral right before he went into hospital for brain surgery. Ogle received his last rites publicly and a party ensued. It was strikingly similar to a wake with the guest of honor present.

But it was a brief passage in the bestselling book *Tuesdays with Morrie: An Old Man, a Young Man, and Life's Greatest Lesson* that popularized living funerals in America. More than five million copies are in print. It hit bookstores in 1997. Mitch Albom, the author and well-known sports writer, rekindles a relationship with his old sociology professor at Brandeis University, Morrie Schwartz, who is dying of Lou Gehrig's disease. The two meet for "class" every Tuesday for a lesson on how to keep living while dying. In the second chapter of the book, entitled "The Syllabus," Morrie is depressed when he returns home from a colleague's funeral.

"What a waste," he says. "All those people saying all those wonderful things and Irv never got to hear any of it." And so he made some calls and set a date. A small group of friends gathered at his home in West Newton for a living funeral.

Albom goes on to describe the event: "Each of them spoke and paid tribute to my old professor. Some cried. Some laughed. Morrie cried and laughed with them. And all those heartfelt things we never get to say to those we love, Morrie said that day. His living funeral was a rousing success." [4]

It was in the winter of 1998 when I came across *Tuesdays with Morrie* and first read about the concept of a living funeral. The ritual intrigued me because it epitomized a dying person's acceptance of the imminence of death, the refusal of which was my father's failure in his final hour. And I wasn't the only one touched by Morrie's living funeral—that simple account inspired many people approaching death to reinvent their own celebrations of life. Since the book's release in 1997, living funerals, or living wakes, have been reported in New York, New Jersey, Florida, Wisconsin, Missouri, Colorado, and California. The book remained on *The New York Times* best-seller's list for four years. Oprah Winfrey produced a television movie called *Tuesdays with Morrie* based on the book. A scene in the movie portrays the finale of Morrie's living funeral with a performance by a group of gospel singers and Morrie reciting a poem. The movie won an Emmy.

"Morrie made an age-old tradition new and trendy," said Megory Anderson, a scholar in the field of religious studies and dying rites at the University of San Francisco, in an interview with me about the advent of living funerals. She added, "The book showed people a living funeral was a good idea and that it's okay to do it. But the idea behind that—i.e., to come together, to support the person dying, and to really express how much the person meant in your life before he goes—is a tradition that dates back two centuries."[5]

Early forms of these living funerals were called "sendoffs," said Dr. Tony Bell, a sociologist of death and dying at California State University, Fullerton. In the eighteenth and nineteenth centuries, these sendoffs were known as a ceremony of the death in bed, in which the dying person presided over a crowd of friends and relatives.[6] The dying person said his or her last words, sometimes dramatized by long-winded speeches to pass on wisdom to the next generation. The tradition disappeared in the early 1900s, when the place of death moved from the home to the hospital. Death in a hospital was not an occasion for a ritual. The dying person became just a body in decline as the doctors assumed control over the deathbed scene. Feelings expressed at the bedside became repressed. This pattern of taboo and avoidance can cause friends and relatives, as well as caregivers, to abandon the patient, creating a kind of "social death" before the biological death occurs.

A living funeral disintegrates that social death with a gathering of family, relatives, and friends to pay tribute to the person who will soon die. Guests are invited by mail, phone calls, and email. The ceremonies take place in private homes, churches, hotel banquet rooms, and community centers. People with terminal illnesses orchestrate the events from their deathbeds. They arrange the guest list, menu, music, and entertainment. Some invite clergy and hospice chaplains to attend and publicly perform the last rites, whereas others just request friends and family members to recite psalms.

PLANNING A LIVING FUNERAL

On a warm May afternoon, Zella arrived at Marty's hospital room and announced, "Marty Geltman's Life Celebration is set for June 23." Marty buzzed with excitement. They had six weeks to prepare the grandest celebration of his life. Zella noticed color returning to Marty's face as they brainstormed about the guest list and entertainment. The upcoming party gave him focus and a reason to push forward. His despondency turned to the exuberance.

That evening, after Zella returned home from the hospital, Marty called. He percolated with ideas and couldn't possibly wait till the following day to share them with Zella.

"Hey, Z, we should get our friends to perform," Marty said. "And we'll get John Conte to play Pachelbel."

John Conte was the musical director at the fellowship. Johann Pachelbel's Canon in D was Marty's favorite piece of classical music. It's a familiar piece, often played at life rituals like weddings, but also often played at funerals. In a way it was perfect because this celebration was a rite of passage for Marty. He was publicly marking his decision to stop fighting for his life and make peace with his death.

He gradually shattered the hospital barriers that isolated him from his family and community. He reconnected by reaching out to call friends and family members to invite them. Each day Zella arrived at the rehab, he had a list of ideas and people he thought should attend. He wanted his comedian friend, Gerry Nussbaum, to start off the show with "a bit," a stand-up routine, so everyone would know it was meant to be a jolly going-out party, not a somber farewell gathering. He suggested Zella and he perform an opening skit using all his best one-liners, which she had been compiling over the past few months. Marty proudly owned the role of director in this production. Zella was his producer. She called their closest friends and relatives. She had a little spiel. First, she would mention that she and Marty had recently attended a funeral and the honoree missed all the great stories, then she would explain that Marty wanted to have a celebration now. "You can either toast him or roast him," she would say with a chuckle. "We want to have the celebration while he's still here."

Their couples' group, called the Amigos, promised Zella they'd put together a dynamite skit for Marty. Zella and Marty's best friends, Victor and Grace Sperber, asked Zella if they could be the opening act. After talking with their friends, she called Marty's sister, Harriett Popper, and her family in Florida. Then she called his son Steve in Pennsylvania. Although a funeral before his dad died sounded wacky to him, he agreed to participate. She also invited his younger son, David.

One week before the celebration, Marty slipped into severe tremors and out of consciousness. Zella thought she might lose him, but he came to after a few hours, murmuring repeatedly, "June 23, June 23." His health ebbed. Family members began to wonder if the celebration would end up becoming a funeral.

INTERPRETATIONS OF A PRE-DEATH CEREMONIAL FAREWELL

The living funeral, or final farewell gathering, can be a catalyst for restoring estranged relationships. In the 1990s, so many young men were dying of AIDS and their unconventional lives clashed with traditional funeral rites. So they designed their own. Many of these young men chose to throw a farewell party before death and then chose to be cremated with no services. The autobiographical film *It's My Party*, written and directed by Randal Kleiser, tells the story of his partner's battle with AIDS and the choice to have a farewell party after discovering he had an irreversible brain disorder that would render him insensible. The protagonist, Nick Stark, a forty-year-old architect dying of AIDS, calls all of his friends to say, "There won't be any wake or funeral, so come now." When someone arrives wearing all black, Nick immediately jumps all over her, saying, "Why are you wearing black? This isn't a funeral, it's a fiesta."

The gathering becomes a bittersweet festivity of farewell, toasting, dancing, laughing, and storytelling. Nick has one last dance with his mother and reconciles with his father after twenty years of estrangement. His father confesses, "I'm sorry, I was not a good father to you." Nick stops him and says, "You were a good father when I was young. You gave me my first watercolor set." Nick goes on to say that the watercolor set inspired him to become a professional artist.

A similar theme of reconciliation is portrayed in the film *The Weather Man*, screenplay by Steven Conrad. Shortly after Robert Spritzel, played by Michael Caine, is diagnosed with terminal cancer, his wife throws a black-tie living funeral that commences with a warm reception, where the guest of honor, Robert, is seen swooping up his granddaughter in a hug and greeting all of his colleagues in a parlor atmosphere of a grand hotel in Chicago. The event then turns to a sit-down dinner followed by speeches. Robert's son, David Spritz, played by Nicolas Cage, is introduced to say a speech in front of an audience of more than a hundred guests. His speech leads to a reconciliation between father and son.

THE LIVING FUNERAL: A CELEBRATION OF LIFE

At one o'clock in the afternoon on June 23, Zella and Marty, in their green Saturn, pulled into the driveway of a red brick Georgian mansion trimmed with white accents. Maple and oak trees shaded the brick pathways trailing the mansion grounds, which were covered in rose gardens and lush flower patches. The mansion had been converted into a sanctuary and community center for the Morristown Unitarian Fellowship. Wheelchair and all, Marty made a grand red carpet entrance through the double doors and into a crowd of close friends and relatives gathered in the atrium.

"Marty's here," voices echoed through the atrium. The guests lavished him with hugs and kisses. His son Steve, his daughter-in-law Patti, and his granddaughters, Lilli and Izzi, greeted him. Marty threaded through the crowd of friends, family, and colleagues. He was famous for his bear hugs, which all his friends had come to expect upon seeing him. He reunited with colleagues from elementary school and some high school buddies. Marty received rave reviews on his tuxedo-and-sneaker ensemble. He savored every minute in the limelight.

Many were shocked at Marty's condition. Zella aimed to get the celebration started immediately, before Marty's energy drained. She rolled Marty into the sanctuary, which was bursting with sunlight pouring through the long, column-like windows. The room was set like a dome theater, with rows of about 200 chairs facing a wooden platform. She parked Marty center stage; to his left was a piano and on his right, a lectern adorned with the Star of David, the cross, and the yin and yang. An altar decorated with balloons and flowers was set up behind him. He waved and smiled as his friends and relatives flowed in and took their seats.

As everyone settled in, a friend wired Marty with a small microphone. He beamed at his guests. Zella stepped on stage with a handheld microphone.

"Say something to test it out," she urged Marty.

"I don't even know how to express how much we love you all. We are both so happy that you all could come," he said. His eyes widened. He stared out into the room, every seat filled—more than 150 friends and family had come to celebrate his life.

He could only say, "Wow," before twisting his words. He could hear his garbled speech transmitting across the room. He stopped talking. His speech was unpredictable because the brain tumor often caused interference. Zella quickly covered up the distortion by talking into her microphone.

"We decided to have this celebration today, as Marty was in an unusual situation dealing with a catastrophic terminal illness," Zella said. "And he was talking about the memorial serv—"

"Terminal?" Marty said, butting in. "What? Is that why we're here? I'm not going anywhere. Unh-unh."

He raised his right hand in a stop gesture. Zella swiveled from foot to foot and looked out to the audience. She shrugged her shoulders and tossed her hair. "I was counting on him doing that today, giving me surprises. Is there a way we can turn him off?" she said. "Anyway, I said to Marty, 'I don't really want to sit in the meeting room, which is this room we're in right now, at some point down the road and listen to all these great stories at your memorial service without you.' So now we have this guy here, so he can hear what we plan to carry on."

Zella curled into a chair next to Marty. She shared some of the adventures of her great love affair with Marty from the day they first met, to the white water river rafting, to dune buggy riding and sharing grandparenthood. She began talking about their most recent trial—Marty's battle with brain cancer. Marty had rehearsed rattling off punch lines to each anecdote, and so Zella shared the story of sitting in the consultation with the best neurosurgeon in the country.

"I asked, 'How long will he be in surgery?' and the doctor answered, 'Five hours,'" Zella said. She paused. It was Marty's cue to deliver his line, but when he opened his mouth out poured a bunch of jumbled sounds. He frowned with frustration. He shook his head and tried one more time, and it was worse than the first.

"And Marty said, 'Do you charge by the hour?'" Zella piped in.

The audience shook with laughter. Marty smiled with relief. Showman that he was, he easily disguised his frustration. As she illuminated Marty's spirited effort to make light of his brain cancer, he started to loosen up and he noticed the audience did, too. Zella then turned over the show to members of the audience. She requested people come to the stage and share their Marty stories.

Marty and Zella's friends, the Sperbers—Grace, a dainty blonde in her sixties, and Victor, a smiling ruddy-faced gentleman—popped on their white top hats and stormed the stage. They danced like a couple of smash Broadway musical entertainers while singing the tune "Hello Dolly," but with a twist.

> Hello, Marty!
> Well, hello, Marty!
> It's so good to have you back where you belong.
> You keep hugging, you keep kissing, you keep holding on!
> You can hear us saying
> We have fun playing.
> So, here's our hats, Marty,
> You're as good as it gets, Marty,
> You and Zella will always be our friends.

As they repeated the final note, they threw their arms out and tipped their hats to Marty. The warm welcome-home song reminded Marty that he really was no longer a patient anymore. He was the Master of Ceremonies.

Zella's eldest son, Bobby Pollack, chose to speak on behalf of her children. He was the closest to Marty. Bobby took the seat on stage next to Marty's wheelchair. He was noticeably nervous, wiping his sweaty palms on his jeans. He shared some of the funny stories of watching his mother, whom he referred to as Mother Goose, primping in the mirror to go out on a date with Marty. He reflected on how they fell instantly in love, like two puppy-love teenagers. He was amazed that his mother found someone with as much energy as she had. Then he turned to Marty.

"You definitely take on a handful when you marry someone with five kids," Bobby said.

"A handful," Marty agreed, his words now coming out intact. Zella pulled another chair up on stage to give her son some support.

"Look at Marty," she said to him.

"I don't know if I can," Bobby said. He was fighting back tears. Bobby held on to Marty's arm and looked at him for a short minute and then turned back to the audience.

"We say dignity is so important. It's easy to be dignified when things are going great, your car is clean, you get up in the morning, and you feel okay. You can do what you want to do. But it's a whole other thing to be dignified when you are thrown something really tough," he said, pausing. "It has been breathtaking to watch you. I will take it with me."

Bobby embraced Marty, and as Bobby stood up, Marty pulled him back down and they hugged again. Marty hadn't wanted his production to get too sentimental. In theory, he thought everyone would just roast him. As a jokester, that's what he wanted, but after Bobby spoke, he realized that this celebration would not be as easy as he'd envisioned. Fortunately, he had made arrangements for his comedian friends from his volunteer acting troupe, the Mental Health Players, to interrupt the festivities with some random acts of comedy to bounce the mood. He refused to allow his celebration to flop. But he wouldn't deny himself the rare opportunity to know how he had made an impression on the lives of those he loved.

Michael Popper, Marty's nephew, chose not to deliver a eulogy for fear of sounding morose. He knew Marty didn't want that. So he kept his tribute light and short. He took the stage with his wife, Mo Barnett, and shared that Marty was always the "weird uncle" of the family. Every family has one. But as Michael matured, he came to realize that Marty was the "cool uncle," a trailblazer. With those words, he presented Marty with a plaque engraved with "Best Uncle Award" from all of his nieces and nephews in the audience.

Best Uncle Award
presented to
Marty Geltman

For Outstanding Humor, Kindness,
And Dedication to the Popper Family

The intimate stories shared by Marty's family illuminated a side of him that most of his friends never knew; simultaneously, Marty's friends spotlighted his days of free love, his humanitarian works, his devotion to teaching, and his constant quest for personal growth. Zella also read letters from friends across the country unable to attend. Most of his family had never known that he and Zella were members of a couples group that met every six weeks for themed costume dinner parties that consisted of experiential role-playing skits, intimate talk therapy, and games. For eight years, the Amigos supported each other through the challenges of marriage, empty-nest syndrome, aging, and retirement. One of the Amigos shared the story of their group and then called the other couples on stage. The five couples, Marty and Zella's friends, paraded in a conga line wearing ponchos and sombreros, shaking their wooden maracas, and singing the song "Amigos" with a twist—they had rewritten the lyrics to share some funny Marty memories that they'd never forget.

John Conte, the fellowship musical director, slowed the festive mood with the opening notes of Johann Pachelbel's Canon in D on the piano. Marty could no longer hold in his emotions. Tears poured down his face as he closed his eyes and rocked his head, letting the music infuse him.

As planned, in this quiet moment Zella told a story. She shared Marty's favorite fable of a peasant boy running along the edge of a mountainside with a ferocious tiger on his heels, when suddenly he stumbled and slid off the cliff. As he tumbled down the mountainside, he caught a tree branch. As he dangled from the tree, he spotted a strawberry patch growing on the ledge and reached up to pluck a strawberry. He popped it in his mouth and plunged to his death. "That is the most delicious strawberry I ever ate," he said on the way down. To Marty, each tribute, each note of music, each hug was like that strawberry. In the midst of his meditative reflections, Marty's son Steve joined him on stage. In choosing not to acknowledge one another as father and son, they'd wasted so many years. Steve had even pretended Marty was dead. Now, that illusion had become a reality soon to be reckoned with. Steve traced his father's outline in a wheelchair in front of an audience of family and friends. He felt strangely surreal sitting with his father at his memorial.

"For those of you who don't know me, I'm Steven, Marty's oldest son. I want to thank you all for coming. My dad has really been looking forward to this." Then Steve turned his attention from the audience to his father. "But, Dad, I thought you said that you had a lot of friends."

Marty started laughing at his son, and the full house, more than 150 close friends and family, shook with laughter along with him. It definitely lightened the moment.

"Life takes us all on interesting journeys, and every family has its ups and downs—and ours is no different," Steve said, as a mischievous smirk illuminated his face. "This incredible turn of events takes me back about three months ago, when I got a phone call from my dad. We normally talk all the time, but rarely does he call me at my mom's house in Florida. My dad asked if I was sitting down. I replied, 'Do I need to be?' He said, 'Yes.' He then informed me of the magnitude of his health problems. However, through it all, the surgery at Sloan, the rehab in Morristown, and now at home . . . the sex change operation went quite well."

The whole audience burst into laughter. Steve was a showman, a natural comedian just like his father. He then turned away from the audience, shed his jest, and looked at his father.

"Dad your upbeat attitude, humor, and courage has helped all of us deal with this situation the best we can. Like everyone in the room, I wish we had more time to spend together. I love you," he said.

That was the first time Marty had heard those words from his son in more than a decade. His other son, David, did not give a tribute, but came with his family, who were all sitting in the front row. Marty's life celebration not only magnified his accomplishments but also maybe some of his mistakes.

Judy, Marty's colleague from Gaudineer Elementary School, reminded Marty of the wonder years with his sons. She worked with Marty for three decades and taught both Steve and David. She pointed out that Marty always attended his sons' baseball games—was often a coach—and exalted him for being a good father and teacher.

"I've known Marty so long, he had a full head of hair when we met," Judy chuckled. "Whatever Marty did, he did with his whole heart. He got involved with every kind of activity even then—many kids today surely remember him."

She spoke about Marty's dedication to teaching. He worked many tireless hours inside and outside the classroom. He tutored his students after school and on weekends. "If anything went wrong at school, we always used to blame Marty. Once again, ladies and gentleman, Marty has done it today. He has brought us all here today to laugh and share with him, and for that I love him. Thank you, Marty."

Marty beamed. His crowning moment, though, came when his men's group joined him on stage. They were all in their fifties and sixties, most with bifocals, bald heads, and bellies. They spoke of how Marty always gave the best bear hugs. And how at first it scared many of them because "men don't publicly express emotion and affection." They reminded Marty that his greatest legacy—teaching the men to express their feelings and affection—would live on in the men's group, week after week, year after year. Marty was their inspiration to get in touch with their sensitive side and nurture deeper connections with their wives and families. Marty couldn't hold back his emotions. A few tears trickled down his cheeks. He was so proud of the men. He hoped all of the younger men in the audience, and especially his sons, were paying attention.

Marty received three lifetime achievement awards for his years dedicated to volunteer service. He reveled in being the star of the show and center of attention. All of his life work was honored through awards and tributes, his dedication to friends and family glimpsed through poetry and song, his love for the theater and comedy reflected through the shtick and skits. Marty was proud of his life. He toned down his glee as his sister sat in the chair next to him. He looked at her with the wide eyes of a little boy. She was seven years his senior. Losing her younger brother was, in a word, wrenching. She looked at him and her eyes blurred. She carried a sheet of paper with the lyrics she'd written for Marty. They had no other siblings. She set her feelings aside, so that she might bestow a memorable parting gift. She sang a lovely song for him.

You're the top, you're my favorite brother.
You're the top, there is no other.
You're a super guy, a humanitarian.
You're the top.

After the celebration, there was a receiving line of people bidding Marty farewell. Some lined up to get in one last chuckle before he departed. He told his friends that they had just received his last lesson: to show people how to die, which Marty believed was to focus on the art of living while dying. At that moment, he rose above the wheelchair, his speech impediment, and his paralyzed left side. He was a luminary, totally intoxicated by the surge of adoration.

LIVING FUNERAL THEMES

These gatherings have taken on so many different formats. The mood, atmosphere, and tone are directed by the honoree. Some families have chosen to rename these gatherings a living wake, a celebration of life, and a friendship service because the term "funeral" is off-putting to the dying and their families. They don't want to feel like they are prematurely burying their loved ones.

Like most funeral directors I interviewed, John Hogan, former president of the National Funeral Directors' Association, believes living funerals are still a novelty for funeral directors because they're traditionally called upon post-death.[7] Over his forty-three years devoted to the funeral business, Hogan has become highly adaptive to the needs of his clients at Fogarty Funeral Home in New York City. He recalled fondly a gentleman in his sixties with cancer who, in 2002, came in to organize his funeral arrangements and then made the odd request of renting out the visitation room to have a party before his death. On the day of the living wake, Hogan entered the room, usually reserved to lay out the dead in a casket for a viewing, to find the soon-to-be-departed sitting on a big chair, like a king on a throne surrounded by his court. The room reverberated with laughter, stories, and tributes all afternoon.

On the other side of America, Sharon Mace, a funeral director in Northern California, began offering these ceremonies for the soon-to-be-departed, which she calls living memorials, in 2003 when she left a traditional funeral home to open her own business. A Special Touch Funeral Home and Cremation Service focuses more on the memorialization and personalization of funerary rituals.

She's arranged a few living memorials for pre-need clients with terminal illnesses. Pre-need clients are those who choose to plan and pay for their funeral arrangements before they die, so as not to leave the burden to family members. Sharon has seen a dramatic increase in the trend toward individuals choosing to preplan their own funeral. A woman in her fifties dying of cancer who came in to arrange her cremation and buy twenty keepsake urns to gift to her family and friends was the inspiration. Sharon suggested she give the urns to her family and friends before at a farewell party. Together they wrote the invitations, which included the request that everyone bring something that evoked memories of the honoree. On an autumn evening, amid the vineyards of Napa Valley, about forty family members and friends gathered. After the supper, the revelers sat around in a circle and shared the reasons they brought their little mementos: one was a seashell and the friend spoke about a perfect day spent with the honoree on the Santa Cruz boardwalk. Others brought photographs of special moments they'd shared that will forever remain in their memories.

Sharon also planned a living memorial that took place in a banquet room at the Hilton Hotel in Dublin. The honoree was a doctor and immigrant from the Philippines. The doctor had a terminal illness and came in to arrange her cremation. She quietly talked of how disappointed she was that most of her family and friends from the Philippines would probably wait until the funeral to come. Sharon suggested she have a pre-death funeral. More than a hundred people filled the banquet room at Christmastime 2006. Every table had a white tablecloth and a centerpiece made up of the honoree's favorite flowers. Each place setting had a small card with these words at the top: "I always wished I'd told you . . ." and on the reverse at the top: "I always wished we'd done . . ." After they dined, the honoree's three sisters sang a song, played a slideshow of her life, and one at a time gave a tribute. They opened the microphone for others to talk and then the champagne flowed. They all toasted to her life.

"It was like a big wedding reception," Sharon said. "It felt like a cross between a wedding and funeral."

Novelty or not, the living funeral is an offshoot of the funeral establishment's gradual move from mourning a death toward celebrating a life. The National Funeral Directors' Association launched a campaign in the opening years of the twentieth-first century called Celebrate a Life.

The traditional, cookie-cutter service has been rejected by people desiring to individualize their funerals. Lengthy nontraditional lay eulogies are replacing having the clergy say a few words of remembrance about the dearly departed in part because families have grown discontented with the funeral service's eclipsing the story of the individual who died. In 2003, Robert Vandenbergh, a past president of the National Funeral Directors' Association, said to a *Wall Street Journal* reporter, "Before 1980, fewer than 10 percent of funerals included a eulogy by someone other than a clergyman. By 1990, the percentage had risen to about 25 percent. Now, it's in excess of 50 percent."[8]

James Hitchcock, a St. Louis University historian who has written on the changing trends of eulogies in American funerals, attributes the changes to two flashpoints in the twentieth century: the extinction of the belief that the funeral is a time reserved for the mourners to pray for the soul in purgatory to expiate their sins and go on to heaven and the Second Vatican Council issuing a reform in the funeral rites titled "Order of Christian Funerals" in 1971 that was revised in 1985 to say that any person is permitted to say "a few words in remembrance of the deceased."

"Since it doesn't say one person, the law can be interpreted," said John Melloh, a Catholic priest and theologian who specializes in death rituals.[9] "Like many of Vatican II reforms, they were just responding to the modern world."

I spoke to Justin Holcomb, an Episcopalian priest and sociologist in the field of death and dying, to widen the scope on the shift toward personalizing funerary celebrations. He believes larger cultural patterns that characterize contemporary American society, such as religious pluralism, declining community ties, and heightened individualism, are the drivers of this change.[10]

Gary Laderman pointed to the 1963 release of *The American Way of Death*, Jessica Mitford's account of the corruption in the funeral industry. The book led to an investigation of the funeral industry by the Federal Trade Commission and was the impetus for many changes in America's death rituals. Suddenly, the old customs and authorities were no longer honorable.

"It broke apart in a lot of ways, since the 1960s and 1970s, when the shift went from institutional figures, like funeral directors, to a more democratic kind of understanding of who has the authority to lead funerals," Laderman said.[11] "Like so many elements of our consumer culture, it really has shifted to the consumers themselves."

The rise of the informed consumer movement clobbered the funeral industry. Neither the churches nor the funeral directors could persuade consumers to go back to traditional models.

THE FUNERAL AFTER THE LIVING FUNERAL

Marty glowed for weeks after the celebration. He played back the tributes, poems, and songs in his mind. He and Zella hung all of his lifetime achievement awards, which turned his home office into a shiny hall of fame. He held court most days with friends and family. Both of his sons, Steve and David, came to the house to spend time with their father before his last breath. Marty felt truly complete.

In his last days, he reclined in a hospital bed, but it was in the familiar bosom of his home. Zella cared for him without any assistance from hospice. She filled the five-disc CD player in their bedroom with Marty's favorite classical music.

"I knew I had to be dying before you would put on all classical," Marty said.

Marty Geltman passed away August 15, 2001. Throngs of people turned out for a traditional Jewish funeral at Menorah Chapels in Milburn, New Jersey. All of his friends and family attended the funeral to pay their respects, but there was no comparison to his life celebration. Instead of laughter, wails of grief echoed throughout the audience in the Jewish funeral home. The eulogies were filled with sorrow and re-membrance. The most important distinction was Marty's absence. Zella melded both ceremonies in the eulogy when she sang these last words.

This is a song for my husband Marty
He loved to play and have a party
This is to say I admire you so
I'll take you with me wherever I go.

THREE Her Life Review: Reliving the Past in the Present

My mother granted my wish to return to England—just not in the way I'd envisioned. Our pilgrimage to her birthplace began the chilly October evening after Dr. Garcia breathed the word "hospice." I nestled into a rocking chair by Mom's bed and pushed the record button on my tape recorder. Retracing her life's journey felt increasingly more valuable than moving forward at this juncture. We were in no rush to get to hospice.

You often hear that when you lose your parents, you lose your past, which could explain my growing anxiety to learn about my roots and the grandparents who both died before I could meet them. My mother's history was in fact my history, on the verge of being lost like my father's. In my selfish endeavor to collect her life stories and navigate through my anticipatory grief, I unwittingly tapped into my mother's life review, defined as a looking-back process set in motion by looking forward to death.[1] Dr. Robert Butler, known as the father of gerontology, defined life review as "a naturally occurring, universal mental process characterized by the progressive return to consciousness of past experiences and, particularly, the resurgence of unresolved conflicts; simultaneously and normally, these revived experiences and conflicts can be surveyed and reintegrated."[2]

When I read Butler's first studies on life review, my mother's words echoing her past conflicts—the divorce that disintegrated her family and the bank hostage crisis that crippled her twenty-seven-year career in banking—resonated. I was no longer insulted by her response to my question "What was the most memorable moment of your life?" I shared these stories with Dr. Butler in an interview after I'd transcribed Mom's interviews. He helped me to understand that I wasn't just collecting memories of her life; instead, I'd taken on the role of listener in her life review. It was a complex self-analysis and evaluative process. Recording a life review through interview amplifies, triggers, and taps into the life being lived in reverse as a person takes inventory of his or her life. The life review is often an inner dialogue and has been described as a movie replaying scenes of one's life, except the screen is in your mind rather than a theater. I extracted the vivid pivotal life moments that shaped the social and psychological DNA of my mother as her life culminated.

RECORDING HER LIFE STORY

My mother's bedside became a portal into various dimensions of time where I met my mother as a child, a teenager, and a young adult, all named Linda.

So what are some of your fondest childhood memories going back as far as you can?" I asked.

Her bedroom ebbed as she and I returned to her childhood home. If we'd physically visited England, I'd have missed the rich nuances and inner emotions as we traveled on a mesmerizing inward journey reflected through her lens. Immediately, I noticed her voice heighten and a look of wonderment shining on her face, like that of a five-year-old girl creeping out of her bedroom into the family room of her small, dark house in Manchester on Christmas morning. Her eyes widened as she described spotting the red tricycle parked beneath the tree. The giddiness turned to disappointment and then tears as she recalled pedaling around the front garden on her tricycle.

"It wasn't even a new bike. My parents were so poor they'd bought it secondhand, cleaned it up, and painted it red," she said. As a child, everything she owned was old and used. She hated the hand-me-downs, especially the faded brown and gray uniforms that were two sizes too big for her tiny physique. She cringed when remembering the schoolchildren mocking the tattered uniforms that hung off her small frame. Linda was already the smallest girl in the classroom at Parkview School. The clothes magnified this imperfection and made school a miserable place. Her timid nature exacerbated the other children's teasing.

The little-to-no-sunshine days in dreary, soot-covered Manchester after the war darkened her path as she walked home from school underneath the roaring railway bridge in the early 1950s. She lived in a small house overgrown with weeds at the corner of Hampden Road in Prestwich, a village near Manchester.

"I used to walk past my house because I dreaded the other schoolchildren seeing it," she said.

Instead of stopping her recollections for fear of slipping down a black memory hole, I held her hand and "accompanied" her.

"What embarrassed you about your house?" I asked.

Linda's mum, Grace, never tidied the house, and her dad, Norman, used the living room as his office space, so it was packed from floor to ceiling with paperwork from his printing press business. I felt a shudder of disgust, as if I were standing beside the helpless little girl yearning for order in a damp, unkempt, cramped home. The only furniture was tattered and secondhand, and bill collectors were constantly knocking at her door.

Without any direction from me, Mom lifted herself and me out of the dark hours of childhood and traveled to summertime. My mother recalled the last day of school in July, which commenced the yearly ritual of packing for the family's six-week camping trip. Her parents served as Cub Scout leaders in the local chapter, so together they wielded superior camping skills. The smell of the luggage, a musty, leathery scent, tumbled out of the closet and awakened a tingling of excitement in young Linda. The scent evoked reflections of last year's camping trip and awakened an eager anticipation for the daily activities of farm life. On the train, young Linda felt like a big balloon about to burst as Manchester receded from sight, giving way to the countryside rolling out like a green patchwork blanket.

My mother suggested we look at pictures of her camping trips in Hatfield in her family photo album. Norman, a stocky five-foot-seven bespectacled man looked like a small Frankenstein next to his tall, slender, elegant wife, who stood at nearly five feet, eleven inches. These black-and-white photographs showed Linda's older brother, Barry, a pudgy, fair-skinned boy with his belly poking out from under his shirt, holding her hand and leading her around the campground. He was six years older than she and her protector. Linda, at that time maybe three feet tall, was a freckle-faced child with red locks. I'd seen the photographs before, but never listened to such vivid narration.

When they arrived at the farm, the family pitched the tents. Linda especially liked her own tent, where she could play house with her dolls.

"I can smell inside the tent right now," she said taking a whiff. "It was my own little world."

Linda especially cherished hiking with her mother through the countryside. She held her mother's hand and passed by the milking farms where calves capered about. The pair meandered through the fields full of blooming wildflowers painting the countryside lavender, blue, pink, and white. She picked small bouquets of buttercups, pinky-white daisies, and bluebells. She listened to the song of the skylark, flying high above in the clear sunny sky.

"What was your mom like?" I asked.

Grace Lyons, my grandmother, was born in 1912, the youngest of the wealthy Lyons family's seven children. She glided instead of walked and always dressed in a suit, as though she were just stepping out of a chapel on Sunday. Grace didn't seem of this world. Her nickname was Faye, meaning fairy, given to her by her older sister Lillian. Grace was a classical violinist.

"She would have been better off traveling with the orchestra," Mom said.

Grace grew up in a large estate overlooking a leafy park in the middle of Manchester, which eventually was converted into a block of flats. Their manor hummed with servants at all hours of the day and had living quarters in which to house them. The Lyons family owned a chain of grocery stores in England. Grace's parents died when she was fourteen years old, and the three Lyons brothers took charge of the family business. The sons kept the books so poorly that gradually the chain of stores closed, and the once well-off family slid into poverty, which ultimately forced Grace to leave school. The Lyons family turned out to be better artists than businessmen. James Lyons became a poet and published two books. After leaving school, with seemingly little direction, Grace toured around England by bicycle and became a camping enthusiast, which was a bit liberal for a woman at that time. She met Norman while serving as a Cub Scout leader in Manchester.

Grace and Norman were worlds apart, but shared the same outdoor lifestyle. They married just before Norman left for Africa to serve in the British Armed Forces during World War II. Grace grew up with servants and had studied literature, writing, and classical violin. She created beautiful prose and music, but she knew nothing of how to use a hoover (vacuum), duster, mop, or sponge. Young Linda was constantly tidying the house while Grace spent her days writing fairy tales, journaling, and making music. When Norman was out, Grace filled the house with her angelic voice, singing songs and often playing the violin for Linda.

"What about your father?" I asked.

My mother decided we'd come to a stopping point in the interview that evening. The question quite obviously stirred unwelcome emotions in her.

LIFE REVIEW REVELATIONS, COMPONENTS, AND INSTRUMENTS

The first interview after Dr. Garcia announced a shortened list of options astounded me. It was different from the interviews we'd recorded in the past. Her fresh depth and ability to excavate such sensory-rich stories from her past was uncanny. Dr. Butler talked about the very same experience he had when first discovering life review as a young doctor fresh out of Columbia University medical school. He was researching a community residence of healthy seniors with James Birren, a pioneer in gerontology, for the National Institutes of Health and found himself engaged in interviews that recorded the spellbinding journeys of these elderly people reviewing their past lives.

Physical triggers such as scrapbooks, photo albums, old letters, and other memorabilia can set off a life review. A physical trip, pilgrimages to locations of meaning—birthplace, childhood home, school—and visits to family and friends to collectively reminisce helps a person rediscover his or her own past. Evocative questions can stimulate a return to these places without the dying person ever having to leave the bed. Barbara Haight, professor emeritus at the College of Nursing, Medical University of South Carolina, developed a Life Review and Experiencing Form that deeply guides the process of life review, covering death, grief, fear, religion, school, hardships, sex, work, and relationships over an entire lifespan.[3]

In retrospect, had I been cautioned about or even known what life review was, I probably would have trod more carefully. Instead, I stumbled through the crowded basement of her memories, pulled out the files in the dusty cabinets, and helped her reorganize and synthesize her life. Dr. Butler points out that the emotions accompanying the life review vary, but an element of pain and discomfort often arises as problems surface.

Dr. Butler explains the benefits of completing a life review in "Life Review: An Interpretation of Reminiscence in the Aged." "Reorganization of past experiences may provide a more valid picture, giving new and significant meaning to one's life: it may also prepare one for death, mitigating one's fears."[4] And in an article published in *Geriatrics,* Butler and Myrna Lewis state: "People can become ready to die but in no hurry to die."[5] The future becomes less critical as the present is emphasized. Butler and Lewis gave us the knowledge that "when people resolve their life conflicts, they achieve elementality, a lively capacity to live in the present."[6] They indulge in basic pleasures, such as nature, children, forms, colors, warmth, love, and humor. Life review can engender hard-won serenity, atonement, wisdom, and a philosophical acceptance of what has occurred in the past.[7]

RECONSTRUCTING HER LIFE

On Thursday afternoon, a couple of days later, my mother called me into her room.

"Okay," she said. "I'm ready to talk about my father."

I propped up the video camera on her dresser to record our interview. She reflected on what seemed the loveless childhood of Norman. My mother tried to reason why he was such a bitter man, but I don't think compassion and trying to understand his past was enough to redeem him in her eyes. When Norman returned from the war, he couldn't tolerate any loud noises in the house. Linda grew up in a place where "children could be seen but not heard."

Norman reluctantly took over the family business, a printing press, in Manchester. Every day when Norman arrived home, Linda feared falling victim to one of his violent eruptions. Sometimes, without even knowing why, she became his target. Her mother never defied him or stopped him. His abuse warped Linda, and she became a nervous and anxious child.

At eight years old, she watched American television shows. She dreamed of having an affectionate, fun-loving, supportive father like Jim Anderson in *Father Knows Best* and, later, Steve Douglas in *My Three Sons*. The television shows reflected sunshine, blue skies, perfect fathers, and brand-new, clean suburban homes. Linda sat on her dingy sofa and clung to the hope of one day escaping.

Respite from her father came, at least for a few days a week, when she would join a rapt group of children at her Aunt Lillian's home. Lillian had a reputation as a great storyteller among the neighborhood youngsters.

"I think I get a lot of my positive attitude from my aunt," Linda said about the woman she considered her role model while growing up. "Although I knew she was in constant pain with the arthritis, she would always open her home to other people. She was bound to a wheelchair, but was always open, interested in people, and more especially in me. She was never inward."

As Linda grew into a bold teenager, she rebelled against her father's constant verbal violence. Eventually, her mum knew they all could not live in the same house. One afternoon, shortly after Linda's eighteenth birthday, in the spring of 1966, Grace unfolded her plan to set Linda's dreams of living in America in motion. Grace had sought out an au pair agency and found Linda qualified for a federal work program with an incentive to obtain permanent residence in America. When the plane ticket and temporary visa arrived, leaving England became a reality, but she second-guessed her plan when she noticed her mother's sickly eyes shortly before her departure.

I interrupted my mother.

"So this was only weeks before you were to leave for America? You received the indication that she wasn't right? But you went because she wanted you to?" I asked.

My mother paused and bit her lip, then answered me.

"And because I wanted to go for selfish reasons as well. It was such a release. I'd always been really nervous. I was like a cat on a hot tin roof. You could come up behind me and I'd jump. I just lived on my nerves. Soooo, I got on that plane and it was like, . . . no more. I was in control of my life. I could do just what I wanted. It was a little scary, but it straightened me up and straightened me out. I wouldn't get in trouble, because I realized I had no one to fall back on. It was, I still think, the best move of my life. To see the blue sky and feel the heat."

After a forty-six-hour trip, she arrived in Shaker Heights, Ohio. She could hear the three children screeching as they opened the front door. The family appeared all-American, like those she watched on television. Yet Linda quickly learned that behind the television screen lay an entirely different kind of family story. The husbands always worked while the wives numbed their lives with gin.

They never showed the liquored wife on *My Three Sons*. Linda concluded that the perfect family was not so perfect, and neither was America. She recognized that there was not necessarily a social divide between classes, a strata system, like in England. Instead, Cleveland was racially divided between blacks and whites. In England, Linda's northern, working-class accent impeded her from ever moving up in life. But in America, people fell in love with her accent.

After four months serving this family, Linda noticed her mother's penmanship deteriorating into a child's handwriting. Eventually Grace admitted she'd been diagnosed with breast cancer. In late October of 1966, just a few days before Halloween—

My mother interrupted herself.

"It's just too much," she said, weeping.

We sat there in silence.

"You know, the first time I cried about my mother was after I met your father," she said.

"He made you feel safe," I said.

"Yes," she said, trying to pull a smile through the tears. "Do you want to continue?"

"Sure, Mom," I said.

On an October evening in the Shaker Heights home, her boss came in reeking of booze. She sat on the bed and slurred her words so much that Linda found it difficult to understand what she was saying. But she figured out that the mutters were about a call from England. She breathed intoxicating fumes all over Linda's face as she came in closer to say, "You're mother died." And she tried to hug Linda's stiff body. Linda moved on, never shedding a tear. She worked tirelessly for the next seven months until she attained a green card, a permanent residence card to live indefinitely in America.

In June 1968, at the height of the race riots in Ohio and the raging war in Vietnam, she found a job as a teller at Cleveland Trust Bank amid the civil unrest. On the teller line at Cleveland Trust, she met Beverly Chambers. A year later, they responded to an ad in the newspaper calling for tellers in California. Together, they interviewed with a recruiter from United California Bank. If they could move out to Los Angeles in a month, the recruiter guaranteed work. The girls set out in Beverly's 1956 Buick on Labor Day weekend, the summer of 1969. America seemed to crack wide open that summer—a man landed on the moon, and the hippie movement slammed the Establishment for the war in Vietnam.

They found an apartment in downtown Los Angeles. One evening, they went out dancing with a fellow teller, who introduced them to Richard Carson, at the Manila Sands, a Filipino dance club in Long Beach. Richard asked Linda to dance. She glided out into the dance floor and immediately noted his ability to lead. It felt as though nobody else was on the dance floor but them. She learned that he, too, was an immigrant. He had arrived in America in March 1967. He had a dual citizenship in the Philippines and the United States. His father, James Carson, was a Pennsylvanian soldier in the military during the war. A young native named Noemi Basconcillo captured his heart, and James chose not to return home. Instead, he lived in a village near a river on the province outside Manila. Although they were few, I extracted the stories of my father's early life from my mother's memory that he had shared with her during their courtship.

"When he was born, there were people who wanted to buy him because he was light-skinned with yellow hair. They called him *mestiso*," my mother said. His family moved to Manila, where his father entered a sanatorium for tuberculosis when Richard was only eleven years old. Shortly after his father's death, Richard landed in America. He lived with his mother's sister Peggy and her family in Iowa. The first snowy winter pushed him to buy a Corsair and head west to California in 1968. He signed up to serve in the Navy. His ship was docked in Long Beach, where he was stationed when he met Linda.

Their romance came to an abrupt standstill when his ship set sail for Vietnam. He refused to follow orders from his commander to board the ship for the week restriction. Instead he stayed one last long romantic week with Linda, savoring every minute with her. He climbed aboard ship on the eve before it left the harbor. Consequently, his commander disciplined him by banishing Richard to Captain's mast, which meant grueling, sweaty labor in the steamy engine room, brutal night watch, and extra duties over above his obligations as punishment for disobeying orders.

Mom oozed. "Your dad and I wrote to each other every day," she said, entranced in a love haze. For the first time, I heard my mother speak lovingly of Dad. I clung to her every word, every detail, as if hearing expressions, stories, and emotions that I'd yearned for most of my life. We rarely talked about my father after the divorce, which was especially difficult after his death.

She went on.

One afternoon, she opened her front door and there stood Richard shining in his dress whites. Home at last from Vietnam. He was tanned, muscular, toned, and hot.

"I have a taxi waiting downstairs," he said. "Can I stay?"

"Sure," she said.

A few months later, they exchanged their vows in the Los Angeles County Courthouse. In the days following my birth, my father was quarantined from me because a woman holding a blue baby raced into the ER at St. Vincent's Hospital in Los Angeles where he worked. Without a thought he immediately administered CPR, bringing the baby back from the edge. That wasn't the only life he saved. Mom recalled watching my father jump over rows of seats at a theater to administer CPR to a man suffering from a heart attack. And she remembered receiving thank-you letters from others.

Listening to my mother talk about my father gave me a sense of completeness. I wanted more, as if she were filling in the holes of my past. Three years after my birth in 1978, my father bought her a brand-new four-bedroom home with a big backyard and front yard in a suburb of Los Angeles. The house was everything my mother dreamed of while growing up in Manchester. Most mothers in the neighborhood stayed home to care for the children and fathers went off to work. But in the Carson home, they both left for work in the morning. Equality in the household led to a fifty-fifty split in household chores.

"Mom, tell me about your career," I asked.

"No, let's talk about something else," she said.

"What could you have done differently with Dad?" I asked.

"Communicate. We just stopped talking," she said.

She paused. "I do remember your dad and I including you in the decision to have another child. 'Denise', we asked, 'would you be willing to give up your playroom so you can have a TV set in your bedroom and a baby sibling?'"

My father also promised that she could quit work and become a stay-at-home mother when they planned to have another baby. But three months following the birth of their baby boy, this proud father severed their marriage. As my mother recalled those horrific hours of having to return to work after a shortened maternity leave and her husband walking out, tears flowed uncontrollably. She had prepared to leave the workforce and suddenly she was back—with a newborn baby *and* no husband. When she begged my father to return, he confessed to cheating on her for years.

Her breaking point came in the spring of 1985 when Ryan, her baby boy, started calling Brenda, the replacement, "Mommy" and her husband announced his September wedding to take place in the home he had once bought for her. The divorce papers ended any hope of saving her family. The combination of blows literally dropped my mother to her knees. One weekend night in March, she collapsed on her bedroom floor. She writhed, no longer wishing to go on. Her bedroom was like a cold, lonely tomb. She hadn't prayed or spoken to God since her childhood. She heard herself crying out loud, pleading with God for mercy.

In the midst of her breakdown, she crawled down the stairs and looked up churches in the Yellow Pages. She found Glenkirk Presbyterian with a Divorce Recovery group. The next morning she went to church and sat in the back. She wept through the whole service. That week, she attended the divorce recovery and found others also in the same alienated, outskirts of society, suddenly single. She gradually climbed out of her tomb. Her home in San Dimas became the refuge to rebuild, start again. Her faith in Jesus rose as the cornerstone of her healing.

Mom reveled in her reflections about the renewal years, when she grew close to Ryan and me. I was about nine and Ryan was a toddler.

"You kids and I did a lot of things," she reflected. "We really didn't have limitations except money. We would go to the hands-on exhibition at the Natural History Museum. I just thought that was the most fascinating thing for a child, also going up to the mountains for picnics and looking at nature rather than just looking at the TV. I think having children brings so much joy to a person's life because you can share. You can go out in the world and think to yourself, what a beautiful world, but you don't have anyone to share it with. You might be married, but they've seen it. To share it for the first time with somebody is very different. I thought museums and zoos were exciting places for kids . . . not boring."

She giddily recalled her most memorable Disneyland trip, the night of the *Captain E.O.* premiere, a Michael Jackson 3-D film, in 1986.

"I didn't tell you kids, but I knew Disneyland was going to be open for twenty-four hours," she giggled. "Admission after midnight was half price. So, it was a Friday night and I said you had to sleep or to rest and to wear warm clothes to bed because we were going somewhere in the middle of the night. I woke you up at about eleven. And I didn't tell you we were driving to Disneyland in the middle of the night.

"It was one of the best times we had at Disneyland. We were exhausted. It was one of those exciting little trips that didn't cost that much, just an entrance to Disney. One of those things that children, I think, would keep in their mind."

As I listened to her, I realized she worked hard her whole life to give us the things she lacked: financial security, new clothes, a clean home I could feel proud of and invite my friends to. She threw me birthday, slumber, and New Year's parties all the time. Those magical years faded in shadow of Gil Lisko, whom she married after I graduated from high school. She found a man similar in nature to her father. The open house that my mother nurtured for me, Ryan, and our friends collapsed under the tyranny of Gil. This was a period in her life I had difficulties reflecting on. Two major turning points continued to surface in our interviews. One, of course, was the divorce, which she had many years to contemplate, but the other pivotal moment came one year after she married Gil.

She described that June morning in 1996 when a security guard approached her in the empty bank parking lot where she worked in Pomona, a Los Angeles suburb probably more appropriately described as a ghetto, inhabited by two major gangs, the Crips and the Bloods. She'd worked in South Central Los Angeles and in banks centered in poverty-stricken neighborhoods over the twenty-seven years devoted to United California Bank, which later became First Interstate and at that time became Wells Fargo.

She'd arrived at seven o'clock in the morning to the bank as usual, to get a head start on her paperwork before her team of tellers arrived at eight thirty. A stranger dressed as a security guard approached her reporting news of a robbery at Pep Boys, an auto shop across the street, and then asked to enter the bank. Upon her refusal, he opened his jacket to brandish his gun and quietly breathed a threat on her life. Sheer terror triggered an uncontrollable stream of urine to saturate her panties and pantyhose. He followed her to the front door of the bank. As they walked through the double doors, he spoke to an accomplice on a walkie-talkie.

She glimpsed his face and noticed he was no older than eighteen. Her eyes zeroed in on his trembling finger curled over the trigger as he shoved it into her head and demanded money. A calm voice arose from a primal place deep within her. She explained that two people needed to open the vault. One person held the combinations and another person used a key. He then yelled at her not to look at his face.

He growled, "If you ever rat on me, I'll kill your son."

He held the gun to her head, threatening to shoot her and continually demanding her to open the vault, until finally he knocked her to the floor. They'd obviously been casing the bank for at least a week because Mom had been taking Ryan into work in the morning before dropping him off at basketball camp. The gunman tied her up in computer cords while waiting for another bank officer to enter. A half-hour later, a scratchy voice sputtered over the radio that another woman was entering the bank. He knocked the arriving woman down and her coffee spilled all over the floor where Mom lay. Then he pulled up the women. Under pistol pressure, the other manager forgot her combinations to the vault. Forty-five minutes with a gun barrel rocking the side of her head, she tried to find ways to please this criminal. Mom suggested the ATM but the combos failed, then a teller drawer. His voice roared, he threatened their lives, clicking the trigger.

In the parking lot, a visiting bank manager arrived for a morning meeting at the branch. He noticed the bank door ajar before opening time and called the police. Minutes later, the police charged through the back door. The assailant ran out the front door with a bit of cash from the teller drawer.

Mom went into work the next day and acted as if nothing had oc-curred. She arrived each morning consumed in a quiet, unexpressed fear and was reminded daily of the incident by the coffee stain still in the carpet at the front door. She had to face her assailants in court to testify a few months later, which caused many sleepless nights.

Could she have ignited the cancer at that time? She asked the question again.

For nine months, she continued the masquerade until another gang of gunmen entered the bank. The second hostage crisis drew a comatose Linda to her knees. She visited a psychologist. He diagnosed her with severe post-traumatic stress syndrome that disabled her from ever entering a bank again. The powers at Wells Fargo Bank voted against granting her early retirement. She'd worked for that bank, which was acquired twice over her tenure, since she was twenty-one years old. At age forty-eight, she was forced to start all over again.

Once she'd purged the soiled past, she began formulating reasons for the major course-corrections that shaped her life. Our discussions about Gil and her marriage focused less on memories and more on confessions. Mom apologized for allowing Gil into our home. He terrorized my brother and me, mostly behind her back. She sided with him, which eventually drove us away. For years, this period remained an "untouchable." My hurt and anger over her inability to protect us against Gil began to melt away in listening to Mom admit her shortcomings. She confessed her failure at being a modern woman, that she was unable to balance a married life, career, and children. That was eye-opening to me because Mom projected an air of being able to handle it all, with the exception of "things breaking down around the house."

Together we dared to point out the positive outcome of my parents' destructive divorce for the first time. She rationalized the divorce by justifying that Brenda caring for my father during his battle with cancer was a blessing in disguise so that Mom was able to provide a refuge for my brother and me. My mother also accepted that the divorce gave her the opportunity to develop an intimate relationship with Ryan and me. She cultivated a deep faith in God and joined Glenkirk Presbyterian Church, which she felt replaced the absence of a family support system and sustained her in facing cancer.

The open forum interviews were inadvertently therapeutic that consequently diffused any isolation or denial in this transitional period as death hovered nearby. The deep reflections naturally segued into Mom speaking openly about her needs, fears, and last wishes. I listened and followed her subtle cues.

In late October, she asked me to help her organize and sort through her paperwork. I opened the filing cabinet in her closet and we pored over the mortgage, bills, and health and life insurance papers. At that time, we decided to have a will and a living will drawn up so that I could serve as her advocate in the event that she couldn't make decisions for herself.

She didn't even need to leave her bedroom. I had the papers drawn up with an attorney and brought them home for her to sign. I valued her courage and strength to plan a smooth exit. We also drew up official divorce papers to legalize the split between my mother and Gil. He still hung around, and I feared dealing with him when my mother was no longer able to serve as a buffer between us. She listened to and respected my wishes. The life review led to another forward-thinking request.

CLEANING OUT HER CLOSET

On the last Sunday in October, I entered her bedroom with some raspberry iced tea. The afternoon sun blazed through the balcony window. Mom was propped up in the hospital bed. She wore a black T-shirt and black pants, from a new wardrobe that I picked out for her to conceal the tube and ostomy bag above her stomach.

"Are you in the mood for an interview?" I asked casually.

She smiled slyly at me.

"What?" I said. "You have something else in mind."

"Yeah, I think I want you to clean the clothes out of my closet," she said.

I opened the sliding glass door to let in a bit of fresh air. Cleaning out the closet is usually a task performed after a person dies. The ritual marks a stage of acceptance that the deceased will not be returning.[8] After the funeral and after everyone stops coming around, you are left to enter the wardrobe wafting with scents of your loved one. And by then, the clothes are just clothes, and the books are just books, but what if you cleaned out the closet with the person there? I believe the life review helped us together reach this revelatory stage of acceptance before her death.

"Go on in and decide which ones you want to keep and which clothes you want to get rid of," she said. Mom and I were the same size—five feet, two inches, twenty-six-inch waist, and size 6 shoe. I stepped into her walk-in closet and began pulling out her suits. The business suits instantly awakened memories of her recruitment as one of the first women in the management-training program at United California Bank in the 1970s. She was poised to emerge as a corporate woman in a man's world during the women's movement.

"You see, I was one of the first women in management at the bank," she said. "They wanted women in management. But back then you had to wear skirts—can you imagine the discrimination?"

She rose on the fast track because she possessed the inner qualities of a hard-working, hungry immigrant in the sophisticated shell of a businesswoman able to adapt to her surroundings. At the time, my father was going to college, so there was no money for her to buy suits to fit in with the other management trainees. She disguised her lack of professional attire by wearing blazers over dresses, which she had sewn herself.

"I still looked nice," she said. "I had a few dresses and jackets to get me through the week. And I would interchange them."

She slid her hands across an array of bright-colored wool suits laying on the bed and returned to those days just after the divorce when she discovered a newfound freedom to pursue her career and a financial freedom she'd never experienced while living with him. She remembered waltzing into Petite Sophisticate with enough money to invest in her first wool suit—it was four pieces, emerald-green, with a spidery patterned black and emerald silk skirt and blouse. The royal blue wool suit with a pebble pattern of black, red, and blue and high-neck blouse came next. She punctuated her ensembles with multicolored beads, gold necklaces, and pearls that expressed her femininity. Her suits were like a fanned peacock in a boardroom of black suits.

We talked about her eye for balancing professionalism with a feminine flare. Short hair complemented the suits, and long hair, she said, was considered unprofessional. Mom worked in the tallest skyscraper in downtown Los Angeles, the Bunker Hill Building, the UCB headquarters that became First Interstate. She rose physically and professionally to the top floors of the sixty-two-story building and corporation.

"I could do no wrong. But, Denise, you know, once you reach the top there's only one place to go," she said, remembering that message resonating in her mind in Marina del Rey on a harbor cruise in the company of all the First Interstate Bank executives when the champagne flutes raised in a toast to her name. She served on an elite team qualified to go into any bank branch to root out the inefficiencies and unearth internal corruption.

The suits symbolized her liberation after the divorce and defining moments in her career. I chose to keep the royal blue and emerald green suits. They reminded me of her wings, multicolored like those of a butterfly.

At that moment, I realized just how much her career meant. I'd never really paid much attention to the outside persona, Linda Carson. If we didn't clean out her closet together, I most likely would have hastily shoved all of her business clothes into a plastic bag to be donated to a women's shelter.

Her closet and oak drawers smelled of her favorite scent, Beautiful, by Estee Lauder. I lifted a lavender and charcoal sweater that she'd knitted herself from a drawer.

"Mom, why did you stop knitting?" I asked.

Time became a commodity once she moved into management. I placed the sweater back in the drawer. It was the only sweater that survived my mother's domestic years. I treasured this sweater together with a baby blanket she knitted for me. I asked about the blanket. She pointed to a box in her closet that stored the blanket, along with my dolls, which she imagined I'd one day share with my own daughter.

I wasn't ready to go there.

I tried on some of her dresses and danced around the room to lift the mood. She was a disco dancer in the late 1970s and 1980s. She and my father used to clear the dance floor when they discoed.

"So, do I have your rhythm?" I asked, gyrating my hips in her slinky, black dress patterned with fuchsia and teal flowers.

"No, you have your father's rhythm." This was a compliment.

"Your dad was the best dancer," she continued. "I loved dancing with your father. I just followed his lead."

Smiling and following me around the room with her eyes, she said, "I'm content. I feel like I'm doing the right thing, having you do this. I don't know how to say this—one of the hardest things after a person dies is to go through their personal effects. I think I want you to know my personal effects before I die. I think you are learning everything. Everything. So the aftermath . . . there really won't be too much to do in the aftermath. I don't know, I just want to make it easy for you. I don't know what I'll be like when it gets near the end."

FOUR

Legacy of Memories: Telling
Life Stories and Last Wishes

Elizabeth Vega, a life review guide and ghostwriter for the dying, invited me to a legacy celebration for a hospice patient in St. Louis, Missouri, around Thanksgiving 2004. Elizabeth's mission of leading hospice patients on a tour of their past life to create life-story books for posterity and, more important, to rewrite the last chapter of their life, deepened my quest. I couldn't resist the invitation upon learning about her first encounter with death a decade prior.

It was January 1994, and she was pushing through her contractions on a bed at Norton Hospital in Louisville, Kentucky, breathing in "one-two-three" and out "one-two-three." As she counted breaths with her baby's father, a couple of nurses scurried about the delivery room monitoring her vital signs. Although she had recently turned twenty-five and this baby was her third child, Elizabeth didn't feel like a veteran at childbirth. This one was even more difficult. The baby was not helping or moving in the birth canal. Stiff, she thought.

Elizabeth clenched her fists. Thrusting her pelvis up, she pushed for the last time. The doctor pulled out the baby. Elizabeth flopped down on the bed. Silence fell over the delivery room. She looked down at the doctor holding the blue baby girl. Elizabeth had signed a "Do Not Resuscitate" order before rolling into the delivery room. She knew that her baby suffered from an aggressive, malignant brain tumor. Rather than have a partial abortion, Elizabeth had chosen to deliver despite the grim diagnosis. She struggled to focus, waiting to hear the sound of her daughter cry, then she started slipping into unconsciousness.

"Hold on," Elizabeth heard a nurse say. "Your blood pressure is really low."

Through the haze, she watched the doctor place her daughter into the father's arms. His long blond hair framed his ruddy face.

Tears trickled down his cheeks and dropped onto the still baby. Only minutes had passed by, yet it seemed liked hours.

Suddenly, the baby girl quivered and choked into a cry.

"She's crying," the nurses cheered. "She's crying."

He placed the baby into Elizabeth's arms. Elizabeth looked down at her daughter's dark eyes and fuzzy dark hair, which covered an unusually large head. She had Elizabeth's olive complexion and long brown locks. Elizabeth called her Gabrielle, which means "God is my strength." Minutes later, the doctor swept Gabrielle out of the room to insert a shunt in her head to drain the fluids percolating around the brain tumor.

A flurry of encounters with physicians delivering differing pieces of advice followed. Elizabeth found herself in the midst of trying to choose between the better of two deaths for her daughter. She could die in hospital or at home. With the shunt, doctors predicted Gabrielle might survive a couple of months in a vegetative state.

"What if we take the shunt out?" Elizabeth asked.

"Maybe a couple of weeks," the doctors replied.

Elizabeth opted to remove the shunt, then swaddled the baby to go home. That afternoon a hospice nurse waved a magnolia blossom over the face of Gabrielle as Elizabeth cradled the baby in her arms on the couch in the dimly lit living room. Gabrielle gurgled for the first time like a normal baby. As Elizabeth watched her dying daughter respond to the aromatic flower, she realized that a life was not measured by days or even years, but by the experiences created in its wake. Upon their return from school, Elizabeth's sons, seven-year-old Christopher and five-year-old Joey, gathered around to see their new sister.

Elizabeth explained Gabrielle would live a short life, like that of a butterfly, so they needed to share all of their favorite things with their sister before her death. The next day the boys brought home fluffy pink cotton candy for Gabrielle to taste. The boys played music for Gabrielle. Elizabeth sung lullabies and read books to her daughter from sunrise to sundown. She was thankful she had decided to bring Gabrielle home, rather than watch her struggle for life in an incubator in the hospital. The hospital meant a slightly longer life, but it also meant separation for two months—and it would have led to the same outcome.

On the fifteenth day, the twinkle in Gabrielle's eyes began to fade and her breathing declined to a labored wheeze. Elizabeth took Gabrielle to the park that afternoon. The wind tickled Gabrielle's pale face and her cloudy eyes squinted in the sunshine. It was her first and last swing in the park. Gabrielle died on the sixteenth day.

For the next nine years, Elizabeth focused on journalism, something she had long wanted to do. She moved to St. Louis, a larger market. She landed a feature writer position at the *St. Louis Riverfront Times.* Gabrielle's sixteen days of life often filled her daydreams. She wanted to pass on the magnolia blossom to other people, but wondered how. Although she had served in a hospital as a birthing assistant in the U.S. Navy, she wasn't a nurse. She wasn't a doctor or a social worker. What could she do as a journalist to help hospice patients?

In the summer of 2003, she returned to Louisville and sat in the cemetery atop her daughter's small grave, recollecting the white-and-pink-trimmed casket below. She recalled the hundreds of people she had met and interviewed over the last decade. Many people she interviewed had said, "Gosh, I've never been asked that question before in my life." She thought it tragic how many people had never talked about their life stories.

She believed, like the ancient Aztecs, that we die three deaths. The first death occurs when your body exhales the last breath of life and the heart stops beating. The second death is marked when your body is lowered into the ground, slipping from the sight of the living, returned to the elements of Mother Earth. The most definitive of the three is when the memory of you in the minds of others vanishes and there is no one left to remember you. As a journalist, she certainly couldn't prevent the first and second, but she might be able to delay the third. Just as the idea formed in her head, she jumped to her feet. "I could interview hospice patients and write their life stories to leave behind for their family," she thought.

Upon her return to St. Louis, she contacted a local hospice, BJC Hospice, and met with the director, Barbara Westland. She came from pediatrics, the other side of life care, and was known as a progressive in the field of hospice. Barbara believed fervently that hospice was about continuing to live while dying. She funded music therapists, harpists, and reminiscent therapists to help bring positive closure to the lives of her patients and their families. Elizabeth's plan cultivated a seed already planted in Barbara's mind. Just the previous year, the National Hospice Foundation drove a nationwide campaign heralding life review and releasing a book and videotape titled *A Guide to Recalling and Telling Your Life Story*. The book is filled with instrumental questions to trigger memories from all stages of life, birth to childhood, youth to adulthood, marriage to parenthood, career to retirement. The book suggests that a younger family member or outside guide accompany the journey back in time to capture these life stories using a pen, audio recorder, or video camera.

Before sending this journalist out on her first assignment, Barbara asked one question: "What is your previous experience with hospice?" Gabrielle's life story touched her.

Barbara sent Elizabeth to visit Jim Wells. Equipped with the same tools she used as a reporter—a pen, a notebook, and a tape recorder—Elizabeth arrived at the front door of Jim and Beverly Wells's home in Chesterfield, a suburb of St. Louis. Jim had recently entered hospice after surrendering to a three-year battle with cancer. He was fifty-nine. His social worker suggested Elizabeth chronicle his life story to pass on to his fifteen-year-old daughter. Jim was concerned about leaving behind his daughter. She was so young—how would she remember him? Had they experienced enough together to preserve his memory in her mind or would he just fade with time as she grew older, graduated from high school and went off to college?

The walls of his home looked like a modern art museum. Elizabeth's eyes strolled along the canvases. Jim spied, silently thrilled by the stranger's admiration. She was also an artist, so she could appreciate the collection. Elizabeth noted the art came from the same hand and even commented on the artist's maturing style. A smile peeked through the bushy, auburn-speckled beard that disguised the gauntness of his face. He humbly admitted to painting most of the pieces. As a reporter, she'd been in the homes of many strangers, and through her keen observations and interviews, Elizabeth often knew more about the strangers she talked to after one meeting than did most people who had known them for much longer.

Jim pointed out the watercolor of a silhouetted tree along the jagged cliffs of the sparkling California coast, which he had painted while still in school and for which *Time* magazine had recognized him as a promising young artist. Instantly, Elizabeth saw a portal into his past. She detected a note of unfinished business and treaded carefully in guiding him to talk about the dawn of his artistic life. She spotted an abstract of John Lennon and Yoko Ono, icons of the peace movement. Jim led her into his basement art studio as he relived his experiences of attending art school in the 1960s and reminisced about receiving a national art award upon graduation. His style was abstract expressionist. He explained how he used all sorts of unconventional materials to achieve the perfect texture.

In his basement art studio, which was full of canvases atop easels, he found solace. He had introduced his daughter to painting, and they had spent many weekends creating side-by-side. She was a natural, just like him. Her artwork adorned the walls of their home and his studio. Since his own youth, Jim dreamed of becoming a professional artist. But his father saw art as a hobby, not a profession. Eventually, pressure from his father and the pull of a stable income offered by corporate America foiled his dreams. Jim harbored aspirations of entering the professional art world when he retired. But the cancer struck first.

A dark shadow of regret eclipsed him. Elizabeth noticed a sway in his fragile, slender frame. He'd lost forty pounds in the last few months. The cancer had managed not only to shatter a lifelong dream, but also to destroy his body. Elizabeth realized writing his life story wouldn't help Jim at this juncture; he still had work to do. He probably had a month or less to live, but it wasn't time to raise the white flag. A cunning smile glowed on her face.

"Why didn't you have an art show?" She cajoled him.

"Oh, I just thought I didn't have time," he said. And then he paused. "Now, I'm out of time."

"Why don't we have an art show for your life celebration?" she said to him, raising her voice to that of a cheerleading soprano. Elizabeth exuded a vitality that often rubbed off on others.

"Yeah," he said getting caught up in her zest. His eyes panned the studio. He worried out loud that there wasn't enough art to carry an entire show. Simultaneously, both suggested showing Ashley's art, too. The brainstorm escalated to new heights as Jim imagined sharing an art show with his daughter.

"It's something she'll never forget," he said.

Elizabeth watched something inside him ignite.

"We can do this," he chanted repeatedly.

At that moment, she witnessed the rapidly ticking countdown on his life stop. Elizabeth had turned his focus from dying to the limitless possibilities of transforming his regret into a monumental achievement. She figured the father and daughter art show could be called "Tributaries: The Legacy That Keeps Flowing On."

THE FIRST LEGACY CELEBRATION: AN ART SHOW

The Wells family bound together and focused on the art show in last weeks of Jim's life. His wife, Beverly, matted and pounded his canvases into frames for his art show. Jim and Ashley collaborated on how they wanted to weave their art pieces together for display at the show. They laid them all out on the living room floor.

Elizabeth made call after call to one art studio and then another in town. No studio would show an unknown artist on short notice. What if Jim died before completing his last wish? Her last call was Mad Art Gallery, an old 1930s converted police substation. She explained her plight and Jim's wish to the owner of the studio. He had recently lost his father to cancer. He managed to fit the art show in on a Friday evening. Elizabeth then pitched Jim's story to a reporter at the *St. Louis Post Dispatch*.[1]

The day of the art show, Elizabeth hammered in nails, rearranging frames and canvases, seeking to carry the eye from one painting to the other. She sat silently absorbing what was before her. It was more than just art. This was an intersection of lives—the artistic outline of a father and a daughter, Elizabeth thought. Her thoughts turned toward her own daughter.

At dusk, Jim and his family entered the doors of Mad Art Gallery. Elizabeth greeted him and instantly saw his eyes widen with awe. Elizabeth thought about how Gabrielle's legacy gave her the courage to help Jim and his family to keep living in the midst of dying.

"You have a decision to make—you can focus on dying or you can focus on living," Elizabeth thought to herself as she watched Jim, arm-in-arm with Beverly and Ashley, walking around the gallery. The seamless presentation of Ashley's pieces married with Jim's canvases mesmerized the family. They showed twenty-nine pieces. The exhibit displayed a progression through the natural life cycle of a father and daughter. Ashley chose to display an early piece drawn in second grade of a bird hovering above her nest full of eggs. Her more colorful works, like the one of a boy and his dog running in a field beneath a violet and blue sky punctuated with red/orange beams of sunlight, fit beautifully with Jim's plain-air collection from his teenage years. A portrait of Beverly in a red hat, entitled "Rose," was a memento of their instant love affair that began in 1979. Jim reveled in seeing his art exhibited with his daughter's art in a gallery.

The evening crowd swept in shortly after his arrival.

He watched people standing in front of the father and daughter artwork. They made comparisons and discussed his style the way he had seen other patrons do in other artists' show. But he wasn't a quiet observer for long. Elizabeth introduced Jim and Ashley to the crowd.

More than 300 people turned their eyes on Jim, Ashley, and Beverly. There were very few dry eyes in the room. Many in the audience were relatives and longtime friends and some were just people in the community who came to support a dying man's last wish. Friends with whom Jim had lost contact over the years had spotted the article in the local newspaper and came to see him. Rather than see his obituary, they saw the article on his life celebration and jumped at the chance to reconnect with him before time ran out. The owner of the studio followed Elizabeth's introduction of the guest of honor with an announcement to the community that he was opening a museum of contemporary local artists and Jim's Western piece would inaugurate it.

Jim glowed in the midst of the fanfare. He was experiencing the realization of a lifelong dream. Elizabeth watched as Beverly, Ashley, Jim's mother, and friends together expressed a range of profound emotions from crying to laughing simultaneously. It was bittersweet. New fans waited in line for more than an hour to meet him. They were honored to meet a man at the end of his life willing to share his love for art with his daughter and his community.

The afterglow of the celebration kept Jim going and talking nonstop about the art show for about two weeks. His energy waned and Jim, the local artist, took his last breath.

Elizabeth attended his memorial service. After the ceremony, she saw a crowd gathered around Ashley and Beverly. She moved in closer to see the photos circulating of Jim glowing in the limelight at his first and only art show. As she gazed upon the pictures of Jim and thought about the more than 300 participants at his art show and visualized people across St. Louis hanging Jim's art in their homes and sharing his story with their families, she knew that his legacy lived on beyond the walls of his basement art studio. But most important, he'd secured his legacy and the love of art in the memory of his daughter.

Barbara, the director of BJC Hospice, attended the show and the memorial service. She was amazed at the outreach. Elizabeth continued volunteering for BJC Hospice while Barbara worked out a way to retain her services full time. She set aside a $200 donation per patient to help Elizabeth devote her talents full time to hospice.

A MESSENGER FOR THE DYING

Elizabeth launched a nonprofit organization based in St. Louis called La Loba Life Services. She repurposed her journalistic interviewing techniques toward a mission of helping people review their lives, write their life stories, define their legacies and plan life celebrations.

Shortly after she launched La Loba, I heard about Elizabeth from a volunteer coordinator at Visiting Nurses Association Hospice in California. Upon our meeting, I felt an instant kindred spirit in Elizabeth. She had the kind of verve that invigorates you at her first "hello." In the year I followed Elizabeth, she made many last wishes come true. I liken her mission to that of the Make-a-Wish Foundation for children, except for adults.

Some may call Elizabeth an end-of-life planner in that she provides the map, organizes the resources, and hands over the tools for people to articulate and then complete their mission before their last breath. She wrote recipes attached with childhood memories and holiday traditions bound in books for grandmothers to pass on to their grandchildren. She accompanied an eighty-year-old woman who wished to ride the Ferris wheel one last time in Forest Park. Elizabeth arranged for an equestrian lover to go for one last cantor in her final days. For a patient with a big family and small living quarters, Elizabeth found an owner of a bed and breakfast to donate her venue for a last supper for the entire family. Elizabeth rented a tutu for a dying ballet dancer to circle around her living room one last time at the completion of writing her memoirs for her daughter.

One evening after visiting patients with Elizabeth, I asked her what La Loba means. We were in her St. Louis home, sitting at a large oak dining table, dimly lit by a chandelier, in a bohemian-style room with creaky wood floors and walls colored by paintings.

"Ah, La Loba," she said, as her conversational voice dropped in key. She sounded like an ancient storyteller as she explained that La Loba was a bedtime story her *Lolita*, grandmother, used to tell her. The story had been passed down through her family for generations and speaks about the cycles of life.

"La Loba is the story of the wolf woman who goes to the desert, and she collects the bones of dead wolves. She pieces them together and on the night of the full moon, she sings and chants over them. The legend says if you hear her song this night, it carries the weight of 10,000 mothers' tears, and if you hear it again, it carries the joy of 100,000 children. It has in it all the elements of life that transform the bones into living, breathing wolves. The legend also says that if you ever run into a wolf, you will see La Loba dancing by the fire in their eyes, and if you look into La Loba's eyes, you will see the wolf there as well." Metaphorically, Elizabeth imagines herself as the wolf woman incarnate—except instead of using bones, she cobbles together life stories.

Elizabeth embarks on an expedition of people's pasts like an archaeologist, excavating personal history and jewels of wisdom for posterity. Then she cleverly weaves together the collection of memories, often into a book, but not always. Sometimes she writes letters for parents to send messages from the grave to their children at those missed milestone moments in life.

This part of her mission really resonated with me. As a child, I endured the absence of my father at many milestone moments. My high school graduation at San Dimas High School in 1993, six years after his death, turned out to be an unexpectedly excruciating experience as I looked up to the stands yearning for my father to be clapping and smiling proudly in the audience. Had I received a letter, words of encouragement, or even a video message from my father that acknowledged the gravity of my reaching that milestone without him, the torment might have been assuaged. I chose not to go to my college graduation for fear of encountering a similar heartbreak. As a child, I knew the value and solace these letters could provide. As an adult, I understood how dying parents could find consolation in writing these letters.

Elizabeth met many young parents in hospice needing to leave words behind for their daughters and sons, but every time they took pen to paper the blank sheet was daunting and every word seemed wrong, out of place. How do you write a letter to your children that will describe your dreams for them, that will express how proud of them you are now, that will comfort them in times of pain and advise them in their hour of confusion or despair? This overwhelming task often resulted, Elizabeth said, in crinkled-up paper being tossed into the trash.

She collaborates with mothers and fathers to help them articulate their message with sentimental and personal touches. Elizabeth's patients review their lives while finding the words of encouragement and wisdom to impart to their children. She tells the stories of their children's births and namesakes. Parents reveal candid stories of failures and mistakes that turned out to be instrumental life lessons. Elizabeth also has an angelic postal service that mails off letters after her patients depart so their loved ones receive a message from beyond in their darkest hours of mourning. Families are stunned when receiving letters with a postmark after the death, but find solace in the unexpected words of a poetic farewell. Elizabeth is a master in finding a voice to author her patients' letters and life stories in first person. Here is a taste—this is a letter Elizabeth wrote for Marilyn Noonan, a wife, mother, and remarkable woman of faith. Elizabeth interviewed Marilyn just a few days before she died. Elizabeth was indeed honored when Ed, Marilyn's husband, requested she read the letter at the funeral.

Dearest family and friends,
I am sending this dispatch from the other side to let you know of my safe arrival. I would have called, but as it turns out . . . angels do not have access to cell phones. I decided to write this letter because I still have some lessons I want to pass on.

I want you to know that despite my physical absence, I am with you today. Somewhere in a place you can only see with your heart, I am watching and celebrating my connection with you at the same time you are celebrating your connection with me. I am doing this free of disease, pain, and the constraints of cancer. Right at this moment, I feel absolutely blessed because I am joyfully in the presence of God while I am joyfully present with you.

I would also like to thank you for the many letters and e-mails you sent me. Late at night when I couldn't sleep, Ed would read me your kind words. Each and every one affirmed my life even as my body weakened. It was as if you were reflecting back to me the impact of all my talents and gifts, including my wit, creativity, faith, and openness. More than anything, I was delighted to know that my life encouraged so many of you to be open as well . . . For this reason, I think the cancer has been a gift, granted, one that came wrapped in tears, but a gift nonetheless. The cancer has given me a chance to come to a peaceful place with my own death, allowed me time to say all my good-byes and finish what I needed to do. It has been the vehicle for many lessons about love, faith in God, the power of hope, and the bliss of living in the moment. As you leave here today, I want you to make a conscious effort to carry on these gifts for me. I want you to live your lives with the freedom and openness to say the things that need to be said. I want you to embrace this idea, not just when someone is dying, but in every living moment. Tell those you love how you feel and then show them . . .

Each time you shared a memory with me, it allowed me to revisit another beautiful moment in my life. You wouldn't believe all the places I traveled just sitting in my bed.

I could go back with Ed to our lucky Las Vegas trip, the one that started with Ed and me shaking President Gerald Ford's hand and ended up with us winning so much on Black Jack that I was able to buy a new car . . .

I rode on horseback through the mountains with Michael one more time. I was free in my mind to be the Scout Lady and have Ed my faithful Scoutmaster by my side. My memories allowed me to see Michael become a leader and just as quickly I was able to stand proudly beside him as he received his Eagle Scout award.

If I was in pain, I could close my eyes and I would be riding in my red convertible with Ed and the boys at the Cardinals' World Series Parade. I could laugh once again on how our search for parking ended up with us being directed into the parade . . .

Our stories keep memories alive long after hearts have stopped beating. So thank you for all the wonderful times I shared with each one of you. I carry them with me. Use your memories of me to accompany you on the rest of your journey . . . I know at this moment you are grieving. When the ones we love move out of our sight and into our hearts, initially there is a sense of powerlessness. Nothing we can do will bring them back. You do however have a choice in how you live in the midst of this sorrow. I want you to choose life. I want you to take all of our memories out into the world. So as my final lesson to you, I am giving you homework of sorts. In those moments you miss me, I want you to do some things.

I want you to write down a memory, take a photo, or tell a good story to a friend or stranger. I want you to start a scrapbook of these memories and interactions so that you will have something to pass on.

I want you to tell someone you love how you feel. Be specific about how they give you joy. I want you to do this every day.

When you are really sad, do a random act of kindness in my name and know I am watching.

Go to a lake, throw a stone in the water, and watch the ripples, then live your life that way—let your every action show the power of kindness, joy, and love spreading out exponentially.

Go to a public place and sing "Margaritaville" at the top of your lungs. Celebrate laughter and silliness and know somewhere I'm singing along.

> *I love you always,*
> *Marilyn*

DIGNITY THERAPY: CREATING A LEGACY THAT LIVES ON AFTER DEATH

Across America, family members, hospice volunteers, nurses, and even doctors are encouraging hospice patients to leave a legacy of memories, or as one psychologist called it, "a heart will," to their family.[2] As described above, some parents leave letters and gifts for the child to open on holidays and milestones such as birthdays and graduations. These efforts help to ward off the feelings of helplessness as the dying person confronts the insurmountable pain of parting with a child and family. Many terminal patients think about it, but would much rather focus on living, fighting for life rather than engaging in an act that symbolizes resignation, which is exactly how my father felt when my mother asked him to write a letter to us about his life and his hopes for our lives. The "hope for the best, prepare for the worse" attitude might be most operative in these situations and is one that palliative care physicians gently encourage.

"The most meaningful legacies are not that concrete," said Dr. Susan Block, associate professor of psychiatry and medicine at Harvard Medical School with a research focus on psychosocial oncology and palliative care.[3] "They have to do with memories, and that is where the life review can be helpful in transmitting stories, also values. And that is enormously helpful for people." Doctors have only recently begun researching the benefits of such legacies.

Dr. Harvey Chochinov, director of the Manitoba Palliative Care Research Unit in Winnipeg, Manitoba, and a psychiatry professor at the University of Manitoba, said that leaving a spoken legacy is important to both patients and family members.[4] He led an international clinical trial, supported by the U.S. National Institutes of Health, to explore the impact of "dignity therapy," an individualized psychotherapeutic intervention, on terminal patients dealing with psychosocial and existential issues.

Dignity therapy engages patients in extended conversations about issues that matter most to them, dreams for their loved ones, last words they want to express before they die, and particular achievements or qualities they would most want remembered. These meaningful discussions are recorded, transcribed, and edited, with a final version returned to the patient to bequeath to their kindred. Researchers call this transcript a generativity document whose purpose is to provide a permanent record that will live on when the person dies.

In August 2005, the results of a pilot trial were published in the *Journal of Clinical Oncology*. Ninety-one percent reported being satisfied with the study and 76 percent reported that the dignity therapy heightened their sense of purpose and will to live.[5] Eighty-one percent said their family members cherished the transcribed oral legacies.[6] Post-intervention showed significant improvement in symptoms of distress and depression and in will to live.

Dr. Chochinov and his co-researchers came up with the idea of a permanent record of the spoken legacy following their research on defining dignity for the dying. The evidence reports that patients suffer deep angst from an assault on generativity, that is, the idea that "nothing of who or what I am will last beyond this lifetime, that I will soon die and my memory will fade."

The generativity document has many parallels to a will that contains how material possessions are distributed or dispensed, but instead it records how the deposits entered one's spiritual, psychosocial, or existential bank and how they should be dispensed. But we must not forget that it's often material possessions that help us make contact with the legacies we wish to pass on to the next generation.

In the book *The Past in the Present: Using Reminiscence in Health and Social Care,* Faith Gibson writes that personal possessions stimulate reminiscence in service to a life review or a legacy. She informs us that clothes, jewelry, shoes, scarves, hats, handbags, luggage, sports equipment, music collections, old letters, medals from war, artwork, books, and old newspaper clippings may be tucked away in parents' and grandparents' closets and attics just waiting for the moment when the younger generation comes along to ask questions about the life attached to these relics.[7]

THE TREE OF LIFE LEGACY CELEBRATION

Elizabeth is the first person to say that what she does is not magic. Each one of us can do this for those we love, but first we need to sit down, listen, and ask questions about the person's life. But as she learned in the summer of 2004, legacies are often hidden in unexpected places. A tricky assignment arrived in June from a social worker at BJC Hospice about a patient named Mary Dexter living in Chesterfield Villas, an assisted living facility on the outskirts of St. Louis, Missouri. Her only instruction was: "Ask Mary about the jewelry collection."

Mary Dexter was hovering somewhere between life and death. After four months with BJC Hospice, her social worker suggested to Mary that she meet with Elizabeth. The social worker recognized that Mary's sharp mind was trapped, a prisoner inside a declining body and the isolation of her living quarters. At first Mary disagreed, feeling like a life review seemed a bit egotistical. As her sixty-third birthday neared, Mary saw no reason to celebrate or reflect on her life. She had lived beyond every terminal prognosis the oncologists had delivered to her over her debilitating, five-year-long war with lung cancer. She had been revived twice against her will. She felt like a vagabond, having zigzagged from her home in Nebraska to California to Missouri to live near family members willing to accept the burden of caring for her.

Every morning Mary awoke to the dissonant whir of the ventilator and realized death has failed once again to visit her in the night, but she just couldn't bring herself to pull the plug. The act defied every lesson she had ever instilled in her special ed students throughout her thirty-year teaching career. That teacher, "Mrs. D," had vanished long ago; now she was just the woman dying slowly of lung cancer in Room 303.

Such was her existence, until Elizabeth knocked on the door of Room 303.

Elizabeth stepped into a quasi-hospital chamber where Mary, a thin, tanned, frail woman with mousy brown hair and wide wire-framed glasses, lay in a hospital bed. Within the first few minutes of their conversation, Mary told Elizabeth about how she'd been peeping out of her bedroom window upon hearing the rumble of the school bus below. The flap of the automatic doors swung open and the harmonious hum of chattering special ed students floated up to Mary's window. They arrived after high school for their work-study program of serving food to the residents. They'd become the highlight of her day because they reminded her of the students she left behind in Omaha, Nebraska.

Elizabeth asked Mary how she came to be in St. Louis. Struggling to project her voice over a wheeze, Mary told Elizabeth about the spring semester of 2000 when her bones turned brittle from the radiation. One day after school, she was whisking around the kitchen whipping up dinner for her menagerie of pets when she slipped and shattered her back. She could no longer care for her beloved Omaha ranch home. Her home was more than just a place where she resided and had raised her sons. The house also sheltered her 288 pets. She volunteered for the local veterinarian and cared for many animals in recovery. Mary was the neighborhood Dr. Doolittle, a Saint Francis incarnate.

One by one, she painstakingly found new homes for them. She reluctantly packed her suitcases. She moved across the country to live with her eldest son in Silicon Valley, California.

"What was it like?" Elizabeth asked.

Mary looked bewildered. No one had ever bothered to ask that.

The harrowing farewells stripped Mary of everything she worked for, lived for, and cared for. She had fostered long relationships with her students; some she had taught since kindergarten. Her progress with each of her forty-nine students, all with various learning disabilities, ended. In California, she endured two years of grueling chemotherapy, then made the decision to go off curative treatments. Mary and her family made the decision that she should enroll in hospice in St. Louis and move to Chesterfield Villas because her octogenarian mother resided there and her younger sister lived down the street. Mary clammed up and seemed reticent to share more. She feared crying, for the mucus would clog her nasal passages and lungs, making it even harder to breath. The multiple losses she suffered now overwhelmed her. She shook her head, signaling Elizabeth to stop. Elizabeth laid her hand on Mary's cold hand. She asked Mary about her jewelry collection.

Mary slipped off the oxygen cannula wired in her nose and hobbled to the closet. She pulled out a box and opened it up. For months Mary had worried about her jewelry collection. She had already picked out a few pieces to bequeath to her sons, their wives, and her sister but she was unsure where the rest of collection would go after her death.

She opened the box. Strings of amber, glass beads, silver rings, Native American bone pendants of the sun and moon, and bracelets embedded with rainbow moonstones sparkled in the afternoon sunlight. Mary lifted a necklace of multicolored beads and recalled teaching her special ed students how to count, add, and subtract. Another loop of pastel beads she used to teach them how to multiply and divide.

Once the precious stones warmed Mary's clammy hands, her painful bedridden condition receded. She stood in front of the classroom where she supplanted math textbooks with touchable, eye-catching, shiny stones. Elizabeth guided Mary with questions to deepen the reminiscences awakened by the jewelry—Mary's teaching instruments.

Mary shared how her interventions using jewelry restored the confidence of the children whose families and communities cast aside as rejects. She remembered being so proud of a little girl who learned how to count to two and then to five and who eventually mastered her times tables. Mary believed and constantly instilled into the children a philosophy of "Doing the best with what you have, rather than focusing on what you don't have." She quashed all quitter attitudes and believed in their abilities while working around their disabilities.

Mary lifted a tree of life pendant and earrings. The symbol gave her students an illustration of community. The roots of the tree created a single unbroken line from the root to the top limb and symbolized for the students their link to everything in their past generations and the future. Mary had bought several tree of life pieces and used them as classroom incentives. The students received points for achieving specific behavioral and educational goals. After totaling a certain number of points, they received a piece of jewelry as their reward. Mary recalled how proud she was when the students pooled all of their earned points together to win a tree of life pendant and earrings for their guidance counselor. They'd discovered the collective power of community and how to give to others.

Elizabeth realized these dusty relics were not just a jewelry collection, but a conduit to Mary's past. It occurred to Elizabeth that she should record a story for each piece of jewelry. Mary's life spun within these precious stones. Elizabeth loved buying antique jewelry at estate sales because she believed that old stones and rings held a person's energy. Most people held estate sales after someone died. The departed's life story would disappear without a trace. Jewelry with a story connected would personalize "Mary Dexter's Jewelry Tale and Sale." As Elizabeth breathed those words, the anxiety drained instantly from Mary's face. Elizabeth shared Jim's art legacy with Mary.

For the first time since Elizabeth arrived, she saw Mary smile.

Elizabeth suggested they invite teachers from the area school districts and the community. Mary thought she could donate the proceeds to purchase T-shirts for the work-study special ed students that brought joy to her each afternoon. She knew the T-shirts would make them feel like they belonged to a workforce, to a community. Mary began to realize that she still had a few more lessons left to teach. Elizabeth and Mary arranged to meet on Tuesday and Thursday afternoons. Mary called her son to have him send the jewelry collection in storage at his home.

On a warm summer afternoon, Elizabeth watched as Mary lifted a tiny gold band that Mary's mother had slipped on her finger shortly after she was born on October 10, 1941, in Sultan, Washington. Mary reminisced and Elizabeth recorded. A silver bangle returned Mary to the school playground in Anchorage, Alaska, where her first boyfriend, Valentine, gave her the gift for her twelfth birthday. She recalled her love for animals starting in Anchorage when she was eighteen years old and volunteered for a local veterinarian. She worked tirelessly beside a team of veterinarians for two days trying to save two beached humpback whales. The mother died, but they managed to safely return the baby to the deep icy waters off the coast of Alaska. She even made her debut on the local evening news in an interview about the rescue.

After high school, Mary married an artist in the Coast Guard and together they lived in San Francisco's Haight-Ashbury district during the hippie movement. She found many of the shield rings embedded with precious stones while jewelry hunting in estate shops and fairs during that era. Full of pride, she recalled standing side-by-side with hundreds of young spirited teachers working toward integration of the black and white public schools after the *Brown vs. Board of Education* decision. She remembered that the Omaha district was one of the only districts to integrate silently without disrupting the learning environment.

Just by touching the jewelry, Mary flashed forward and backward in time. She recounted the surprise of receiving the copper bangle etched with a bird from a student who thoughtfully picked it out while on a trip to Mexico, his homeland. Mary indulged in countless stories of receiving gifts of jewelry from her students. They became treasure hunters like their teacher.

As Mary spoke, she modeled the jewelry on her fingers or around her neck. She ran her fingers over a parrot necklace that inspired a play entitled *The Parrot Queen* that her students wrote and performed in. They repeated the play many times so each student could play the lead role and be crowned Parrot Queen. Elizabeth giggled and then placed the necklace around Mary's neck to crown her "The Last Parrot Queen."

Over the ten weeks they spent together, Elizabeth recognized Mary tapping a wellspring of positive episodes in her life that began overpowering her corrosive despair and negativity. Mary transformed before Elizabeth's eyes as she reconnected to her past life untouched by the cancer. She could return to her classroom or walk hand-in-hand with her boys or cuddle her animals once more.

A silver dolphin ring brought on recollections of her koi fish, Beauty. "Beauty was more like a dog than a fish," Mary said. Every time Mary entered the room, Beauty whacked himself against the tank to get her attention. Mary blissfully relived the evenings when Beauty would jump out of the tank and land on the floor. She simulated to Elizabeth how she wrapped her hands around a slippery five-pound fish and muscled it back into the tank. Elizabeth knew that for a brief moment, Mary was back in her home.

Mary looked forward to Elizabeth's visits until one dim October day. Elizabeth's schedule began stacking up with patients at BJC Hospice, and she was finding it difficult to juggle her patient load. She showed up two hours late. Mary shouted at Elizabeth.

"Do you know what it's like to wait, to just sit here and wait?" Mary said.

Elizabeth apologized for not calling. Mary described her frustration of always having to wait for her meals, wait for people to come visit her, wait to die.

Elizabeth had treated her like a living person, not a dying person, until that point.

Elizabeth was afraid. She sat down on the edge of the bed as Mary relived the traumatic encounters of waiting for death and being revived twice, although a signed Do Not Resuscitate order was in her file at Stanford Medical Center.

"Were you angry?" Elizabeth asked.

"Yes, very angry," Mary steamed.

The third time all systems in her body shut down, she awoke needing to go to the bathroom. Mary startled the nurse preparing her body for transport to what Mary believes was the morgue. The nurse mumbled something about being dead, Mary said.

Elizabeth left that day and cried on the way home. Even though she helped people tell their life stories, she couldn't shield them from death. Elizabeth realized in the three months she had been spending with Mary, she had given Mary the magnolia blossom, but Mary had taught Elizabeth about the gradual wilting of that blossom.

After the fourth large FedEx box arrived from California, Elizabeth grew discouraged. The task proved too big to complete in time for the

November sale date. They scaled back on writing a story for each piece of jewelry and instead grouped them. Mary worried that they would not make enough money to pay for the T-shirts. Elizabeth looked at a room full of jewelry numbering in the high hundreds and knew they would make enough. She struggled to convince the nervous Mary that people would in fact attend the sale.

Outside Mary's window, the trees had shed their colorful fall coats and now looked like skeletons beneath the looming winter sky. As the jewelry sale neared, Elizabeth and Mary polished all the jewelry and priced the pieces. Elizabeth saved the tough job for last. How do you put a price on jewelry bound with your life story? Elizabeth laughed when Mary tossed a gold ring with diamonds from her ex-husband in the five-dollar batch.

"Someone will get a surprise," she giggled.

And then in the same breath, she placed a beaded necklace that a student gave her in the twenty-dollar pile. They encased the pieces in small bags. Elizabeth sent special invitations to all teachers in the local districts.

On the morning of the jewelry sale, an army of hospice and nursing home volunteers helped set out the displays of jewelry on a maze of long rectangular dinner tables covered with white linen tablecloths. The skylight in the hall ceiling filtered in the sunshine, drenching the jewelry exhibits in natural light. At the cash register, Elizabeth placed a letter from Mary and a journal for each person to write where the pieces of jewelry would land next.

Upstairs on the third floor, Mary strapped on her portable oxygen tanks and anxiously sat in the wheelchair waiting to leave her room for the first time in months. She rolled down the hallways. When the elevator doors opened she heard the familiar buzz of people sounding like a crowd at a country fair. Her mother, a woman resembling Mary with white hair, turned the wheelchair around the bend into the atrium. Mary gasped. Hundreds of mothers, daughters, sisters, and teachers circulated the displays. They read her life stories and thoughtfully picked out pieces. She saw glimmers of smiles and a few tears on their faces. Elizabeth introduced Ms. Mary Dexter to the crowd. She was overwhelmed with emotion. She no longer felt like the woman in 303 dying of lung cancer. They were all there for her.

The crowd began to stir anxiety and she felt a shortness of breath. Teachers came up and thanked her. One by one, they exalted her creativity in teaching special needs students. Some shared how these pieces would return to the classroom and live on in teaching special needs students locally. But the triumph was short lived. Mary felt a surge of panic and urged her mother to roll her back to her room. Mary hoped to go down one more time, but just could not drum up the courage.

In the first hour of the jewelry sale, a businessman from the community introduced himself to Elizabeth as Don. The round, jolly fellow had read the news story about Mary in the morning paper and felt so inspired that he drove to Chesterfield Villas to participate. Don owned a local T-shirt business and offered to donate the shirts for Mary to give to the students.

Elizabeth visited Mary after the sale, bearing gifts and good news. Most of the jewelry had been sold. They made more than a thousand dollars plus the donation of the T-shirts. Mary suggested that they donate the extra money to the students so that they could donate to their favorite charity. Then Elizabeth surprised Mary with a book of pictures she'd secretly taken of all the jewelry displays, bound with Mary's life stories. She also gave Mary the journal, packed with stories from teachers, mothers, daughters, and sisters who would carry on her memory. Young teachers described their challenges in working with special needs students and found inspiration in Mary's classroom lessons and rewards. Some told how they selected a string of beads to reuse for counting and math in their classrooms. Others wrote about using the bone jewelry as touchable folk art for their history and social studies classes.

In January 2005, after the students returned from their winter break, the work-study special-education teacher, Barbara, came up to Mary's room to say thank you and report on how the students responded to her gifts. Elizabeth, Barbara, and Don, the T-shirt guy, gathered in Mary's room. Don delivered the T-shirts. The gold shirts were adorned with the tree of life logo and read "All Life and Learning Is Connected."

Elizabeth helped Mary into her shirt, then handed the rest to the teacher for her students.

Barbara smiled and said, "I told them how you observed the students getting off the bus outside your window each day and how you had previously taught special ed. Suddenly, I watched these restless kids settle down. They really realized you were giving so much to them. Then I went on to tell them how you orchestrated the jewelry sale and how so many of your friends and family members volunteered to help. I explained how a whole lot of people chipped in to make this work. All this love going around because you wanted to do something for them."

"Have you figured out what to do with the extra money?" Mary asked.

"Yes, as a matter of fact, the group I really like is Heifer International."

Heifer donates an animal, like a cow, to an impoverished family, then that family must donate so much milk or the first calf to another family. Everyone who is a recipient must then become a donor. This establishes a chain of giving that keeps going around the village. It's helping people to help themselves—precisely in accordance with Mary's teaching philosophy.

"I showed the kids the catalogue and they each decided what animal they wanted to give," the teacher said. They pooled their share of the money to donate a goat, some rabbits, and a heifer. "There was so much giving that went into them getting the shirts, but it's not too often that they get to give something concrete, something tangible. They get to hold the money and choose how to give it to somebody who really needs it."

Mary's spirit brightened. She turned to Elizabeth.

"Look what we started," Mary said as her voice cracked and tears of joy flowed.

Elizabeth threw her arms around Mary and squeezed her tight.

"What a seed you planted," Elizabeth said to Mary.

"I think it's a forest," Mary said. "It's growing."

After Barbara left, Elizabeth took hold of Mary's hand.

"I feel selfishly glad that they did resuscitate you because I got to meet you," Elizabeth said.

"Yeah," Mary said.

Elizabeth kneeled beside Mary.

"Remember I told you about the Aztec culture, that there are three kinds of deaths?"

"Yeah," Mary said.

"And by the last standard, you know, you are going to live a long, long, long time," Elizabeth said.

FIVE Her Season of Lasts: Traditional, Seasonal, Communal Rituals

On a still, overcast afternoon in November 2001, I noticed my mother's life cycle had strangely begun to mirror the annual changing seasons. The sun-filled days dimmed, giving way to longer, drearier nights. Winter, nature's end, and the rapidly approaching holidays sparked me to contemplate her lasts. We often celebrate a person's firsts—the first cry, the first word, the first step, the first birthday. Thoughts about a person's lasts are often reflections rather than plans of action, but if you knew, as we did, then logic or intuition told me her lasts must be momentous. How do you celebrate the last Thanksgiving? The last Christmas? The last New Year? The last birthday?

I sat down at the computer and composed my next list of interview questions about family traditions. I had no idea whether Mom had brought English traditions across the Atlantic or had adapted and replaced them with American traditions. Exploring her roots could help orchestrate a season of memorable lasts.

Traditions link generations, bond families, and live on after death. Before excavating the roots of traditions celebrated in our home that were brought over from England, I needed to get our upcoming American holiday under way. My mother had always handled cooking the bird and the fixings, just asking me to do simple things like set the dinner table. This year, Mom wouldn't be doing much cooking—or eating, for that matter. All of a sudden I had an idea.

I left my cursor idling on the computer and ran downstairs to the kitchen. Mom kept all her holiday recipes on index cards filed inside the sacred green box. I climbed up on the counter.

There in the cupboard above the oven was the vault of our secret family recipes. I carried it like one might hold the family jewels into my mother's room.

"What are you doing with that?" she asked.

"We're going to plan Thanksgiving dinner," I said. "Let's put together a grocery list. You will have to teach me how to make Thanksgiving dinner this year."

She opened up her box and smiled so proudly that you would've thought I had just asked her to teach me about the secrets of motherhood. Together, we sifted through her recipes. She dictated the ingredients while I wrote a grocery list.

Thanksgiving morning began early. Mom warned me that Thanksgiving dinner is a methodically timed mission. She'd aced the process, and in order for this to be a success, she needed me to carry out her instructions. So like a good soldier, I followed her orders. Over the course of six hours, I learned how to prepare a whole turkey for roasting plus all the secrets, shortcuts, and addenda to her recipes. I discovered her special casserole serving dishes, each bought specially for this annual dinner, and their hiding places in the depths of our cupboards where they hibernated year around. At four o'clock, just as planned, the turkey and all the fixings arrived on the dinner table, cooked and seasoned to perfection, just like Mom's.

Beverly, Mom, Ryan, Simon, Gil, and I sat around the dinner table. I led the prayer of Thanksgiving. Mom usually did that, but I figured the time had come to assume the role. Afterward I suggested each one of us take a moment to reflect on the year and share one to three things we were thankful for. As I sat back in my chair, exhausted, a windfall of memories from the year invigorated me. I was most grateful for my mother's openness, her willingness to share her life with me. Emerging out of a semiconscious reverie, I felt the cool tears rolling down my cheeks. Mom reached over and placed her hand on mine.

"Thank you, my love," she said.

She then thanked each one of us for taking care of her. As the matriarch of our family, she rarely showed vulnerability long enough to admit the need for our devotion.

I felt the pull of the changing of the guard, a calling to fill the matriarch's duties, on the eve of Advent. One of the unspoken customs in our home on the first day of Advent was to sweep away all the troubles that plagued us throughout the year. Physically and mentally, we cleaned our home and cleansed our minds. Advent brought a time for renewal and preparation to unite in a mission to make Christmas the shining shared family memory of the year. Mom always gave us an Advent calendar to spark excitement, drum up anticipation, and begin the countdown to Christmas morning. She would collect our Christmas wish lists and commence the secret shopping for gifts to stuff our stockings and gifts for beneath our tree.

The dark days of late fall would fly by, culminating in the Advent weekend festivities—created and nurtured by Mom to lift us out of the bleakness of the days—that embodied the spirit of Mother Christmas for her children. The first weekend of Advent, she would reclaim the boxes marked "Christmas decorations" from the garage, play carols, toast Advent with eggnog and apple cider, and transform our home into a winter wonderland. We would roam the Christmas tree lot in search of the perfect evergreen to bring home and dress it in lights and ornaments. The scent of pine would fill the house while we rolled dough, cut cookies, and baked batches of sugary treats to deliver to friends.

On Christmas Eve, we would read passages from the bible's nativity story and verses from *Twas the Night Before Christmas*. Both stories were so ingrained that to this day, I can recite them by heart. After our reading, we would congregate at the church an hour before midnight for the candlelight service. Following carols, a single flame would pass from one person to another, each person lighting the next person's candle, and together we would proceed outside singing "Peace, Peace, Peace." The glowing candles would illuminate the midnight skies as we sang "Silent Night." Christmas Day, my brother and I would awake to the sounds of presents rustling in a bulging stocking at the foot of our beds, reminding us that Christmas had arrived. Even after we discovered Santa Claus was really our mom, we continued to be the beneficiaries of all this enchantment she stirred.

As visions of past Christmases swirled about me, I poked my head into Mom's room to request an interview about our family's seasonal rituals. She turned down the Christian praise music that converted her sickroom into a sanctuary of calm. I knew she missed singing hymns with the choir at church on Sundays. The CD player had become her surrogate. I turned on the tape recorder and camcorder, and she unfolded the genesis of our family traditions.

She said, "Oh, I began to cling onto traditions much more once my life was brought to a standstill after the divorce. I think I was building new traditions and wanted them to be meaningful because I was trying to make it okay to be single."

This was a revelation as I realized Mom had reinvented our holidays after Dad left. Most of the Advent traditions to which I'd become accustomed started when I was seven, my brother's first Christmas. She had planned the festivities to revolve around my brother and me to disguise the absence of our father. It dawned on me that the spirit of Christmas, the magic, was in reality a true illusion born out of my mother's spirit of survival.

She went on.

"I tried not to focus so much on the emptiness, the bleakness. You and Ryan made my life. You saved me from the loneliness after the divorce," she said.

"Children's wonderment of Santa Claus makes Christmas. I would collect all the gifts, some would be stocking stuffers from Santa Claus and some would be from me under the tree. I would always make sure I had separate wrapping paper from Santa Claus," she said.

"Yeah, Dad always made that mistake," I quipped.

We both laughed, but then her giggles gave way to unabated tears. The mention of my dad brought reminders of her first Christmas after the divorce. Ryan and I, her only family, spent the holiday with our dad and his new fiancée. For her, it was the longest, darkest, and most devastating Christmas she'd ever experienced. For the first time in her life, she actually entertained the idea of moving home to England. Instead, she combated her feelings by opening our home to other single people the following year, and every year after that. Although she ran the divorce recovery group at church, I'd discovered the source of why our home was the default destination for many single people at Thanksgiving and Christmas. My mother never wanted anyone to be alone at Christmas.

"What about in England, what traditions made Christmas important to you?" I asked.

"All the good food my dad cooked to surround an enormous chicken," she said. "My fondest memories were the excitement of what the gifts were in my stocking at the foot of my bed Christmas morning. And then there was one big present under the tree from my parents."

It sounded familiar.

As Advent approached, I found myself subconsciously trying to invoke the spirit of Christmas. I could hardly fathom Christmas without my mother igniting the season. I scrubbed the floors and dusted the furniture while trying to reconfigure the forthcoming Advent to bolster my own spirit of survival. To be honest, Advent held no meaning without her, but reviewing her life gave me the will to keep pushing on when I just wanted to wallow. She had done it for me. I could now do it for her.

I thought about how ritual saved my mother at her life's lowest point. I began to understand the meaning of rituals and how they provide structure, actions, and a way to uplift the spirit wearied by chaos and unwanted changes. Rituals permeate our lives, orient us in changing conditions, and observe transitions in the cycles of our existence. The late anthropologist Arnold Van Gannep, author of *The Rites of Passage: A Classic Study of Cultural Celebrations,* said that throughout our history, humans have turned to rituals to cope with moments of crisis.[1] This patterned and/or symbolic set of behaviors focuses on balance in the midst of chaos as we pause, reflect, and release old routines, welcoming new ones and moving forward.

My cleaning ritual rid our home not only of the dust, but also of the residual shadows of pains, failures, and losses of the last year. I stepped outside into the cold fresh air and looked at my reflection in the sparkling sliding glass door.

"Okay, you can do it," I thought to myself. I turned to open the garage door. I rummaged through the dim garage searching for the boxes of Christmas decorations. I dragged them inside and turned on the Christmas music. I climbed the stairs and found Mom listening to hymns in bed with her eyes closed. I know she missed singing hymns in church on Sunday.

I invited Mom downstairs to help decorate. She resisted. It was the first time I'd witnessed a dispirited "Mother Christmas" on Advent's first day. I momentarily faced yet another crisis. I could give in to her and weep for what had been or plead with her to join me. I chose the latter. She sucked on a lollipop filled with morphine for breakthrough pain and came down. I retrieved the decorations and she told me where to place them. Afterward, I made her some raspberry tea and poured myself a glass of wine. Toasting the first day of Advent didn't feel the same, but at least we were warming up.

On the second week of Advent, I carved out a path in the dense thicket of trees that appeared to be sprouting out of the asphalt in this suburban neighborhood where I grew up, La Verne. Mom gave me the address of the Christmas tree lot we'd been going to since I was a toddler. Simon, my boyfriend, followed close behind me. "This is it," I hollered back to him. I happened on an extraordinary hybrid tree—a cross between a Noble and Douglas fir. Ironically, I'd always chosen the Noble, whereas my mom preferred the traditional Douglas. We switched each year. This hybrid was the *perfect* mascot for our special Christmas, especially considering the true meaning of the symbolic evergreen is immortality in the winter season.

As we trimmed the tree, Mom entertained Simon and me with stories of how the many ornaments had entered our vast family heirloom collection.

"You know I made sure to get the Christmas decorations in the divorce," she said.

"I'm so glad you did, Mom, because each one is a piece of our family's traditions," I said.

I realized at that moment, and I think she did, too, that each year from this Christmas forward, I will pull out these boxes and make sure to celebrate no matter how debilitated I would be by her absence. These decorations and traditions will invoke not just the spirit of Christmas, but also the spirit of my mother. The stories attached to the ornaments will inevitably become family lore to pass on to her grandchildren and great-grandchildren as we sit around the Christmas tree in the future years.

Whilst decorating, we talked about English Christmas traditions that Simon and my mother missed. They reveled about Christmas pudding, custard, Christmas crackers—a cardboard tube filled with a paper hat, a toy, a joke, and a banger (two thin lengths of cardboard with a bit of gunpowder) that pops when pulled—and all sorts of customs my mother had never mentioned. For the first time, I felt like an American in the company of Mom and Simon. I'd rarely heard them romanticize England. Christmas made her nostalgic for home.

Her reminiscence gave me an idea.

THE LAST CHRISTMAS

Late Christmas morning, I assisted my mother as she gingerly descended the stairs. She followed the sounds of clanging pots and pans that grew louder with each step. Her eyes widened at the luminescent living room. Beneath the twinkling tree, mounds of gifts addressed "To Mom" sparkled in her favorite colors, lavender and violet. Her best china adorned the dining table, together with the English Christmas crackers she'd reminisced about.

As she entered the family room, Nat King Cole's voice reverberated the "Christmas Song." She turned toward the clatter in the kitchen to see a sight any mother would be proud to behold. She gasped.

Flames lit up the stove as Ryan whirled around the kitchen sautéing the shrimp *diabla*. Ryan and his fellow culinary artists worked in a four-star exhibition kitchen at the Napa Rose at the Disneyland Resort. So he was a pro at choreographing a culinary show. Since our mom was unable to visit him at the Napa Rose, he brought the show home. Her kitchen looked like a set from the Food Channel Network. Every pan on the burner sizzled. Balsamic vinegar reduction bubbled on the stove next to a simmering white wine and butter sauce. The roast, decorated in fresh herbs and painted in English mustard, sat idle like a piece of artwork on the island. The blender swirled fresh basil and garlic into a bright green pesto sauce.

Mom settled into her recliner. Ryan carried a saucepan over to her.

"Smell this," he said.

"Ahhhhhh, that smells delicious," she said.

He impressed her with his presentation and rich, aromatic master-pieces. She feasted with her eyes and nose. He dazzled her by explaining in eloquent detail each step in sculpting his artwork.

"Everyone, let's move to the living room," I called out to Mom, Ryan, Simon, Gil, and Beverly. We planned to eat Ryan's appetizers while opening presents; that way Mom wouldn't just be sitting and salivating while we ate. He described the anatomy of each dish.

"We don't make dishes with recipes in a fine dining restaurant. That's why you always see a chef with a pocket full spoons—you always taste as you go along," he said.

In the midst of all his presentation, Mom dove in. She took small bites.

"Ummmm," she said. "This is good, love."

Ryan stopped talking to watch his Mom relish his creation. She hadn't eaten anything since June, but couldn't resist a nibble. I threw on the Santa hat and passed out the gifts. Purposely, Mom received the most gifts. She gave me a thank-you kiss for each one. It was fabulous.

Ryan dished up the dinner. As we gathered at the table, I directed everyone to lift up their Christmas cracker, cross their arms, and, in unison, tug hard on the person's cracker either side of them. Loud bangs triggered an explosion of wrapping paper, cardboard, and toys spraying across the table. We all slipped on our silly crown-shaped crepe-paper hats.

"Okay, everyone has to read their Christmas cracker joke—you'll find it inside the tube you just burst open. And then I want you all to share a Christmas memory or tradition," I said.

"Okay," Mom said. "What did the astronaut see as he was cooking?"

We called out silly answers, but none were correct.

"No, an unidentified frying object," Mom said.

"Just remember, never fry an egg naked," Ryan said, making us all laugh at his obvious mistake.

"Ohhh," Mom said. "Never fry anything naked." We each proceed to tell our joke, then I said, "Okay, a memory—all of my Christmases were magical and special because of you, Mom, but I'd have to say waking up at dawn every Christmas morning to the crackling of wrapping paper and gifts in my stocking at the foot of my bed is by far my favorite memory. Thank you."

"I agree," Ryan said, raising his glass for a toast to Mother Christmas.

We spent hours sitting and bonding around the dinner table, followed by wordplay games. Simon served dessert, the famous English Bird's custard and Christmas pudding. Mom indulged in all of the nostalgic scents and activities of English Christmas past.

The next morning when I woke up, Mom called me into her bedroom.

"Denise, I want you to come in here with your tape recorder," she said.

Now, this was a first. I always initiated the interviews. And this is what she said: "Christmas 2001, I didn't do one thing. Usually I am the one who plans everything and does everything, and this time I just lay in bed or lay around the house and didn't do a thing. And my daughter from November on was rushing here and there buying gifts, wrapping gifts, and planning the food. Everything I would normally do, she did it and did it in style."

"What are your first memories of Christmas morning?" I asked.

"I suppose seeing my bleary-eyed son at about five in the morning having to get up because he had an early shift so he could spend Christmas with me, which was really touching . . . Having Ryan do the cooking, that was something special."

She giddily recounted his exquisite creations. After she came up for air from exhaling all of her memories, she turned to me.

"Well, I just wanted to get that down so we wouldn't forget, because it was so special," she said.

"What made it so special?" I asked.

"Seeing my children in the kitchen doing everything that I'd always done. Who would have thought three years ago that Ryan would be cooking the Christmas dinner?"

THE LAST NEW YEAR

For New Year's Eve, I booked a room at the Hotel Laguna. With the sunroof open and fresh sea air on our faces, we cruised south on Pacific Coast Highway.

Freedom.

We arrived in Laguna Beach just after two o'clock. I rearranged the bright, airy room to give Mom the perfect comfortable perch to recline on the bed and gaze out the window—at the waves crashing onto the shore, children playing in the park, and couples walking hand-in-hand on Main Beach.

Serenity engulfed us. We played cards on the bed. After a few hours, I draped a sweater over her shoulders and wheeled her into the elevator and down to the oceanfront café. We joined the dozens of spectators gathered to watch the last sunset of 2001. The sun glided across the lavender and tangerine sky and slipped elegantly, like a curtsy, into the Pacific Ocean. Everyone clapped and whistled at nature's grandest finale.

At dusk, I was a bit nervous as I set up Mom's IV feed life-support system. I connected the IV to her open port and held my breath as the machine booted up. The waves rumbling toward the shore echoed in our room. We watched the New Year's Eve special with Dick Clark on television and witnessed the ball drop in New York's Times Square, ringing in 2002. I felt a rush of joy and triumph for again refusing to surrender to this cancer. I flopped down on the bed across from Mom and looked at the moonlight illuminating the ocean below.

I heard the rumbling sound again, but it wasn't coming from outside. I looked across the room to see the bed rocking against the wall. In California, small tremors weren't unusual, but this wasn't an earthquake.

My mother was convulsing. Her face was as white as the moon and her eyes were nearly black. I leapt up.

"Oh, my God, what's going on?" I cried.

I'd never seen anyone have a seizure before. I was terrified.

"I feel cold inside," she quivered repeatedly.

"I'm going to call 911," I said in a panic.

"No, no, please, Denise," she begged me.

"If you go unconscious, I'm going to call 911," I said.

I called Norris Cancer Hospital at USC and the operator said she would page the on-call doctor. I tried to stay calm, but I couldn't disguise my own trembling voice. The operator asked me what was going on. After I explained, she gave some advice.

I cradled my mom's body as she continued to tell me she was going cold inside. I thought, "This is it. My mom is going to die in this hotel room and I'm alone." I aligned my breathing with hers and began rubbing the middle of her back for what seemed like an eternity before the doctor called back. He didn't help much, but the shaking had subsided.

Twenty minutes later, the shaking escalated again. Midnight struck. Everyone was celebrating the arrival of the New Year as I prepared myself for the inevitable.

"I love you, Mom," I said.

"We're going to get through this," I said, assuring myself more than her.

"I'm so cold inside," she said repeatedly until the shaking stopped.

She drifted off to sleep. I stayed awake to keep watch.

Finally the rising sun blinded me on the first morning of 2002. For the first time, thoughts about my mother's last breath, the actual moment, left me breathless. The episode rocked me. Its magnitude felt like the kind of earthquake that scares a native Californian enough to move out of state.

The following day we visited Dr. Garcia, who discovered an infection in the open intravenous line that spread to the blood in her veins. Despair and hopelessness attacked me in the aftermath. I awaited the fatal aftershock. I found myself constantly entering her bedroom while she slept to check if she was still breathing.

My best friend, Denise Noble, called me about plans for Mom's upcoming fifty-fourth birthday, which was on January 9. Denise asked me to meet her at a local coffee shop to strategize. I slipped out of the house that afternoon. Having the same name and born three days apart, we'd been best friends since junior high. My mom was like a second mom to her. People often asked us if we were twins. We were the same height and wore the same dress and shoe size, but she had brown eyes and heaps of curly locks.

That afternoon in a quiet corner of the café, I relived the terrifying New Year. For the first time, I felt truly defeated by the cancer. Festivities no longer sounded appealing. Reluctantly, I agreed to collaborate on a plan of action for this last bash. There was no time for invitations and RSVPs. Instead, I telephoned all of my mother's friends. Each phone call forced me to reach out, and as a result, my despondency faded.

THE LAST INTERVIEW

Mom's 2002 birthday fell on a Wednesday. In the morning I orchestrated a petite bedroom birthday celebration. My brother and I tied a dozen balloons on my mother's bed and placed two vases of fresh cut irises in the room before she woke up.

I led the "Happy Birthday" wakeup song as I carried in a delicious cake topped with whole fresh fruit and lit birthday candles. Mom sat up in bed and rubbed the newly grown fuzz atop her bald head.

"Should I put my wig on?" she asked.

"No, you look pretty without it," I said. "So, how does it feel to be fifty-four?"

"No different," Mom said. "I have to do mathematics to figure out my birthday—I don't remember how old I am. You know, I watch the television commercials, and there are so many fifty-, sixty- and seventy-year-olds. Now, I know I'm at the end of my life, and I'm only in my fifties, and there are so many out there in their eighties and they're still vibrant."

She was overwhelmed with these thoughts of missing out on growing old. Tears cascaded down her face. She was referring to all the pharmaceutical commercials that show energetic seniors pushing their grandchildren on the swings at the park. Others show seniors hiking in the mountains and enjoying nature in their golden years.

"I'm not going to be one of those people," she said. "Well, I've really looked at life, the older people, since I've been diagnosed. I realize I'm young and yet I've had enough of this life."

She paused, rethinking her bold statement, and amended, "Not enough of it."

Beverly, my mother's best friend, interrupted her, "You've enjoyed what you had."

"But I've enjoyed what I've had," she agreed. "I've done what I was meant to do here."

"Leave a couple of leftovers," Beverly said.

"Yes, I have raised two children, to carry the smile on," she said, emanating a smile as bright as the first ray of light after a long, dark, sleepless night.

THE LAST BIRTHDAY PARTY

The following Sunday after her birthday, she stepped out of the shower and slipped into her new maroon fleece sweat suit, which succeeded in concealing the external tube that dumped a florescent green fluid from her intestines into an ostomy bag that hung at her side. Her face, arms, and legs were swollen, a reaction to the antibiotics.

Just before noon, I escorted the birthday girl down the stairs. She stopped in the living room decorated with bouquets of balloons, lilac flower arrangements, and a feast of meats, cheeses, vegetables, and a breadbasket.

The walk downstairs stirred a bit of nausea, causing her to labor in her breathing and vomit all over her pink turtleneck. I quickly changed her shirt and quieted her worries about it happening again in front of all of her guests.

"No one is going to care if you throw up, Mom," I said. "As long as you don't barf when you're blowing out the candles on the birthday cake." She burst into laughter.

"Yeah, they all know I'm sick," she said.

I admired her courage.

Around one o'clock, the doorbell rang and in strode families and elders from my mother's church, many of her single friends from the divorce recovery group and their kids, our neighbors from my childhood home, my closest friends, and her bible study group. We hadn't entertained this many people in our home since before my mother's diagnosis. She sat like a queen in the family room, against the backdrop of her sunlit garden.

In the midst of chatting with her friends, a Christian praise music band—five strolling singers and a strumming guitar player—entered and passed through the living room to encircle her. She gasped, recognizing one of the singers, David Ayala, Denise's friend from college. David, a twenty-six-year-old civil engineer studying to be a minister, had visited my mom a couple times to pray and read the Bible with her and sing to her, but this time he brought his band. Mom missed the live praise music at church on Sundays.

It was a delightful surprise.

The guitar player led the group in singing the powerful hymn "Amazing Grace," which instantly triggered a volcanic eruption of tears to stream down my cheeks. Mom turned her head up to me and reached out. I knelt down beside her. I remembered singing these words at my father's funeral. It felt strangely visceral to be singing this song in my family room with a choir of intimates. I saw each person gradually join in the chorus. I'd never witnessed anything like this before. The singing transmuted the atmosphere in our home from trepidation to reverence.

The rising symphony of voices publicly acknowledged the lament and celebration of Mom's last birthday. I saw tears in the eyes of every person around the room. They raised their voices to mirror the guitarist, who led them higher and higher until the mournful hymn burst into a crescendo of hallelujahs. Mom's eyes were closed, tears rolled down to her mouth, which was curved upward in a smile, and she was singing "Hallelujah." Our voices felt like angels' hands lifting her up on a chair swinging higher, higher toward the heavens. Overwhelmed by the transcendent emotions around me, I held tighter onto her hand, not ready to let go. For an instant I felt as I had on my first day of preschool, when I was not ready to enter a new world without her. She opened her eyes and turned to me. She was singing the lyrics "God will make a way, where there seems to be no way." At that moment, I released my iron grip and smiled back.

As the music swung low, David turned his attention on my mom. "We just wanted to come by and wish you encouragement on your birthday. Do you have any requests?" he asked.

"As a Deer," she said. The guitarist and the group sang the intro and then led us into another rhythmic pattern of repeating the chorus after him. The melody carried us to her next request, which Mom led, the guitarist following. Her voice lifted in key as if rejoicing in the face of death.

I turned to the clock and what had seemed like ten minutes was in reality more than an hour. Then David asked us all to gather around my mother. Ken Daignault, a church elder who led the Sunday evening healing services, knelt in front of her and called upon everyone to lay their hands on Mom.

"Let's bow our heads. Thank you, Lord, for this time to come here. We ask that you keep Linda and Denise in your strong loving arms so they may continue to experience the fullness of your joy and love. Let them grow in their bond with each other and encourage one another even during this time when they might feel weary."

His prayer gave words to my deepest needs. My mother gripped my hand tightly. Others joined, praying aloud. I'd never experienced being the center of a community of prayers. I yielded to this solidarity enfolding us. I no longer felt alone in taking this journey—we'd been joined by a number of willing passengers on our train as it moved to my mother's final destination. Ken closed the prayer with an "Amen."

"Wow," Mom said, wiping her face. "I didn't expect that."

I lunged in and gave her a bear hug.

"So, is this what you do at every birthday party?" I said to David while mopping my tear-stained face. I asked him for one more song.

I lit the five-candle and the four-candle atop a gleaming white cake decorated with lavender roses and the words "Happy Birthday Linda." Beverly carried the cake over to my mother as David led us in singing "Happy Birthday."

Mom craned her head over the cake to get a better look. Beverly leaned forward a bit, and the cake tipped and splattered in Linda's lap. Everyone scrambled to rescue the cake.

When Beverly finally stood triumphantly with the cake in her hands and the candles still lit, we exhaled and the entire room shook with laughter. The comic relief cracked the solemn mood. Denise passed out a quiz called "All About Linda." It was a lengthy multiple-choice quiz that tested how well people really knew my mom. The quiz spurred curiosity about her early life, which she rarely talked about. I opened the photo albums we'd recently been poring over to show off my mom as a little girl and an adventurous teenager. I retold stories that were fresh in my mind, entertaining our friends as the sun dipped beneath the hills outside.

FINDING STRENGTH IN COMMUNAL RITUALS

Admittedly, I'm not a devoted churchgoing type like my mother, but certainly the communal gathering, singing, and then praying for my family shifted my perspective. The support encircling us was palpable and led me to a deeper appreciation for rituals steeped in communal bonds and fellowship with which Americans in pre-modern society confronted death.[2]

In his book *Confronting Death: Values, Institutions, and Human Mortality*, David Moller captures the essence and benefits of gathering together to celebrate a last birthday or holiday with the family and community instead of dwelling in isolation while awaiting death's arrival.

"Rituals function to facilitate a sense of well-being. Anyone who has taken part in a community ritual of prayer and song . . . has felt strengthened, perhaps even gained a sense of elation from doing so . . ." Moller writes. "The individual is able to transcend, at least temporarily, his or her fears, vulnerabilities, and anxieties. This state is achieved by becoming part of something greater and more vital than oneself and by absorbing the energy and vitality that are generated by the group rituals of worship."[3]

After the frightening close call on New Year's Eve compared with the reinvigorating birthday celebration, I valued the strength drawn from the presence of our friends and family.

Most doctors, psychologists, and hospice practitioners suggest that families gather together for one last birthday or holiday celebration when death is near. Sometimes this is a bit easier for all involved in lieu of organizing a "ceremonial farewell" and/or living funeral. We can depend on birthday traditions or holiday traditions to guide us into rituals that cue us to gather for a memorable occasion and embrace the magic we unwittingly experienced. Thomas Driver, author of *The Magic of Ritual: Our Need for Liberating Rites That Transform Our Lives and Our Communities,* appropriately describes the revelatory moments of my mother's last bash.

"Ritual controls emotion while releasing it and guides it while letting it run. Even in a time of grief, ritual lets joy be present through the permission to cry, lets tears become laughter, if they will, by making place for the fullness of tears' intensity—all this in presence of communal assertiveness. A ritual is a party at which emotions are welcome."[4]

The afterglow of the party didn't last long in the wake of the seizure aftershocks. This time, she slipped into unconsciousness. Ryan and Beverly carried her to the car and raced her to Norris Hospital. When I reached my mother, she reclined in a hospital bed. She told me that she'd been having waking dreams of someone tapping her hand, telling her it was time to go. Beverly and I both asked if she felt like all of her business was complete. She answered with a lukewarm "Yes."

A few minutes later, a nurse connected my mother to a morphine drip to minimize breakthrough pain. By the next morning, my mother was completely disoriented. She faded in and out of consciousness. She breathlessly asked me over and over to gather everyone together.

"I'm going to die," she warned. The disorientation steadily increased.

I tried to get a hospital release, but Dr. Garcia refused because she had a lingering fever, but he tapered the morphine. She was restless and her whispers became pleas for me not to leave her in hospital to die alone. I ordered a rollout bed and set up camp in her room. I promised Mom that I'd stay in the hospital room with her until we could both be released. My constant presence cleared her distant, cloudy state of panic.

By Sunday, seventy-two hours later, we still awaited discharge. I finally understood why she was miserable in the hospital. The endless pokes and prods from the staff around the clock with no concern about her sleep made her feel like a prisoner instead of a person. At two, three, four o'clock in the morning, they were in the room taking her temperature or checking other vitals. The daily rituals and rhythms of the hospital robbed my mother of her dignity. In a way, I felt like I learned this truth too late.

LAST WISHES

At dusk, Simon and I sat around her bedside in the cold hospital room. My mother reclined in bed and wore oxygen tubes in her nose. She'd come out of the tunnel in a heightened state of awareness. She began to talk at length with Simon about her decision to give up the intravenous feeding.

"Do you think it's giving up?" she asked him, while I sat in the corner of the room reading *Death, the Final Stage of Growth* by Elisabeth Kübler-Ross. I looked over the top of my book but decided to stay out of this conversation.

"I think you have done all that you can do to fight it," he said. "Denise and Ryan know you have fought hard. But you must be tired."

"Yes, I know, but is it giving up?" She asked again, almost rhetorically.

"Denise," she said.

"Yes, Mom?"

"You're going to need to take care of Ryan, be tough on him," she said. "Don't let him spend all the money. At least wait until he is twenty-five years old before he has access to it. Except for school. He can have the money early for college."

"Don't worry about it, Mom," I said. She was talking about the life insurance monies and retirement plans. We'd arranged to place all of my mother's assets in a living trust that would automatically go to us, her beneficiaries, in the event of her death. The living trust protected her estate from the lengthy process of probate when the courts assume the decedent's estate and distribute the assets according to the will. Probate can often take a year or more to file through the system. The living trust cost us close to $2,000 to put in place, but it was a wise investment. Basically, it protected Ryan and me from having to deal with probate courts and lawyers in the aftermath, when we would most certainly be overwhelmed by our grief. She knew our shortcomings and planned to protect us in her absence.

"You now have the reserves to travel and write that book," she said. "I just want you to get that travel bug out of your system, my love."

"Are you going to be okay, my love?" she asked, concerned. I knew what she was asking, and I wanted to say "No, just stay, we'll figure it out together." Instead, I got up, pulled down the guardrail on the bed, and sat next to her. I wrapped my arm around her and squeezed her tight. I felt my body temperature rise as I held back a torrent of tears welling up from some dark underground well in my gut. This was not the time for *my* tears, *my* grief.

"Yes, Mom, don't worry. Ryan and I will be okay," I said. "Come on, you raised us to be independent, right?"

She smiled and then closed her eyes to rest, as if finally receiving some peace of mind after a terrifying week of confusion.

I later came to recognize that last conversation as her oral ethical will, which summed up her wishes of how she expected me to live on in her absence and finalized her life review. She advised me to always seek God's guidance. She blessed my aspirations to travel and write while bestowing the responsibility of mothering my brother. Her instructions served as a spiritual and ethical compass.

The next morning, I woke at dawn in a haze on the cold vinyl hospital rollout. My mother was asking the nurse taking her morning vitals whether she could go home.

"Mom, I'll be right back. Don't worry. We'll take care of it today," I said.

"Okay, love," she said, trusting. She had total faith in me. The eldest at twenty-six, I was officially her primary caretaker, but we were a team. She made the decisions. I carried them out. Walking out of her room, I tried to devise a plan to inconspicuously get her out. Juggling three different escape routes in my head, I bumped into the resident intern in the hallway. I pleaded my case. His unibrow rhythmically bounced up and down to a series of "ahs" and "hmms." After hearing me out, he smiled and promised to take care of it. At four o'clock that afternoon, an ambulance crew arrived in Mom's room with a clipboard—the "golden" patient release papers. We were out. I gripped the gurney rail with one hand and called home to let everyone know we were free. We barreled down the hall and exited the building. The "liberation" crew helped my mother into the back of the ambulance. I hopped in the front seat with the driver. I craned my head back as the ambulance turned out of the Norris parking lot.

"Are you okay back there, Mom?"

"Yes, love, I'm just glad to be going home."

SIX

Oral Ethical Will: Video Recording
Valuable Last Words

The last words video recorded of John Marting, a member of our Greatest Generation, resembled an oral ethical will delivered to his sons surrounding his deathbed on a rainy afternoon in Irvine, California. As
the clock ticked loudly toward his eleventh hour, he reminded me of a
modern-day Jacob poignantly sharing what was most important to him,
his regrets in life and how he wished them to live on after his death. I sat
in awe realizing that here in the early years of the twenty-first century,
John, a true man of his generation, short on words, shorter on compli-
ments and self-reflections, reawakened a Jewish custom that dates back
to Biblical times when "parents used ethical wills to leave instructional
accounts of what they wanted most both for and from their children
while expressing what they learned in life."[1] It was reminiscent of the
passage in the Hebrew bible, Genesis, chapter 49: Jacob's sons gather

around their patriarch's deathbed, as he tries to pass on instructions on how they should conduct their lives after he dies.

Jack Riemer, known as America's rabbi, wisely warns parents in the book *Ethical Wills: A Jewish Modern Treasury* that "if parents don't take the time to share their life stories and the stories of those from whom they come then the stories will disappear and "our kids will be deprived. Parents would leave these wills behind because they believed that the wisdom they had acquired was just as much a part of the legacy for their children as all the material possessions," noted Rabbi Riemer.[2] In these wills, "parents reflected on their life experiences often through the prism of God's teachings to impart spiritual wisdom, values, morals, and life lessons onto their children and future generations."[3]

This custom is not only Jewish but also Christian and Muslim. In the book *Western Attitudes Toward Death From the Middle Ages to the Present*, social historian Philippe Ariès states that the oral custom survived throughout the eighteenth and nineteenth centuries. He specifies that a person on his or her deathbed delivered the will, which he describes in that period was more than a legal document to dispose of the property.

"The will was the means for a person to express his deep thoughts; his religious faith; his attachment to his possessions, to the beings he loved, to God; and the decisions he had made to assure the salvation of his soul and the repose of his body. This ritual assured the dying person that his or her life's wisdom would survive the physical death."[4] The ethical will became nearly extinct in the early twentieth century, when people edged toward death in hospitals rather than in the company of family and community.

In 2005, I discovered technology has revived a valuable social/familial deathbed ritual of recording treasured last words when answering an ad at Volunteermatch.org for a life review interviewer with a video camera to spend time talking to hospice patients in service of producing a life story video. In the past, *oral* exhortations survived through the generations of families and societies via memorization, rehearsal, and repetition. Today, video and audio technology replace these modes of transmission while also providing families with an opportunity to participate in the ancient custom of gathering around the dying family member to heed his or her last words.

The ad connected me to Donna Miller, a coordinator of volunteer services, at Solari Hospice in Orange County, California. She recruited and trained a volunteer corps to visit with hospice patients in need of a friendly visitor to read books to them, play music, or just sit so the family can take a break. In her late forties, with blond hair and a playful nature that could always turn a smile, Donna was reminiscent of an aging surfer girl. On a portable DVD player, she played the video of Raymond Long recounting vivid tales of his life, which spanned ninety-four years, from the early twentieth century and into the twenty-first century. His tales were intermingled with a montage of biographical photos and music. The life review interview ended with a simple oral ethical will to his daughters, who sat beside him during the filming. I'd seen personal history documentaries, but this one was different. It was a raw conversation at the end of this man's life.

Donna knew from experience that caring for a family member drains physical and mental energy, often depriving the family from spending time just sitting and reminiscing. In fact, she knew more about Raymond's life than she did about the lives of her own in-laws, who had recently died. With their last breaths went two lifetimes of rich family history never to be shared or passed on to the next generations—to their children, grandchildren, and great-grandchildren. Her personal convictions and years of listening to hundreds of hospice patients reliving episodes of their lives led to recruiting community volunteers to preserve these reminiscences as a gift to the families who would be losing this life in the not-too-distant future.

Shortly after our first meeting, Donna launched a new hospice volunteer program at Hospice Care of the West, where I underwent hospice volunteer training and had the required tuberculosis and drug test. For two years, I followed Donna and her volunteers from bedside to bedside, family to family, recording life story interviews and consequently oral ethical wills. I quickly learned that these videos were not an easy task. The average stay of a hospice patient was less than three weeks. Of course, there were exceptions, but for the most part patients died within weeks or days of their admission to a hospice. For months it seemed like every other time we scheduled a life review video interview, the patient slipped into decline or, worse, died before we made it. I was disheartened as I came to witness what I already knew. Most physicians gave hospice referrals a few weeks or less before the patient was expected to die, leaving little time for the family to prepare. In many ways, a hospice referral marks the time when the family and the patient come to a peaceful understanding that the death is near, which often motivates a desire to preserve family history—but sometimes that revelation or referral comes too late.

In the case of the Marting family, their patriarch's last breath neared. He'd just returned from a long stay in the hospital, where they almost lost him, giving the already-scheduled interview tender significance. On the eve of the interview, as was customary, Donna sent the questions to the family and asked them to look through old family photo albums to ignite memories.

On a gray January afternoon in 2007, John sat poised on an oversized chair surrounded by his family. He was eighty-nine with lung cancer and Alzheimer's disease that he fought like a bull for more than two years. His memory was starting to fade along with the rapid deterioration of his body.

"Alright, everyone," Donna said, drawing the attention of John's wife, two sons, two daughters-in-law, and grandson, who were gathered in a small apartment in an assisted living community. He emanated a stalwart fatherly presence.

"Before we start the interview, I want each of you to give John a hug and kiss and say anything you'd like while we roll the camera," she said, calling the family to action. She craned over to view the monitor atop a digital video camera on a tripod operated by the cameraman, Robert Ostmann, a fifty-four-year-old high school teacher and hospice volunteer. She gave him the cue. He hit the record button.

John sat against a backdrop of his prized possessions—framed pictures of his sons, Larry and Richard, at their college graduations—now both are in their mid-fifties—and his fiftieth wedding anniversary picture with his wife.

His face animated to a smile, radiating his laugh lines, whiting temples, and creases on his bald head, when his daughter-in-law approached him. The attractive blonde in her late forties commenced the parade of love and affection.

"You're a movie star today, Dad," she said, upon embracing John. He proudly accepted his role.

"Thank you," he responded.

She straightened John's blue button-up shirt, and he lifted his eyeglasses on his face.

"You're a superstar to us every day. We love you, Dad," she said.

His wife, Marjorie, a petite woman exuding a regal presence, white hair, brown button eyes, pink lips matching her pink pantsuit, sashayed up to John and pursed her lips together. She was a year his junior. They sweetly kissed each other, and she said in a soft voice, "I love you."

"I love you, too," John said. He beamed up at Marjorie and then turned to the camera. "I'm glad I married this woman."

Richard, John's youngest son, standing six-foot-four and dressed as if he were attending a board meeting, bent down to kiss and hug his father. It was obvious to everyone that he was relishing the long embrace. Larry, a brawny, rugged guy in a flannel shirt, gingerly approached his father and uncomfortably stuck out his hand for their usual handshake. Instead of hugging, they sort of awkwardly rubbed cheeks. Richard lived nearby in Newport Beach, but Larry's family had driven more than a hundred miles to participate in this special event.

John carefully took a long gaze at each of his family members and surprisingly remarked, "I've never felt so much warmth and love in this room." He was right. The warmth emanating between the family members instantly melted the winter chill outside. John and Marjorie had lived in the retirement community for twenty years, but had never hosted so many visitors.

Larry's wife, Carla, followed, and then John's grandson, twenty-one-year-old Dan Marting, swooped in and whispered, "I love you, Grandpa," and hugged him.

"Are you ready, John?" Donna asked.

"Yeah," he said, with a big grin. "I don't have any secrets, so go ahead."

"Well, if you have secrets, they might make this even better," she said, sparking his family to laugh nervously. As the clock ticked closer to John's final hour, Donna tried to preserve his life story, in his own voice. Before she started, she invited the family to jump in and ask questions whenever they felt inspired to do so. The video would be their last chance to collect on a permanent record any memories they wanted him to share.

Donna introduced herself and then asked John to introduce himself.

"Tell me your full name," she asked.

"John Clifford Marting," he proudly announced.

"Where and when were you born?"

"July 25, 1917, in St. Louis, Missouri."

"Were you named after anyone?"

"Yes, coincidentally, I was named after both grandfathers," he said. "And I'm proud of it."

John was the third child of seven children born to his mother, Estella, who was a stay-at-home mother, "which was traditional in those days," John said. And his father, George Marting, was a General Electric appliance salesman. John spoke of how beautiful his mother was and how she played piano. "She could've been a professional," he said. He told stories of visiting his grandparents and of growing up in St. Louis.

"What kind of a child were you?" Donna asked.

John looked around at his sons and grandson to draw inspiration for how to describe himself as a boy.

"Small," he said, breaking the silence into laughter. His childhood painted a picture of Americana with a big family in the Midwest, days and times swept away by the modern world.

"Were you a good student in school?" Donna asked.

"Medium. I was not brilliant, but I did manage good grades overall," he said.

"Did you play sports in high school?" Donna asked.

Both of his sons piped in. "Dad, didn't you play some basketball in high school?" Richard said. Larry reminded his father of his days on the diving team. They riffed on the sports reminiscences because it was something their father had shared with his sons.

"Did you have a girlfriend?" Donna asked.

"Did I have a girlfriend? I wouldn't remember her name," John smiled in Marjorie's direction, making everyone burst with laughter

"You're pleading the Fifth, Dad," his daughter-in-law said.

"That's true," John said.

"Did you serve in the military?" Donna asked.

"Yes, they got a hold of me for four years."

"What branch?"

"The Marine Corps. As soon as Pearl Harbor was bombed, I was at the front door of the enlistment office," he said. The question spawned a distant gaze as he recalled lining up with hundreds of young men eager to enlist at the recruitment office in St. Louis and serve the country after the surprise attack on Pearl Harbor, December 7, 1941.

"People really felt they needed to come forward for their country at that time. I can't say I didn't enjoy it. It was something I knew and I excelled at."

"Dad," Richard said. "Weren't you a riflery instructor?"

"I was a riflery instructor. At that time, those who were expert shots were singled out. I was chosen for my record."

John began to doze between his deep guttural coughs. The interview was mentally exhausting for him. Robert asked Marjorie to join him in the interview around the time that she entered his life. Marjorie sat beside him and held his hand.

"John, when did you meet Marjorie? Do you remember what year it was?" Donna asked.

"Nineteen forty-five."

"No, we were married in '45," Marjorie slyly corrected him with a grin.

"So, I guess it was before that," John said.

"Yes, two years before," Marjorie said.

"Was it that long?" he asked, bewildered. He turned and smirked at Marjorie. He decided it was best she told the story. He didn't want to get himself in any trouble. They had the classic love story. John and Marjorie met at the wedding of Marjorie's sister. Marjorie was the maid of honor. He was the best man. He was one year older than she. They wrote every day while he served overseas. Marjorie joined the Navy WAVES, Women Accepted for Volunteer Emergency Service, and rose to officer before John returned. John and Marjorie found themselves in a quandary. Military rules state that enlisted men are prohibited to fraternize with higher-ranking officers. So, he removed his uniform and slipped into a suit to marry the officer, hence their song from the soundtrack of the film *An Officer and a Gentleman*.

"Can you describe your wedding?" Donna asked.

"It was quite simple. Things were not very plentiful then," Marjorie said.

They married on a foggy night, at a small church without a center aisle. Marjorie wore a borrowed wedding dress and walked down an off-center aisle to meet John at the altar. The flowers for the entire wedding cost seventy-five dollars.

"Where was your first home?" Donna asked.

"Parking Lot C for LAX, now," Marjorie said. "It was a tiny Marlow Burns tract house that we paid $3,700 for, a little two-bedroom house with a tiny kitchen. If the bread drawer and oven door were open at the same time, they overlapped. After the birth of our second baby, we decided we needed some more space. We moved to Sherman Oaks into a new home with two bedrooms, a living room, and den. It was a one-bath house. We stayed in San Fernando Valley until we moved to Irvine in 1989."

"Dad, when you bought the house in Woodland Hills, you built the patio cover, you built the walls, and did construction around the house," Richard interjected to reflect on his father's devotion to building a space for accommodating family gatherings and playing ball.

John and Marjorie held hands as they reminisced about the births of Larry and Richard, born twenty-one months apart. Marjorie sent them off to preschool, and she went back to school to get her master's degree. She became a high school teacher and then assistant principal at Van Nuys High School. They were Little League parents. Marjorie kept score and John announced from the sidelines of the baseball and football fields. They attended all the chalk talks. And when their sons matured and moved on to high school, Marjorie clocked times and John judged at the boys' swim meets.

"John," Donna said, trying to awake him from a doze. Donna told John that when her husband, George, dozes and she wakes him, he always makes the excuse "I'm just resting my eyes." John said he really liked that one.

"So, John, what was your primary career?" Donna asked.

"Draftsman," John said proudly.

"What company?" Donna asked.

"What they called Generous Petroleum, or rather General Petroleum, which eventually became a part of Mobile Oil," John said. Marjorie pointed out that he inherited his artistic talents from his mother. He excelled in mechanical drawing in high school, so a draftsman seemed like a natural fit for John when he began searching for his career path after leaving the military.

"If you had to do the same job again, would you?" Donna asked.

"Yes, because it was something I knew," John assured himself and his family.

"John, do you have any hobbies?" Donna asked.

"Well, how would you say it . . ." John paused looking for the right words.

"Family," he said. "Yep, that pretty much sums it up."

"What about gardening?" Marjorie prompted.

"That's not a hobby," John grinned.

The family collectively reminisced about holidays, traditions, and family vacations. They spoke about their sons growing up and eventually leaving home to go off to college. Donna then turned the life review toward retirement.

"So, you said you like to travel. Where have you been?"

"Well, we retired after the boys were out of school. Our first cruise was Alaska, and we were bitten by the bug of cruising. We went on eighteen cruises," Marjorie said.

"What was your favorite cruise, John?" Donna asked.

"Pearl Harbor—I wanted to go back and see it as a civilian," he said and then leaned forward, reliving the tour of Pearl Harbor. "It was an adventure."

A look of satisfaction shined on his face.

"So looking back on your life, do you have any regrets?" Donna asked.

John sat back in the chair as all his family members leaned in to make sure they heard him clearly. He closed his eyes to ponder the question.

"I didn't follow through on my goal," John said.

"What goal?" Marjorie asked, with a look of puzzlement.

"Following up on my education. Of course, the biggest obstacle was money," John said. John's sons looked at each other in bewilderment. Marjorie looked confused

"John, is there anything you want your family to know?" Donna asked.

The family patiently waited. The questions they wanted to ask but didn't have the heart to, Donna asked. John sat silently, pensively, for a long moment. For a man short on words, finding the voice to express what lay heavy on his heart was challenging. John closed his eyes for so long that Donna thought he'd fallen asleep again.

"John," she said.

"Well," John said. "I'm just glad they put up with me. I hope I was a good father because that's what's important to me."

He paused to peer into the eyes of his wife, his sons, his daughters-in-law, and his grandson.

"I'm proud of our family. You've all done well and I'm proud of what you've accomplished," he said.

At that moment the room was silent except for the sound of sniffles. Robert looked up from his camera to wipe his own glistening eyes. Donna paused to wipe her eyes. Robert turned the camera to pan the room.

Richard choked back his tears to respond to his father's praise.

"Even when Dad's been feeling pain, in the hospital, he's always thinking of others, he's apologizing for his coughing, he's been humble, and family's the most important thing to him. He always thinks of other people before himself," he said as tears glinted in the corners of his eyes and then rolled down his face. Robert focused the camera on Larry's ruddy face and quivering lip. Larry tried without success not to cry. Through a tearful gaze at his father he said, "It's been really interesting to listen to what you have to say. I heard a lot of new things today; my respect for you and my love for you just grows."

He then bowed his head and looked to his mother. Marjorie's shaking hand cupped on John's, she looked at her husband's endearing face. "We've had sixty-one wonderful years together, and there's nothing I would have changed. We started with a promise till death do us part, and we kept the promise all the way without really ever having a hard time. We started with nothing, but we were satisfied. We never bought anything we couldn't afford. We tried to make things we did an example to our family."

Donna watched the Marting family console one another in long embraces, and Robert turned off the camera. Donna could never predict what might transpire during a two-and-a-half hour interview, but gathering the family together at the end usually pushed heartfelt emotions to the surface. That's really her goal, to create an opportunity for her patient to share his or her life story and for the family to sit, listen, and respond. The video camera and interview helps everyone focus on the present reality. It's hard to avoid that your father is dying when he's expressing his last words in a filmed interview for posterity.

Robert and Donna talked with Marjorie and John about the music they really liked. John always sang the lyrics "a bicycle built for two" to Marjorie. They also, of course, mentioned the soundtrack of *An Officer and Gentleman*. And John loved hymns, traditional Christian hymns.

Robert also collected photographs of John's life from family photo albums. The raw video footage would now return to Robert's classroom at Laurel High School where his students would help him edit the video. Time was against Robert.

That evening, the Marting family went out for dinner at Spaghetti Bender, a restaurant in Newport Beach. Around the diner table, Larry and Richard both talked about how much they'd learned by participating in the interview. These kinds of introspective conversations had never sprung up around the dinner table, not when they were growing up and not in later life during the holidays. His sons hadn't thought to ask him some of the questions that today had unearthed many revelations about their father's life.

As with most children, they'd kind of just taken Dad for granted. The filming of the video turned out to be an unexpected discovery process for John's sons. After learning his father had always wished to go to college, Richard had a newfound appreciation for his University of Southern California education, which launched his career as a chief financial officer of a Fortune 500 company. His father had never once mentioned concern over the investment in his son's future or the sacrifices made in his own life to provide for his sons. The interview also garnered some unexpected delights. They'd never been particularly affectionate with their father. In fact, Richard recalled that John used to tuck them into bed with a kiss and hug every night until they reached adolescence and then the affection vanished. Richard was particularly pleased that John openly embraced the hugs and kisses that afternoon.

In the hours after the interview, John steadily declined. Twelve days later, Donna received an urgent call.

MAKING A LIVING PORTRAIT

Andy Rooney once said, "The best classroom in the world is at the feet of an elderly person." In the winter of 2006/2007, I spent many mornings at Laurel High School in Los Alamitos to meet up with Robert Ostmann and the students in charge of creating what they called "life movies" of the hospice patients.

At 9:01 a.m., at the sound of the first bell, the students, mostly boys, poured through the doors of Mr. Ostmann's classroom, which looked more like a buzzing television newsroom, stacked wall to wall with computers stations, video editing equipment, and video cameras.

John Maxwell, a blond blue-eyed surfer wearing a baseball cap, rode in on his skateboard a bit late and sat pensively in the corner of the studio. He turned the pages of Jack Chernobeiff's family photo albums, which his teacher, Mr. Ostmann, and Donna had collected at Jack's life review interview the day before in Whittier, California. The family marked with medical tape the photos they wished to include in the documentary. John began scanning the marked photos into the computer. Jack was a ninety-one-year-old Russian American who served as the cantor at the Molokan Church in East Los Angeles. He had lived through two world wars, the rollout of the first automobile, the Great Depression, and the advent of television, and he reflected on his personal journey through the century, which in many ways captured the kind of history John only read about in books. Jack remembered the union battles that improved the hazardous conditions in the factories he had toiled in as a machinist throughout his life.

John's curiosity seized him, and he stopped scanning to look through the entire photo album. He pointed out Jack next to a Model T.

"Wow, this must have been taken in the 1920s," he said. "That car is insanely old—it's got wooden spokes and a leather roof. And look, they have an American flag flying from it."

He scanned in the photo even though it wasn't marked.

"I really like using stills because it makes the movie a lot better when you have pictures showing what his life was rather than him just describing it in his own words," John said to me. The pictures John selected provided visual context for the interview.

His co-producer of the life movie, Dan, a quiet eighteen-year-old with curly brown hair, sat at a computer station next to John. He wore a pair of large professional headphones. He intently watched the video interview of Jack. John used Photoshop to scan in and perfect the photos, and Dan used Final Cut Pro to input and edit the video interview.

Robert, in jeans with longish sandy-brown hair, looked more like a film director than a teacher. He came over to remind John and Dan of their tasks.

"I want you to listen to the interview all the way through and then break up the raw footage, into stories, into anecdotes with descriptive labels such as meeting his wife, getting his first job, going to war," he said. "Think about how best to tell the story. Do you want to tell it chronologically or thematically?"

At the end of the process, they will have a catalog of short video clips to splice together with photographs to visually anchor Jack's reminiscences. Dan unplugs the earphones so that we can hear some of the passages that will make the final cut. On a computer screen, Jack, a tall man with an oval face and long beard, sat beside his wife, Ana, a tiny woman with a white bob, in their living room just the day before. He had a thick Russian accent and a strong patriotic love for America. Jack described witnessing sleepy Los Angeles rise from dirt streets to the metropolis it is today. With awe in his eyes, he recalled the hustle and bustle of hard-hats paving the sidewalks and streets, erecting skyscrapers and whole neighborhoods blooming with trees.

"Gas was just a nickel—do you even know what a nickel is?" Jack asked, peering out of the computer screen as if asking Dan and John if they'd ever used a nickel to pay for anything. He even sang patriotic songs a cappella, one of his favorite pastimes when hanging out with his friends.

"I like what he says about the Model T and three pedals," Dan said. "This is like a California history lesson from orange groves to high rises."

I was moved by this intergenerational conversation, and that it wasn't in real time made it all the more special. Another student interrupted.

"Whose photo album?" he asked.

"It's a guy name Jack. We're filming him for his life video," John said.

"The guy is passing away soon, so we're filming it," Dan said.

"That's nutty, man," the student said. "Is it hard to watch?"

"He can't speak or hear very well, but his wife is helping him out," Dan said.

"He's really had a long life," Dan paused. "You know he's remembering it in his mind—he's pointing out pictures, saying names, he misses everything."

Mr. Ostmann looked on and was noticeably impressed by his students' observations. He uses the life review videos as way to broaden his students' experiences. It's a teaching tool about story and life progression— showing the students how these people's lives develop from being young kids playing in school, growing into young single adults starting careers or going off to war, taking on the responsibility of nurturing a family, being good parents, building a home, dealing with crises and illness.

This model of family life is missing from many of these students' lives because the majority of the students at Laurel High School, a continuation—also known as an alternative—high school, come from broken, abusive homes. In many cases, one of the parents has tragically died. These crises send the kids into a tailspin and they can't cope in high school. The continuation school is a second chance for them to catch up in their credits at their own pace in a nurturing environment where the teachers, like Mr. Ostmann, find creative ways to get around their learning obstacles rather than berate them for their failures.

Robert relies on his students to create a rough cut of the video. This boosts their confidence and independence. They are generally not big novel readers, and these videos create a new way of learning how to assemble the building blocks of a good story. The life review videos draw on strands of history, psychology, biology, and technology to weave together an interactive project that helps students think outside themselves and craft something special to give to others in the midst of a difficult situation.

I returned to the classroom a few days later to check on John's progress. The young Jack in the albums had aged into a graying, bearded man. Between the interview and the photographs, the life review video had begun to shape into a story told through Jack's reminiscences, but refined by John's intuition, which he used to find the perfect chronology of photographs to visually breathe imagery into Jack's words. John was on his thirteenth year of school. He lived with his father and his octogenarian grandmother in Seal Beach.

"John," I said lowering my voice. "Has anyone close to you died?"

He stopped flipping through the photo album.

"Yeah," he turned his eyes up at me. "My mom, when I was five."

John, like me, spent many hours poring over photo albums of his deceased parent. When your parent dies at a young age, as you get older, you desperately try to hold on to your own memories of them. Sooner or later, the only memories you have are those attached to photographs, and you can't summon your parent's face without the visual aid. Eventually, the memory of your parent's voice fades. That's difficult to contend with. You cherish the photo albums and the contents within because they are the only physical presence and connection to your parent. Even if John didn't fully understand that, he tapped a reservoir of sensitivity and intuition to provide other families with the images that would spark memories after death. John and I both agreed we'd love to have had such a video of our deceased parents.

After spending time with the students, I returned home with a collection of life review videos they'd edited over the course of a year. I had been at most of the interviews, but I wanted to watch the finished video. Like it or not, these videos are bittersweet. Sometimes family secrets escaped and Donna would need the students to edit out parts of the interview. The questions stir a rollercoaster of emotions when people at the end of their life venture to live it in reverse. Memories are attached to emotions and some of the most searing life experiences are those linked to fear.

I was particularly impressed with the depth in some of the memories linked to fright. A little old lady name Toni had a life review recorded by Donna's pet therapy volunteer, Shelley Smith, and Katie, a fifty-one-pound golden retriever, whose presence unleashed some childhood terrors. Because of Katie, Toni was able to retrieve memories from her early childhood. She recalled hiding her puppy in the cellar from her father because she feared he'd beat the dog. Toni shuddered when returning to the cold shed in which she had hidden from her strict Austrian father. She'd grown up on a farm in Minnesota with ten siblings. She said, "We used to call him Hitler, before Hitler got famous." However, she lamented, "I feel sorry for him because he missed out on everything. He was a mean man." She sighed and happily announced that all the children survived his wrath. In contrast, the stories of her mother making *pizzia* were filled with wonderment. Toni demonstrated the step-by-step process. "She'd spread a nice clean white sheet on the table, pour flour on it, and then she'd roll the dough and throw apple slices and walnuts on to it. We'd straighten them out even though we didn't have to. But we wanted to be a part of it. Then she'd roll it up and put it in a baking dish to cook. It was deeeliiiiiciiious."

Toni imagined herself in her mother's kitchen making her favorite dish. If the recorded life review had occurred earlier in her illness, she may even have taken the opportunity to demonstrate these recipes for her family on video camera, which would be preserving a memory while simultaneously creating a new experience for the family to participate in. This idea could stretch beyond the kitchen. A younger member of the family, like a son or granddaughter, could take the dying person to her old neighborhood or her favorite park. An intergenerational connection is made whilst recording some family history. The obstacle to organizing such an enriching family experience is not necessarily the technology, but rather that it requires confronting mortality, finality. As a society, we've become so overly concerned with avoiding death that we even avoid conversations that may stir thoughts about death. If you choose to film these stories, it means you're acknowledging that the interviewee will not be here sometime in the future.

Dr. Harvey Chochinov, psychiatrist and director of the Manitoba Palliative Care Research Unit in Winnipeg, Manitoba, where he is lead researcher on dignity therapy, studied the value of these legacies for the beneficiaries. The study, Dignity Therapy: Family Members Perspective, published in *The Journal of Palliative Medicine*, sheds light empirically on the therapeutic benefits. As I mentioned in Chapter Four, Dr. Chochinov developed a novel intervention to record the spoken legacies of hospice patients to bequeath to their family members. Dr. Chochinov interviewed the bereaved family members six to nine months after the patient died in early 2006. Ninety-five percent reported that the dignity therapy helped the family member who was dying.[5] Sixty-five percent of the families believed the dignity therapy helped their loved one prepare for death. Close to 80 percent of the families believed the intervention helped them during grief. Ninety-five percent of the family members would recommend dignity therapy to others. The results informed me that not only does the interviewee benefit from producing a permanent legacy to pass on to survivors, but also the families receive sustenance from this parting gift in the aftermath, their grief.

If time to record a last interview and oral ethical will is short, Dr. Diane Meier, director of Hertzberg Palliative Care Institute at Mount Sinai School of Medicine, offers five expressions for patients to meditate on when thinking about important things to say to those they love.

1. "Thank you for being my father or thank you for being my son."
2. "Please forgive me for anything that I may have done that caused you pain."
3. "I forgive you for anything that you may have done that caused me pain."
4. "I love you."
5. "Good-bye."

A LIVING TRIBUTE

At nine o'clock on Monday night, January 29, 2007, John Marting took his last breath in his home in the company of his family. One of John's daughters-in-law called Donna to ask if it was possible to have the video to play at John's funeral, which was set for Saturday, February 3. Donna called Robert right away. He said it would be a tight squeeze but would try to finish the video in time for the service.

The following Saturday morning, I joined Donna at the memorial service at Creekside Christian Fellowship in Irvine. We entered the sanctuary, which was dimly lit with candles. Just over a hundred people filled the pews. Richard and Larry stepped up on stage to give talks, which they titled "Remembering Dad." As I listened to them share memories of their father, I couldn't help but notice some of the same stories that John and Marjorie had told, but this time they were told through a son's eyes.

The open-mic testimonials filled in the portrait of John from the perspective of friends. They distilled their memories in an effort to make John's genuine character, his humor, his strength as a family man, and his faith come alive. Many spoke about how John and Marjorie's marriage was an example of true love that we all should try to emulate. After the dozen tributes, the lights dimmed, John appeared on a four-foot-by-four-foot screen at the front of the sanctuary to complete the portrait of him that everyone had tried so desperately to re-create. The song "I Will Remember You," by Sarah McLachlan, played as a larger-than-life still photo of John smiling at his fiftieth wedding anniversary illuminated the silver screen at the front of the church. The still photo faded to black, and John, looking very dapper, appeared on screen.

Against the backdrop of his home, John introduced himself, then launched into his birth story and childhood reminiscence, which were complemented by a montage of baby photos. A black and white baby picture of him in a sailor suit glowed on a black screen followed by a picture of John at three years old next to his tricycle in the front yard. Photos of John on his father's shoulders and holding onto his mother's hand strolled across the screen to the faint hymn of "Amazing Grace" as he shared fond childhood memories.

Donna asked, "What kind of child were you?"

John said, "Small."

The laughter of his family on screen was joined by the chuckles of those in the sanctuary. As John spoke about his years going off to war, images of the young Marine, bent on one knee and then lying down on his belly aiming his rifle, shot across the screen. A close-up of John and Marjorie's hands folded into one another came into focus as the song "A Bicycle Built for Two" played. Marjorie narrated their love story.

"We were thrown together," she smiled, and then she squeezed John's hand.

Marjorie and John's commentary enlivened the medley of still photos of their courtship, wedding, and early years of parenthood. They sat on the front porch of their first home, held the hands of their sons while hiking on camping trips in Yosemite.

As the documentary came to a close, John rested his head back in the chair and then leaned forward as if talking directly to the audience and said, "Looking back, I think I've done pretty well."

His words were marked by the family bathing him in love and affection followed by a slideshow harmonized by the Beatles song "In My Life: There Are Places I Remember," sung by Judy Collins. At the end of the slideshow, a black screen darkened the sanctuary and Donna's voice could be heard saying, "Hey, John, hey, John."

The dark sanctuary was once more illuminated by John popping up his head from a blissful doze on screen and his voice exclaimed, "I'm just resting my eyes," followed by his familiar guttural belly laugh. The audience laughed along with John and then stood for an ovation as the credits rolled. It was spectacular.

Tears of joy slid out of Donna's eyes. "That was amazing," she whispered under her breath.

The pastor took the stage and was noticeably affected by the video.

"Wow, that was remarkable," he said. "I don't know if you all were thinking about what I was thinking, but I have to ask—are we really saying the things we need to say to those we love? Are we leading the lives that we'd be proud of if we were in John's shoes being asked these questions at the end of life?"

After the service, Larry approached Donna in a long embrace.

"Thank you . . . you're timing was perfect. We said the things we needed to say and heard the things we needed to hear at the right time," Larry said. In that moment of loss, the family gained. They gained John's life story told through his reflections and not hand-me-down stories. People came up to the Marting family to offer their condolences, but also to express their awe over such a wonderfully told life story.

"I really felt like I got to know John," one woman said.

"This was the best service I've ever been to," said one man, and everyone crowded around agreed.

"It beautifully captured everything great about John—his smile, his humor, and his love for family," another man said.

Richard and his family gathered around Donna to again express their gratitude.

"His voice and his life story will be forever preserved," Richard said, hugging Donna and almost sweeping her off her feet. "Thank you so much. Years from now my grandchildren will be able to meet and learn about their great-grandfather John Marting and the incredible life he led."

A couple of months later, the Los Alamitos School Board invited Robert and his students to be recognized for their devotion to hospice patients and their families. Before the ceremony, they gathered with Donna and the Marting family for dinner to celebrate. The Marting family spoke of how the video was the highlight of the memorial service. Richard had watched the video a few times after the funeral and now recapped his thoughts.

"In your mind, you remember things from the past, you can look at still pictures," he said. "But having the video, it's like he's right here, since it's a conversation that we were involved in, it's not an eight-millimeter home movie of him pushing us on our bikes from years ago. It was so close to the end, so it has real poignant meaning for us."

At the school board meeting, Robert introduced a sampler video that included the interview with John. The students rose for their honors, and John Maxwell stood, like a director on Oscar night, to accept the certificate and standing ovation. Then Richard Marting took the microphone.

"Excuse me for my misty eyes," Richard said. "We really wanted to come and give our thanks publicly to Robert Ostmann and his students for creating this life video of my father . . . The videotaped interview provided us with a chance to turn the light on him, focus and listen to our father recollect sixty-one years of marriage and raising a family. We were able to learn about his greatest joys and regrets. When he was asked, 'What are you most proud of in your life?' It was the first time I ever heard him say 'family.' And he was asked, 'What was your greatest regret?' I'd never thought to ask him this, so having this forum really taught us something as well. His response was that he never went to college . . . I'm sure Robert's students learned a lot of technical skills from this process and walked away with a sense of accomplishment that all of us receive when we finish a project, but I also hope that they took away a greater understanding of family and the love of a father, and that's a lesson that would make my dad proud."

SEVEN Her Living Wake: Reminiscing and Farewell Party

On our way home, I stretched out on the front seat of the ambulance driving east on Interstate 10. The Los Angeles skyline receded from view. As the white divider lines blurred by, I contemplated the parallels in my parents' lives and their polar opposite approaches to death. In my father's last hours, an ambulance crew entered our home. They lifted him onto a gurney, loaded him in the ambulance, and raced, sirens blaring, to the hospital. Isolated in an antiseptic chamber of a hospital, he died. Fourteen years separated their final days. The sirens were silent on our ambulance, and instead of going to the hospital, we were leaving the hospital—we were going home.

I asked Simon, my boyfriend, to ready the house for my mother's homecoming. He prepared her deathbed with as much care and concern as a father might build the crib for the arrival of his newborn. He knew she wished to lie in the living room looking out at the winding road lining the sunlit amber hills covered in pines and wild flowers that stretched to the horizon. We had talked about her last view on a few occasions. As we had discussed, he replaced the dining room table with her hospital bed. The bed faced the wide panoramic wall of windows and a semicircle of dining table chairs, including my rocking chair for visitors. Her CD player rested in her reach on a nightstand on the left and a lamp and medical supplies were on her right. He selected framed family photographs that adorned the walls and surfaces of our home and brought them down to rest on the table at the foot of her bed.

We arrived home at 4:59 p.m. One member of the ambulance crew walked inside with me to check out the home and plan a route. I gasped upon walking in to see the dimmed glass chandelier set to a warm golden glow and china cabinet lights illuminating her prized possessions and artifacts collected over her lifetime. I thanked Simon. He was in film production and had a special talent for creating sets that memorable moments are made on. It was so inviting, but the moment was interrupted.

"Where are the oxygen tanks?" the EMT asked me.

Beverly walked in. "They haven't arrived yet," she said.

"Well, we'll have to wait before we bring Linda in," the EMT said.

I started laughing, thinking it was a joke. They weren't going to hold my mother hostage. But the look on this woman's face was serious. She opened her mobile phone to call her people. I opened my phone to call mine. Three hours later, Dr. Garcia dispatched a nurse from the Visiting Nurses Association to free my mother from ambulance care. The nurse and the oxygen tanks arrived simultaneously, at eight o'clock.

I wondered if we should chant "We Shall Overcome" as the ambulance crew marched her across the threshold of our home. Just at the moment of victory, she whispered to me, "I'm in pain."

My mother squirmed in pain around the bed as the nurse gave her an examination. Like clockwork, each time she met a new healthcare practitioner, we had to answer a battery of questions regarding her medical background, family history, and lifestyle. I delivered all of the dates and descriptions of all her past surgeries and medications, which I had memorized like the alphabet. She deferred to me during these interviews, but when the nurse asked about her current treatments, I said "Just TPN."

Mom sat up in the hospital bed and made an announcement.

"I want to refuse TPN and go into hospice if that's okay with my daughter."

I lost my breath.

"Is that okay with you, Denise?"

My mother asked as if she'd just ordered an appetizer for me at restaurant and then casually asked if that sounded good. Seven days or less. Sitting here watching my mom die slowly was impossible, unimaginable.

The nurse was caught in a force field of tension encircling all of us. I looked at my mother's weary eyes filled with pain, concern, love, and worry. Her hand touched mine.

"Love," I think she said, but I couldn't hear her clearly. Silence enveloped me. From that quiet came my voice choking and stumbling, "Ah, yeah."

Then, "Mom, okay, that's okay with me," I said with cool and calm.

The nurse was saying something, but I couldn't hear her clearly. Seven days. I tried to calculate how many sunrises, how many sunsets we had left. Then my voice again emerged, repeating the nurse's words to my mother.

"You realize in hospice you can't have TPN," I said.

"Yes," my mother said. "I know I will go in seven days or less. I know."

Then my frenetic thoughts turned to my brother. The nurse pulled away from the bedside and turned off the TPN machine. I called Ryan from the family room to the bedside. He looked so young, innocent.

"Mom is going to quit the TPN," I whispered. He pushed the bar down on the bed and lay next to her.

A hospice team from the Visiting Nurses Association arrived the next morning. The hospice nurse connected my mother to an IV line attached to a small morphine-dispensing machine about the size of a Walkman. She could hit the "bolus" button when she needed to self-medicate. The hospice nurse suggested that my mother be watched around the clock until her last breath. I took the early nightshift, and Beverly offered to take the slot from two o'clock to seven o'clock in the morning. I kneeled down by the side of my mother's bed.

"Mom, I will stay here with you until you pass," I said.

"Okay, my love," she said, reaching for my hand.

Later I read a book left by the hospice nurse that described the signs to watch for when death is near. It talked about how she would sleep more deeply, sometimes one eye at half mast and the other closed, as if half of her were with the living and the other half were focused on the beyond, the afterlife. The booklet also spoke about how the person may see or talk about someone who has already died and might be disoriented about what time and place he or she is in. Physical indicators included kidney failure and labored breathing, sometimes called the "death rattle," occurring as death is imminent. The book also pointed out that hearing is the last sense to go when a person enters a coma and even after the last breath.

The following afternoon, Beverly and I called all my mother's friends and family to inform them she'd made the decision to go.

THE LIVING WAKE

They came on a day's notice from San Francisco, San Diego, Las Vegas, Santa Barbara, and other local cities. The procession of visitors—my mother's friends from church, divorce recovery, and Parents without Partners, her colleagues from the bank, our neighbors from the home where we lived with my father, my cousins and aunts—all arrived like a parade stamping out the silence that once surrounded death. They carried casseroles, bouquets of flowers, and baskets of plants.

A shimmering veil of bright winter sunlight draped the doorway, momentarily blinding me as I stepped out onto the front porch of our San Dimas home. The trepidation in their gaits reflected my apprehension, but it melted as I embraced a group of attractive women in their mid-fifties, whom my mother had affectionately nicknamed her "prayer warriors," followed by Pastor Tom Naylor and his wife, Buffy, and Ken Daignault, our close family friends from church. We saw a few from my father's side of the family and some of his friends, many of whom we hadn't seen since his funeral. Most remembered Ryan, my brother, as a toddler and didn't recognize this nineteen-year-old young man standing by my side, greeting them. It's funny how death brings people together.

Jane Herges, formerly Daignault, my best friend from childhood, who'd recently married a Dodger, brought enough food in grocery bags to feed at least two baseball teams. I helped her carry in the bags through the living room. This was a sight to behold. My bald, ivory, emaciated mother lay on lavender-billowing air mattress encircled by friends and family showering her with hugs, kisses, and flowers. I could hear her voice asking for everyone's latest life headlines and saying to one colleague, "You must be working hard—I look better than you and I'm dying."

The aroma of simmering casseroles wafting from the kitchen gave off the nostalgic scent of a holiday festivity. Poignant tears turned to laughter as I threaded through dozens of familiar faces, many of my family and friends who stood by me when my father died.

Although Mom was the atypical life of the party in a hospital bed, her magnetic presence commanded the room. Just two days previously, the living room had looked like an untouchable glass museum. Mom had decorated her favorite room in the 1980s, when black lacquer furniture, smoked glass coffee tables, decorative wall mirrors, and pastel silk flowers were in style. It was the center of activity for all special occasions.

Pastor Tom, a handsome man in his sixties with silver hair, sat in the rocking chair at her bedside. My mother sucked on some ice chips while they discussed the details of her memorial service. She wanted the praise singers from her birthday party to sing the same lineup of songs. She also requested that her favorite piano player, Dwayne Condon, play at the service because "his voice is right from heaven," she said. Pastor Tom jotted down all of her requests. I stood behind the rocking chair eavesdropping on their conversation. After Tom took care of his business, he read her biblical passages about living on in heaven.

"You will soon be in the presence of Jesus," Tom said while anointing her forehead with a thumb smudge of oil. "You will have no more pain, hunger, thirst, or tears. You will party around the table of the wedding supper of the Lamb and be in the presence of those whom you have loved and who loved Christ, including, most of all, Denise and Ryan, who, when their times come, will join you in paradise."

Tom moved from the rocking chair and people began filing up to the chair to sit down and share their memories impromptu with my mother. My thirty-two-year-old cousin, Robert Carson, sat down in the rocking chair and held my mom's hand. He shared how his Auntie Linda taught him to love nature, art, and museums. He reflected on his memories about being a child in tow as Auntie Linda whisked him away on trips to the Natural History Museum, the Los Angeles County Museum of Art, mountain picnics in Angeles Crest, and camping trips in Yosemite. Nature walks were his favorite because she pointed out animal prints in the dirt, birds' nests in the trees, and burrows in the ground.

"It was selfish really—I just loved to see the wonder in your eyes," my mother said. I found myself caught up in his reminiscence and seeing Mom lithe, whole, and healthy picnicking in the mountains.

Friends of my parents echoed recollections about the early days, when my mother and father danced beneath the disco ball and flashing lights at the "Filipino parties" orchestrated every weekend in the 1970s into the 1980s at the homes of my father's clan. Apparently, Linda was quiet and reserved until my father, Richard, swung her out on the dance floor. His panache intoxicated her. I saw her eyes flicker in ecstasy as they spoke.

My mother piped in, "It became easier when everyone suddenly wanted to start practicing English."

I relished listening to her laughter that followed. It sounded like the chimes of a child's blissful, uninhibited amusement. Her spirit brightened with each reflection shared. The collective reminiscence was a welcome respite from my relentless worry about my mother's pain and morphine doses. As I gazed at her from the arm of the couch, I drifted off into much-needed moments of reverie. Recollections of Mom and Dad dancing together flooded my mind. My memories vaporized when Roberto Hernandez, my brother's nineteen-year-old friend, rounded up his crew of friends and they approached the bed.

"I'm speaking for all the guys here," he said. "You have always been and always will be the best mom a guy could ever have. Don't worry, Mom, we'll take good care of Ryan."

I found it hard to draw my eyes from the group of teenage boys standing around her deathbed. She appeared so frail and weak next to them. One by one, the guys leaned down to kiss her head. She beamed and whispered "thank you" to each one.

My boyfriend, Simon, ran his hands through his brown hair, then kneeled down at her bedside.

He quietly asked, "May I have your permission to marry your daughter?"

"Yes, I've always wanted you as a son-in-law," she said. "But only if that's what Denise wants."

Spoken like a true independent, single mother with a feminist edge. She served dual parenting roles to my brother and me. My mother reached out her arms and Simon leaned in to hug her.

A poignant chorus of tears both joy and sorrow erupted from deep within me. I couldn't even envision the future without my mom at that moment. I was so narrowly focused on the present—her next breath, her next words.

"You need to take care of each other," my mother said, peering into my eyes and then turning to look at my brother. Ryan embraced her and I rose from the arm of the couch to join them.

"Don't worry, Mom, we will," Ryan said, turning to Simon for approval. At that moment, I realized a good ending lights the path toward a new beginning, whereas a bad ending leads to a pitch-black tunnel with no beginning in sight.

Ryan rekindled the reminiscing. He, like my mother, always had a knack for injecting levity at just the right moment.

"You know, my mom was the best date I ever had. For one, she always paid," he said. "She usually asked me out on Sunday or Monday and then we would go out on Tuesday nights for a date at Chili's."

"Well, it was the only way I could see you once you bought your truck," our mom said, laughing at her own cunning tactics.

My mother contained the enormity of her impending death with a peaceful demeanor surpassing any that I'd ever witnessed. I felt an overwhelming sense of gratitude because I knew it was for my brother and me. She refused to allow us to let go alone. All the people present were like lifelines to hold onto when she slipped away.

Some comical stories surfaced when my mother's colleagues spoke of her dry or rather "wicked" wit. My mother's boss, Ron Steinberg, a tall, refined white-haired man in his sixties, looked lovingly at her and kissed her head. She was irreplaceable to him. Ron added that she was like a sister to him. Everyone murmured in agreement to every word he breathed.

My brother and I saw our mother reflected through the eyes of others showing deep love and respect. Her friends from church talked about Linda's unwavering faith and endless source of compassion for helping others through lay ministries. The shared memories echoed her love for getting everyone together for a party, no matter what the occasion. My mother confessed she'd always wanted to be a housewife and create fabulous dinner parties for her husband's clients. Instead, she orchestrated dinner parties for her own colleagues and friends.

Sharon Dannels, my mother's closest confidante, talked of sowing the seeds of their sisterhood over many bowls of soup. Linda used to make soup on weekdays and invite her over when they first met in a divorce recovery group at church. Equally, Beverly Chambers, my mother's longest and dearest friend, invited us to gallivant into their past when she and Linda drove across country together in the summer of 1969.

At Mom's request, we pulled out photo albums so everyone could participate in one last shared recollection with Linda. All the guests in our house found their faces between the covers of her photo albums. Photo albums circulated the room and people shared vivid stories of how my mother invited them into her life and left "footprints" they will cherish forever. Some people just wanted to be private and hold her hand and whisper words of love. I witnessed a catharsis more than once at my mother's bedside as the sun slipped behind the hills that evening. Some stayed for hours and hours, others decided to spend the night.

That evening my aunt, Mimi O'Reilly, cooked my mother's favorite Filipino comfort food—chicken adobo. Previously married to my father's only brother, she and my mom were like sisters. After she served me a plate, I sat down in the rocking chair at my mother's bedside.

"Mmmm," Mom said.

"I'll share mine with you," I said.

"I'm just enjoying smelling it," she said, eyeing my plate of stew.

On Thursday morning, Mom began to drift in and out of consciousness. My cousin, Robert, and I decided to take her outside, into the back garden. We lifted her out of bed and carefully seated her in the wheelchair.

She hadn't moved from the bed since Monday. She had a catheter and ostomy bag, so she had no need to get up. We wheeled her out onto the patio and her face lit up. She rubbed her little bald head and inhaled the fresh cold air.

"Mmmm, it's nice to be outside," she said smiling, closing her eyes and shaking her head in the wind. She watched in awe the birds soaring high in the blue sky above our heads. Mom craned her head from the back of the wheelchair and stretched up like an ostrich. "The air is refreshing," she said. She sighed and closed her eyes again. She reveled in the sun smooching her skin and the wind tickling her cheeks. I felt her yearning to embrace everything around her. "Mmmmmm," she sighed. I began to recognize those sighs as hums from deep within her soul. Words could no longer express the emotions welling within her. Around one o'clock, I saw goose bumps forming on her arms.

"It's getting chilly out here," she said. "I'm ready to go in." We wheeled her back to the living room. Robert and I carefully placed her back in bed. The house bustled with more visitors on Thursday afternoon. Robert left for the airport just before sunset. He pulled Ryan and me out to the front porch before he left. He held my face and Ryan's in his hands.

"Your faces remind me so much of your parents," he said. "I see Auntie Linda and Uncle Richard in both of you. And even when it's just us, we'll still have our memories of them. We'll keep them alive and then we'll make our own families and sit around sharing stories of Auntie Linda and Uncle Richard."

I could feel myself crumbling, and I dragged my heavy body back to my mother's bed. I fell into the chair beside her bed, held her hand, and wept. My childhood friend Gina Betancourt sat behind me and held me really tight to make me feel secure while I opened the floodgates that I'd been clenching closed since Monday night. My mother never shed a tear. She just stroked my head and hair, quieting my inconsolable sobs. I could feel aches and pains throbbing in every cell of my body as if I were physically experiencing my mother being torn from me.

"It's okay, my love, let it out," she said repeatedly.

THE VIGIL

At sundown, dozens of friends and family members gathered around for a candlelight vigil presided over by Ken Daignault, a church elder and family friend. The smoked glass chandelier cast a smoky, golden glow in the room.

The candlelight danced in the mirrors on the wall. The room was luminescent. I looked around at the silhouetted faces of nearly thirty of our intimates. We were all bound by my mother, this overflowing source of love in the center of the room.

Mom reclined on her bed and smiled at everyone gathered. She limited her conversations, as her words became jumbled and sometimes lost in translation. Her consciousness was slowly fading. I watched Ken sit down at the rocking chair by mother's bed and hold her hand. He was praying silently for her. Then he stood up and called everyone in the house to encircle Linda's bed. He asked us to lay hands on her. The prayers were no longer asking for a healing, but instead praying for a peaceful passage. As we all joined at Mom's bedside, he prayed for angels to come down and lift Linda out of pain. He asked aloud that the angels go before her and behind her into heaven. In the dim golden light, everyone followed Ken's lead, praying aloud for a safe journey. My mother's friend followed with a prayer and then tapped my hand. I don't know where it came from because I've never prayed publicly in my life. I echoed Ken's prayer asking God to lift my mother into the palm of his safe, loving hand and carry her into heaven. With that I heard myself say aloud, "Thank you for giving me such an amazing, loving, and strong woman for a mother."

Ken closed the prayer after me, and we all said "Amen" in unison.

On the table to the left of my mother's bed, a CD player hummed instrumental praise music. The soothing sounds of a harp, piano, and flutes created feelings of peace and tranquility as she drifted in and out.

"She's going home," said Sharon, as she sat with my mother that night.

Denise and I sat on the bed's edge. The living room and family room were filled with people in meditative prayer and quiet conversation when my mother suddenly raised her head from a doze.

"Why don't you two get out my bible," she said to Denise and me.

We pulled out my mother's weathered brown leather-bound bible from her nightstand drawer, and she guided us to read some of her favorite Psalms. The bookmark in her bible was one I made her when I was in first grade. I colored a rainbow and wrote "Read and Enjoy" twenty years ago on this bookmark. It gave me a smile of nostalgia, and I'm sure the bookmark gave her a similar feeling. My brother sat down on my mother's bed beside me. He seemed a bit uncomfortable, and I noted that tomorrow I would limit visitors so he could have some private Mom time. She cupped her hand on his, then asked Denise to read Psalm 139. Denise took some time finding it. My mother, still wanting to be in control, reached out her hands and Denise handed the Bible to her. She quickly found the page. As I listened to Denise's voice read the words, I realized that this Psalm comforted my mother when thinking about her own death and she wished that comfort would now blanket me as she made her departure.

> O Lord, you have searched me and you know me.
> You know when I sit and when I rise; you perceive my thoughts from afar . . .
> You hem me in—behind and before; you have laid your hand upon me . . .
> For you created my inmost being; you knit me together in my mother's womb.

She placed her hand on Denise's arm. Denise stopped reading. My mother's eyes rested on me. Those words resonated deeply into my bones, the bones "knitted in my mother's womb." I grabbed hold of my mother's bony hand. She stared into my eyes with that ever-present piercing look of knowing, or rather telling me I would be strong and go on without her. We would never really be separated even at the moment of death because I was made in her. She asked me to finish the Psalm. These words I read aloud.

> All the days ordained for me were written in your book before one of them came to be.
> Search me, O God, and know my heart; test me and know my anxious thoughts.
> See if there is any offensive way in me, and lead me in the way everlasting.

As I read the last lines, I felt like I'd read them before. My mother must have read this Psalm to me or maybe she'd included it in one of the many letters she wrote me over the years. We continued reading Psalms like lullabies as Mom drifted off to sleep.

On Friday just before dawn, I crept over to my mother's bed, passing by and/or climbing over her snoring guardians sprawled out in our full house. I noticed the empty catheter bag hanging on the bottom rung of her hospital bed. Her kidneys had ceased. Shortly her heart and lungs would follow. I sat down in the rocking chair. Her eyes opened. She smiled at me. Her spirit seemed to grow brighter as her body withered. I leaned over to embrace my mother and swabbed her mouth with a sponge and moistened her lips with Vaseline.

We sat quietly for a couple hours before I opened the blinds so that we could watch the sunrise over the hills outside.

That afternoon, we gave her a sponge bath while listening to instrumental hymns. She hummed throughout the process and afterward we slid a fresh pink nightgown on her. Ryan and I spent the whole afternoon and evening at her bedside. Beneath the dusty glow of the chandelier lights, my brother crouched down and laid his head and arms spread-eagled on Mom's petite body. He spent the whole night bedside. They played winking games and exchanged many memories. He shared with Mom some of his favorite times, like the Captain E.O. night at Disneyland, flying in a helicopter in Hawaii, soaring high above Utah in a hot air balloon, hiking to the top of Vernal Falls in Yosemite, the Easter egg hunts, and Mom's delicious tuna casserole. It was so tender watching my mother and brother.

I just couldn't get enough hugs and kisses because I knew from experience those are what you miss the most. I heard Mom call Ryan "Richard." Then a bit later she actually called for Richard, my dad, again. I couldn't help but wonder if he might be there. We often hear about somebody from the other side that comes when the time of death is near, but since there is no one who returns from death to report or refute these accounts with the exception of those who've had near-death experiences, I took comfort in hoping my father was there to accompany and ease my mother's passage.

On Saturday morning, I awoke, restless, and walked downstairs to find Beverly sleeping in the rocking chair beside my mother. Mom's eyes opened. She smiled faintly but said nothing. I just sat bedside and stroked her hand. We exchanged no words. She just dozed in and out of consciousness. I listened to our full house as it awakened.

Ryan replaced me at the bedside when Denise and Sharon came to pick me up for an appointment with Forest Lawn Mortuary at one o'clock. It was just ten minutes down the road, and I assumed it would only take me away for forty-five minutes at the most. The foray turned into a dis-combobulating nightmare. We met a pre-need representative short on compassion. She did little to mask her crass sales tactics, which disgusted me. I interrupted her to explain that my mother was dying at home and I really couldn't get home fast enough. She raised her voice to compete with mine.

I exited the office and crushed my plans to know where my mother would go after she died. Just as I entered the lobby and reached for the door, a hand calmly rested on my shoulder. I turned around to see a stately woman with the face of Betty White dressed in a long black dress with a white lace collar. They'd obviously called in the godmother of funeral counseling to quiet me down and stop me from marching out the door.

"Denise," she said in a soft voice. The godmother of funeral counseling introduced herself.

"I'll take care of you," she said.

The only reason I stayed was to right an old wrong from my past. Two excruciating hours later, we left the cemetery with a plan.

On the drive home, I gazed out the window of Sharon's car. I watched busy people driving in and out of Vons grocery store. Life outside felt foreign, a stark contrast to the comforting atmosphere and feeling of suspended time that reigned over our home.

"I shouldn't have left," I said.

"It's good you took care of it," Denise said. Sharon agreed.

"I just want to get home," I said.

Finally we arrived at home. I opened the front door. My eyes dropped on my mother. She was still. I gasped for air, but the wind had been knocked out of me. Ryan stood up from the rocking chair. As my little brother walked toward me, I no longer saw the scared boy. He emanated the confident, strong presence of a man. I shook my head. He wrapped his arms around me and whispered.

"Denise, Mom's slipping into a coma, so you need to say your last words now," he said. The CD player reverberated a harmony of flutes that pierced my ears. I was breathless again and could feel an intense oscillation in my head and chest. He motioned for me to sit on the chair, but I wasn't going to take this one sitting down. I stood over my mother's bed.

"Mom, can you hear me? I love you and I know you love me," I said.

"Mom," I yelled. "You can't go, Mom, before you tell me you love me one more time." I paused.

"Mom," I paused again.

"Please, Mom, don't go," I said as my voice weakened to a near whisper.

She wasn't responding. She had already fallen deep into a coma. I sat down in the rocking chair and tried to hold back my anger. Her eyes rolled in the back of her head.

"Mom," I cried loudly and dropped my head.

From the corner of my eyes, I glimpsed her left arm rise.

"Oh, my God," I said. "Mom."

She struggled to shake the deep sleep. I stood over her body and looked into her eyes as she motioned for me to turn down the music. I raced over to the other side of the bed and turned down the music. And she slipped away again. I walked back to her right side, sat into the rocking chair. I stood back up.

"Mom, please, please, you have to . . ."

I examined her face for a sign, anything. The light suddenly glinted in her blue eyes staring up at me, focusing on my face. Her mouth was dry and she struggled to speak.

"I love you," she whispered and stared so lovingly into my eyes. And then she traced the outline of my face.

"I love you, too, Mom," I said, and my body collapsed on her. There was barely anything left of my mother. I hugged her gently, kissed her, and moistened her lips with a sponge. I sat in constant vigil at her bedside. The sun eventually set as I reflected on our journey that led to this peaceful hour. I felt as if she reflected, too. I watched her eyes fluttering, as if she were in the REM stage of sleep, as if so much activity quaked behind them while the rest of her body lay still. I imagined her traveling rapidly through time. I remembered how they say life flashes before the eyes just before the last breath. It looked as if she'd entered that mind traveler mode. I had no idea how long she would stay in a coma, but I remained vigilant. Just before two o'clock in the morning Beverly suggested I take a break. I refused several times. Finally I left my post and let my heavy head hit the pillow on the air mattress beside my mother's bed where Denise lay. Simon lay on the couch above us and my Aunt Mimi rested on an adjacent couch.

As I slipped into my own REM sleep, my mother's breathing began to rattle and slow. Minutes passed before she took her next breath, then she gasped for another breath and exhaled really deeply. Beverly rested her hand on my mother's hand.

"It's okay, Lin, you can go now," Beverly said.

Two long breaths later, she passed away. My Aunt Mimi pronounced her dead at 2:07 a.m. on Sunday, February 10, 2002.

"She's gone," Beverly said as she shook me awake. The house was still. Beverly changed the CD to Elton John's "Candle in the Wind," a tribute to the British Princess. We bathed my mother with lavender soap and dressed her in the pair of white satin pajamas with gray trimming, the ones Simon gave her the previous Christmas. She said they made her feel like a movie star. After she was all dressed in white, I thought she looked better than a movie star. She looked like an angel.

They say hearing is the last sense to go. I recited the Twenty-third Psalm by heart. Then I opened her bible and read Psalm 139. As I read the first verse, a song came to me, a song I hadn't sung since I was a girl in Sunday school. The song was Psalm 139 called "Search me, Oh God." I sang loudly, like a sorrowful siren expelling my grief from the depths of my soul with every note.

Search me, oh God, you know my heart;
Try me and know my anxious thoughts.
Oh yeah.
See if there be any hurtful way in me and
Lead me in the everlasting way.

I found myself taking mental snapshots of her. We had the same hands. I wondered if she looked at me with same awe when I first emerged from her body. Those were her first looks at me and now these were my last gazes of her. Simon beckoned me to the couch. He cuddled me and softly said, "You remind me of a proud but exhausted mother just after giving birth."

I didn't call the funeral home. Instead we kept watch over her all night long. Sure, we strayed from the tradition of calling the funeral home right after the last breath. In fact, we didn't even call the hospice. At sunrise, white beams of light washed the living room and my mother of color. I lifted myself off the couch.

My mother's friend Sharon had the air of a priestess as she gathered us around the bed and led us in a short farewell prayer of gratitude for my mother's peaceful passing. After the prayer, Sharon turned to me and said, "Denise, are you ready?"

I struggled to draw my eyes away from my mother. She reminded me of a rose when plucked from a garden, still beautiful but no longer alive. She hadn't yet embarked on the process of decay when the petals wilt and turn brown; she had no crawling gangrene like my father; in fact, she looked no different—her eyes set at half-mast, her painted red toenails—from the day before except for the absence of her breath and the half-moons on her fingernails now lavender instead of pink. Hers was the first dead body I'd seen before it was stone cold, preserved by the embalming process for funeral ceremonies.

She had a heavenly smile, bringing to mind her voice reminding me ever so gently, "Carry on the smile."

I released her warmish hand, which I had intertwined with mine. The parting of ways vigil had ended and the practical matters of after-death care lay ahead.

EIGHT Vigil: Holding Hands at
the Eleventh Hour

On a midsummer's day in 2005, Megory Anderson, a death doula, waited
at Alex Cameron's home in San Raphael on the northern coast of California. She's not a medical professional or connected to a hospice. She's a
spiritual escort to death's door.

That week the cardiologist had announced that the pacemaker regu-
lating Alex's heartbeat had been recalled. The replacement would mean
another surgery, a protracted recovery, and one good year of life. Alex
weighed the twelve months of medical dependence that would take him
to age seventy-six. Although he lived alone, home seemed like an infi-
nitely better option. The faulty machine had kept him in the hospital for
most of the spring. He missed the freedom of home. Alex served as the
official greeter at St. Gregory of Nyssa Episcopal Church in San Francisco, a position given to him by the Reverend Lynn Baird after Gus,

Alex's partner of fifty years, died. It gave Alex a reason to wake up every Sunday morning. His familiar handshake, hug, and charming Scottish brogue warmed the congregation. He'd become a prior-like fixture at St. Gregory's. His flowing, ornate, shiny-blue vestment illuminated his rosy cheeks, wire-framed glasses, and wispy white hair. The congregation noticed when Alex was absent. Lately, he'd missed too many Sundays to count.

The cardiologist switched off the pacemaker and predicted it would take about two weeks before Alex's heart would slow to its final beat. Before boarding the ambulance, Alex called Lynn, the pastoral care priest at St. Gregory's, who was his healthcare proxy. Leaving twenty-four-hour hospital care to enter home hospice care, he needed more than a health-care proxy to protect his final decisions.

Alex needed a surrogate family.

That's where Megory came in.

Contrary to current belief, hospice is not twenty-four-hour nursing care. The program relies on family and community to perform daily nursing needs at home. Lynn called on Megory. Her wisdom came from helping numerous people labor out of this life during the AIDS epidemic in her neighborhood of San Francisco. Traditionally, a doula supports the woman in childbirth at home while the midwife guides her baby's safe passage into the world. The Greek word "doula," meaning slave or servant of God, entered the American vernacular in the late twentieth century partly due to the home-birthing movement when women sought to return the human element, mystery, and community support system back to the birthing experience.

Doulas encourage women to trust and listen to their own bodies through relaxation techniques, massage, and emotional and spiritual guidance that assuage pain and decrease fear of labor. Similarly, at the end of life, Megory guides the dying person to release the bonds of mortality, or as William Shakespeare wrote, "shuffle off this mortal coil,"[1] using a practice of she aptly calls Sacred Dying." She described this practice to me as "bringing spirituality, through presence and ritual, into the physical act of dying, which emulates the familial prayerful presence at the bedside in the centuries before the modern-day hospital." She believes no one should die alone. So she holds vigil until the last breath and often for many hours after.

She met Alex, a hospice nurse, and the ambulance team upon his homecoming. Alex assured Megory that he would be fine on his own, shooing her out like a stray cat. Then four evenings later, Alex blacked out and tumbled onto the kitchen floor whilst taking his medication from the refrigerator. Waking later, dazed and sprawled on the tile, he crawled to the telephone, called Lynn Baird, and asked for help.

Megory arrived with her overnight bag and pillow. Although only in her mid-fifties, she exudes the sage-like presence of one who has sat bedside with many departing from this life. She helped Alex back into bed, lit candles, and played soothing instrumental music. She knew nighttime remained the most difficult hour of the day as light faded and darkness closed in. She sensed it was more than the darkness stirring his trepidation. Her calm quieted Alex's nervous energy.

His eyes surveyed Megory's eyeglasses on her round angelic face, which was framed by a cloud of sandy blond locks. He almost said something, but bit his tongue.

On impulse, she cupped her hand around Alex's.

She asked, "Are you prepared to die?"

Alex's outer armor of defensive independence cracked. After four long days of trying to care for himself and then his fall, her candor relieved him. Her question, as it often does, led to a surge of worries about his everyday business. He rattled on about who would pay his car registration and water his garden. When Megory assured him she would care for the garden and other business, his practical concerns gave way to deeper reservations. Her simple question gave him permission to give voice to the unspeakable, to contemplate his own death. Each question he managed to vocalize quivered with a gush of weeping that seemed to flush out his fears like water eager to escape from a cracking dam.

"What's it like to die?" he asked, sobbing. "Will it be painful?"

Just as Megory opened her mouth to share some of her experiences with those on the threshold like him, Alex blurted out: "I don't want to die alone. Please don't leave me alone, just get me where I need to go."

ORIGINS OF A DEATH DOULA AND HER VIGIL

Alex's questions and his last requests weighed heavy on the minds and hearts of many people with whom Megory had sat vigil. She remembered the first time a young man asked her the very same question, "Tell me what's it like to die?" At that time, in the spring of 1991, she had no answer for him. She was forty-one, and she'd never been in close proximity to a dying person or laid eyes on the dead, with the exception of her grandparents in their caskets at their funerals.

Her first date with death started upon her answering a call for help from a friend whose brother was dying of AIDS. He begged to see a priest, but they couldn't reach one on short notice to give the man his last rites, a Catholic ritual that involved confession, absolution of sins, and the giving of the last sacrament, bread and wine. Although Megory had no formal training in last rites, she intended to improvise. She was no stranger to ritual. For five years Megory had served as an Anglican nun in the Order of Saint Helena, New York. She remained steeped in a monastic ritual-led life after leaving the convent in her late twenties to pursue religious studies at American University in Washington, D.C. She continued this cloistered lifestyle on a one-year fellowship at an orthodox Jewish institution in Jerusalem. Upon her return, she joined the Graduate Theological Union in Berkeley, where she was researching a doctoral thesis in comparative religion.

When she arrived at her friend's home, she suggested that first they clear away the medical supplies and clutter. She lit candles, turned on some soothing instrumental music, and turned the burdensome sickbed into a tranquil, sacred space.

Then came the question.

"Tell me what it's like to die," the dying man asked.

She had no answer. So she drew on her own experience when she'd contracted meningitis and teetered for weeks on the threshold between this life and the next. At a visceral level, she related to him. She thought about what she would want at this moment. Someone to hold her hand, listen to her concerns, and quiet her fears with assurances. So that's what she did.

When he asked for a priest, the only person able to give the last rites, she remembered an ancient ceremonial rite called the Anointing of the Sick, which dated back to the time of Christ's death. The priest, family, and community processed around the sickbed to rub olive oil on the person's diseased body. The sick person could confess his or her sins while the community encircled the bed in prayers lasting often a week or more. This physical healing ritual later became the ritual to prepare for death known as the last rites, an abridged version of which is still practiced today. And *in extremis* (a Latin phrase that means "in an extreme situation"), a layperson is allowed to preside over this rite.

Megory reawakened and recast this physical healing ritual into a spiritual healing to prepare for death. She and her friend gave him a sponge bath and then anointed him. She listened to his final confessions and gave him the ceremonial bread and wine. As the dying man drifted off to sleep, she sat in prayerful vigil until he exhaled his last breath in the early hours of the next morning.

Just a week later she picked up the telephone and a hesitant, unfamiliar voice requested she sit with yet another man dying of AIDS. Megory responded. Later she received another call, and another, and another. Megory found herself in the midst of a vanishing community. In the 1990s, she became the angel of the dying in San Francisco, a city transported to a pre-industrialized age when deadly epidemics wiped out huge populations in cities. Most of these men were allowed to die at home because of the strength of hospice in the community. But Megory quickly learned that hospice was not a twenty-four-hour caretaking service, and clergy seemed unable to make house calls on short notice.

Megory recognized this void and answered her phone around the clock. She discovered this tight-knit community of men between the ages of twenty and forty had taught themselves how to "do" death. Suddenly they had become seasoned veterans. From July 1981 to March 1998, 17,198 had died of AIDS in San Francisco.[2] Nearly 70 percent had died at home. This provided space around the deathbed uninhibited by medical professionals or any authority figures. The very nature of this disease dwelled in the dark underbelly of society. In many cases, family banishment had entrenched their alternative lifestyles, and many AIDS sufferers were divorced from religion.

She'd never met any of these men before the shadow of death darkened their lives, but promised to stay to their last breath. Many young men needed more than just sacred space. In their final days, the past wreaked havoc on their tormented souls. This was not the hour to say, "Let's talk about your mother!"

She tailored symbolic, customized rituals to help them come to terms with their life. Often she'd ask them to write down all of their past afflictions on paper, fold it up, and toss it into a bowl. Together they asked for forgiveness and absolution, then set fire to the bowl. Watching these actions, regrets, and grudges turn to ash symbolically nullified unresolved obstacles that prevented them from finding peace. She would then ask them to use visualization to place all the pains, villains, wounds, hardships, and prejudices they'd encountered on a blanket. Then they would shred the blanket. Rage would pour out of them with each rip. Powerful actions like these allowed each man to exhale and "push the reset button," let go of anger, release pain, and forgive the unforgivable. Actions carried more weight than words for these fragile young men. The despair drained from their withered faces and bodies. The transformation was palpable. Soon after, she watched them peacefully exhale the last breath of life.

A University of California at San Francisco study entitled "Death Rites in the San Francisco Gay Community: Cultural Developments of the AIDS Epidemic" defines "sitting vigil" as an improvised ritual practiced by the gay community.[3] "Sitting vigil with the dying person with AIDS was an act of support for the dying partner and for the caregiver. To sit vigil required the recognition and acceptance of death. It was an act of honoring the final stage of life and helped to create a quiet and peaceful environment for death," the UCSF researchers wrote. "During this state of acceptance there were no attempts to resuscitate. Often circles of friends, family, and hospice workers rotated the sittings so as not to overwhelm one individual caregiver.[4]

The vigil included final visitation of friends to say good-bye coupled with ceremonial trimmings—candlelight, an altar displaying pictures of the dying person, and soft, ambient music.[5] The community passed around and reenacted these rituals. Similarly, they passed around Megory's name.

Megory says that by the time she reached the AIDS community, they had systems and rituals in place that harkened back to deathbed traditions in early America, when people died in the bosom of home and community. In the book *Living in the Shadow of Death: Tuberculosis and the Social Experience of Illness in American History,* Sheila Rothman details evocative accounts of dying in the company of family and community before the proliferation of the modern-day hospital. Tuberculosis, like AIDS, had no cure.

Rothman writes that the invalids lived among those in more advanced stages of the disease watching a "preview" of their final hours. Doctors could stave off tuberculosis by suggesting men go on health-restoration voyages to the West Indies for the winter. As a result, many died away from home. Rothman gives us insight into early American dying rituals, stating: "For religious Protestants the thought of not ministering to a family member at the moment of death was a recurring nightmare. It was considered both a privilege and a duty to offer consolation to dying family members, to 'watch' and guide them in their final hours and in this way learn their innermost wishes and execute them in the manner desired."[6]

Rothman describes the death at home of Deborah Vinal. "In the last days of her life she finished all early business, calling in all her friends to say goodbye and handing them a gift. Even during the last night of her illness she was still summoning special watchers, the men and women she wanted to pray and sing with her as she awaited for her final call."[7] This mirrors the final visitation and vigil enacted by Megory and the young men in the AIDS community.

In the book *Western Attitudes Toward Death: From the Middle Ages to the Present,* Philippe Ariès writes of the waning presence of these "watchers," communal and familial, in the 1930s to 1950s as more people died in hospital. People began to look to science and technological interventions, decreasing their dependence on prayers and community presence. I pieced together the changing of the guard from family to medical professionals with some excerpts from Sharon Kaufman's book *. . . And a Time to Die: How American Hospitals Shape the End of Life.* In the 1960s, she references the word "deathwatch," "a term used mostly by nurses to characterize the vigil during which they kept a close watch on patients known to be dying. . . . A deathwatch could be initiated by physicians or nurses and once it began ward nurses arranged almost constant surveillance of the patient, responding immediately and ensuring the patient was not left alone between family visits. This shared deathwatch also enabled nurses to reduce family interference with staff routines and "protect" them from seeing the final moments of life. Families were rarely present at the moment of death."[8]

As Megory moved her ministrations from house to hospital, she dealt with some resistance in the hospitals, but gradually medical professionals saw the benefits in carving out a time for a vigil. In 1996, she founded the Sacred Dying Foundation as an umbrella to recognize a sacred transition filled with grace and mystery that honored all cultural, religious, and family traditions. The rituals were not necessarily rooted in religion but rather in what one believed to be sacred and spiritual. The elements of a Sacred Dying vigil are a union of many death rites.

For example, vigil is a rite observed usually on the third day. It is called a wake in the Roman Catholic tradition. Family and close friends gather around the deceased for a viewing to say their prayers and goodbyes on the eve of the funeral and burial. The premise of keeping watchful prayer, praying someone out, Megory adopted and recast for the end-of-life vigil. Megory repurposed the event into an act, therefore "vigiling" at the bedside.

She incorporates Jewish law, which states, "During the last minutes of life no one in the presence of the deceased may leave, excepting those whose emotions are uncontrollable or who are physically ill. It is a matter of the greatest respect to watch over a person as he passes from this world onto the next." This is the underlining premise of the practice of vigiling and the heart of Sacred Dying. After the person dies, Jewish law calls for the body to be ceremonially washed to help release the soul. Megory recast this purifying ritual by washing a person's body and hair before the death to help release the soul. In vigiling, she often anoints or massages the body with oil. The anointing is a symbolic, public act of marking the person's transformation from one state to another. In the vigil, many believe anointment recognizes the holy, divine, or spiritual presence.

As a former nun, Megory called her time spent vigiling at the death-bed holy work. She never accepted money for her services, but instead decided to turn her experiences into educational opportunities for clergy, hospice, care providers, and families. Megory taught classes about being with the dying and end-of-life rituals at both the University of California at Berkeley and the University of San Francisco.

In speaking to clergy about how to be with the dying, Megory recognized varying religions had a similar response. Clergy were generally trained to deal with the sick, dead, and bereaved, but had never been formally trained to specifically deal with the dying, which is a different experience than dealing with the sick. Dying is a transition to death, it is the in-between that has been left to doctors. But now with home hospice, more and more clergy, family, and community members are called upon to be present. She rolled out a vigiling pilot program to train church communities, hospices, clergy, and laypeople on how to vigil with the dying. As she points out, to sit vigil with someone at the end of life is a gift, which is why Megory's program is for volunteers, or what she likes to call "vigilers." She describes a vigiler as a compassionate listener and bringer of rituals, a prayerful presence bringing stillness and quiet to honor the sacred and personal transition.

In 2000, on the other side of the country, Phyllis Farley, the chairwoman of the Maternity Center Association of America, brought her wisdom in empowering, educating, and caring for women in the beginning of the life cycle to the ending stage. She founded the Doula to Comfort and Assist program to pair trained volunteers, educated in the processes of dying, with dying patients. Farley coined the term "death doula." The program began at the Shira Ruskay Center in New York. She envisioned volunteer nonsectarian doulas trained in the processes of dying, advanced directives, hospice, spirituality at the end of life, and, above all, how to be a compassionate companion. The doula also learned about active creative listening, common misunderstandings about hospice care, and ethical wills to sum up one's life. It is a volunteer program, but differs from vigiling in that the doulas visit with the patient throughout their journey and may or may not be present during the vigil period before death. Another doula program that is a closer relative to Megory's vigiling training is the Eleventh Hour hospice volunteers, or doulas.

As many of these Eleventh Hour, doula, and companion for the dying programs grew across the country, Megory also crisscrossed the nation, training new vigilers in hospices and church congregations from San Francisco to San Diego, Texas to New York, Connecticut to Florida. In the summer of 2005, her teachings underwent a test. Could she teach the tenets of Sacred Dying to members of her own church community?

A COMMUNITY OF VIGILERS

Megory listened to Alex's questions. What is it like to die? Will it be painful? She knew the answers now. Megory quelled those worries. She told him the facts and what to expect. The morphine would more than likely keep the pain at bay. Eventually he would fall into a deep sleep with shorter waking moments and then he would slip into a coma. She assured him that he would not be alone and he would get where he needed to go. As she often did at the deathbed, she shared stories of preparing someone on this side to meet God or a higher power on the other side. For Alex her experiences were like bedtime stories, which eventually carried him into a deep sleep.

In the morning, Megory rose to sunlight pouring onto the lush gardens just beyond a wall of windows that faced Alex's bed. She looked out onto what reminded her of a sunlit rain forest colored by birds of paradise and other equally vibrant, fragrant flowers and shiny, tropical leafy trees. Alex had lived in Hawaii and re-created his garden to remind him of the island paradise. Just four days before, she'd discouraged Alex to set the mechanical hospital bed from Hospice of Marin in his bedroom. Part of the Sacred Dying tenets evangelizes atmosphere and ambiance. The bedroom often creates a claustrophobic, isolating experience, whereas placing the bed in the hub of the house opens the dying experience to boundless opportunity and invites impromptu social interaction. She was happy Alex had followed her advice to set up the bed in the living room.

When Alex awoke, they spoke about his collection of paintings. He was glad to be home among his own watercolors. The showcase of sculptures from around the globe held memories of his life—each piece was an endless conversation piece. Megory listened to many stories and then shifted his voyage from the past into the present. She shared the plan of calling upon members of the church to visit in shifts with Alex through-out his final days. She assured him he would never be alone. This way he could see all those he missed. Another dimension of Sacred Dying is sharing the time spent at the bedside so that everyone in the community can be involved without exhausting one person, one caregiver.

Alex seemed open to her plan. This grand room would accommodate his guests. He promised to be a hospitable host. That afternoon, Megory sent out an email requesting visitors and night-watch visitors to spend time with Alex in his home. She explained each person could find their niche, how he or she desired to be a part of his surrogate family. To-gether they would create a constant vigil presence. Some might want to read him passages from the bible or their favorite book, others may just want to talk or give him a massage or bring over a bowl of fresh-cooked soup or a bag of groceries. Others may want to help straighten up his home or do laundry. Together they could discover their own resourceful ways to accompany Alex. That one email sparked an abundance of return emails, so Megory set an online schedule and circulated it to the group. Each person signed up. She started a log for each visitor to write about what occurred on the visit and update others on what Alex may need. This email log would become the group conversation between them all. She used a system, or a tradition, already set up for pastoral care.

Libby McQuiston, a soft-spoken blond in her fifties, lived down the road from Alex and offered to visit him four times a week. She volun-teered for Zen Hospice and knew how to be with the dying, but as Alex quickly pointed out on one of her first visits, she had a lot to learn. He had a caustic sense of humor and truly spared no one. Alex loved his Scotch. This love increased as the time to enjoy it decreased. When Libby ar-rived at Alex's home, his glass was empty. He offered her some sherry or lemonade. She was not a drinker, but offered to make him a drink.

"Ah, yes," he said in his gravely Scottish accent. "Will you pour me a Scotch?"

She took his empty tumbler into the kitchen and filled it up with Scotch. Alex looked quizzically at the tumbler.

"Call in the neighbors, this woman doesn't know how to make a Scotch," he hollered.

She laughed. He laughed, then gave her the recipe—one ice cube and a dash of water. She became a pro.

As the emails of Alex flew through cyberspace and landed in Megory's inbox, she could see in one glance how Alex was feeling, what he ate that day, what he read, how many Scotch cocktails he'd drunk, and all the activities and conversations that filled his day. It seemed that the company of these visitors rallied Alex. Megory had requested the Eucharist a couple of times a week to keep Alex in a sacred place. The Co-Rector of St. Gregory's Church, Donald Schell, a priest with bifocals and curly brown hair, arrived every other day with the consecrated bread and wine. Instead of just staying for the ritual, he enjoyed talking with Alex about death. Donald saw Alex as a gracious host guiding him into the great unknown—the last frontier. Alex was prepared to meet his maker and "see Gus again." His confessions were few, but his reflections long. Donald felt like a VIP on this journey to life's end. Most of his church congregation were baby boomers and had not yet experienced this stage of life. Alex became the congregation's teacher on how to accept death gracefully. Alex, the official greeter at the doors of St. Gregory, now welcomed the members into another holy sanctuary, the threshold between life and death.

As they learned from Alex, he in turn began to rely on his solid group of caretakers: Megory, Libby, practicing nurse Ruthann Lovetang, massage therapist Kerry Bostrom, Tracey Haughton, and Linda James, his closest confidante. These ladies gave him all the tender love and care he could possibly wish for. Ruthann, a member of the St. Gregory's of Nyssa's choir, suggested to Megory that maybe the choir should come and sing for Alex. Megory had often brought in gospel singers, harpists, and other musicians to perform during a vigil. She knew Alex was holding on beyond the doctors' predictions. She sensed some unfinished business, but in the three weeks since he had been home, nothing seemed to surface. She knew he missed the music at church.

On the fourth week, Alex felt strong enough to walk over to his computer and check his email, only to find an abundance of new messages from the pastoral care people regarding his day-to-day progress. He read email after email detailing the conversations he had with people at the church, what he ate, the food they brought, and the housework chores they performed.

He rang Lynn, shouting, "I don't need the entire bloody church to know when I've had a bowel movement." Although the pacemaker was off, his blood pressure could still rise. Yet his heart thrived on the unfettered attention showered on him by the members of St. Gregory's.

When the choir confirmed their performance date, Ruthann told Alex. From Megory's experience, she'd attest the gay community taught us a lot about how to die and say good-bye. In San Francisco, good-bye parties known as "blowouts" joined the repertoire of end-of-life rituals. When Alex heard the St. Gregory of Nyssa choir planned to sing for him at his home, he took the liberty of organizing a blowout by inviting all his neighbors and friends, near and far.

As the date for the choir performance and blowout neared, Alex coaxed a friend to drive him to Macy's and help him pick out a new pair of pants for the upcoming festivities. He needed a new pair because nothing fit him—he'd become a walking skeleton in the last four weeks. And it was important to him to dress properly for this occasion. St. Gregory of Nyssa's choir, famous for their angelic voices and soothing sounds of heaven, performed all over the nation. And now they were going to perform for Alex in his home. He was so excited.

On the morning of the performance, Alex bathed, combed his hair, and got dressed. His new pants gave him a boost of confidence. He left his bed and sat in his overstuffed chair awaiting the festivities. Friends and neighbors gathered around him for cocktails and appetizers. The forty-member-strong choir descended on his living room and encircled him.

In pure bliss, he sipped his Scotch and sat like a king, listening to the familiar sounds of Sunday mornings. In an instant he was once again transported to the sanctuary of St. Gregory's, where he'd yearned to return for weeks. As he closed his eyes, their voices, uplifted by their united force, sang to him, just him. It was a powerfully moving experience. There were few dry eyes in the room as the music penetrated his soul. Many of the choir members gathered closer and laid hands on Alex as they sang "Amazing Grace" and the "Our Father." Alex felt as if he were surrounded by singing angels. His mind floated in and out of present and past as the music carried him to distant memories. He requested his favorite hymn "How Great Thou Art." His thoughts turned to his youth, and he realized how many people with whom he'd shared his life were absent, most especially his surviving sister in Scotland. He rubbed his prayer beads and tapped rhythmically to the notes that seemed to transport him to another time and place, dancing in the Scottish countryside.

MUSICAL AND PRAYERFUL VIGILS

Megory has quoted from Don Campbell's *The Mozart Effect for Children: Awakening Your Child's Mind, Health, and Creativity with Music,* saying, "Music is a holy place, a cathedral so majestic that we can sense the magnificence of the universe . . . ."[9] Music is universal and uplifts the dying soul. To help a person transcend physical decline is one of the goals of Sacred Dying. There is nothing more powerful than singing or praying aloud for a person in the final days, hours, and minutes of life. Megory often called on gospel singers or harpists to transform a room of burden to hallowed glory. Sometimes she asks the families to sing religious songs or cultural celebratory songs from their youth to invoke good memories, feelings, and familiar home surroundings. For Alex, the Scottish hymns took him back to the amber Highlands. Music is the language of the soul. It needs no interpretation.

Megory had found in sitting bedside with people of varied faiths and communities that certain prayers brought comfort and closure as the last breath drew near. Megory would encourage the dying person to remember songs attached to his or her good memories, like Christmas carols, ethnic or patriotic songs, religious hymns, and family favorites. As Megory points out, there is no instruction for their use, just someone willing to lead the group to create a family gathering where music is the main component. This gesture often inspires unexpected reverence and a sacred place to release combined emotions with no language for expression. Music also leads to a meditative or reflective state and, above all, at a time of flux and frenzy, relaxes the dying person and those gathered. Many songs have prayer-like qualities that guide everyone collectively to reach a prayerful state.

Jewish law calls for the confessing of or atoning for sins, so when Jewish people meet the final hour of life, they will often offer confession or atonement. No rabbi needs to be present for this act. Psalms are often read or sung at the deathbed.

In her book *Sacred Dying: Creating Rituals for Embracing the End of Life*, Megory points out, "Both Judaism and Islam teach that those at the deathbed should turn their thoughts to repentance and divine mercy. Those gathered around must be careful not to engage in any idle talk. This focus brings merit to the dying person. In almost every faith tradition, it is forbidden to speak of mundane things in the deathbed room."[10]

In preparation for death, a Muslim may ask for forgiveness from God and repent all earthly sins.[11] The dying person, or if she or he is unable, a family member, must say aloud, "There is no God but Allah and Muhammad is his prophet."[12] These must be the dying person's last words, and after they are spoken, silence falls over the room until the last breath of life. Sixty to a hundred people at the house surrounding the dying person in prayerful meditation or reflection is common.

Similarly, family and community gather around the deathbed in Hindu and Buddhism traditions; however, these last hours are reserved for positive, uplifting prayers and chants. No confessions about this life are necessary because all are focused on helping the person into the next life.

A SACRED VIGIL: HOLDING ON, LETTING GO

After the choir left and the guests had said their farewells, Alex lay in bed thinking about home. He decided to call his sister in Scotland. A few days later she and her son flew out from Scotland to visit him. The reunion invigorated Alex, giving him unexpected energy to dine out for one last exquisite steak dinner. They spent hours reminiscing about the past, and her visit allowed Alex to finally lay to rest the severed ties he'd left behind when he escaped Glasgow in his early manhood. Coming together with his sister again completed him and gave him the farewell he had longed for on the evening of the choir performance.

Mere hours after his sister and her son departed, Alex began to decline. He'd held on for six weeks longer than expected. As Megory forewarned, he began to sleep for long bouts and barely woke during his conscious hours. On a Saturday in early autumn, Megory, Ruthann, and Libby sat around Alex's bed. Ruthann placed a stethoscope over his heart and listened. She looked at Megory. They needed no words. His heart slowed. His breath followed.

Alex opened his eyes at half-mast; Ruthann whispered to him, "Alex, are you ready to go?" At that moment she felt her own heart stop. She sucked in a deep breath. Why did she wait so long to ask him this question? Megory had already asked the same question six weeks before on the first evening she stayed with Alex. Then he was not ready. Alex raised his eyebrows and curled his lips up into a smile and whispered back to Ruthann, "Yes."

A few other members of St. Gregory's entered Alex's home and encircled his bed. They sang soft hymns from the hymnbook. Upon Megory's request, Donald Schell, the priest, arrived with consecrated bread and wine. The praise singers parted their circle to allow Donald to stand by Alex's bedside. Donald united them in prayer and then gave Alex the last rites. For the last time, Alex ate the bread and sipped the wine as his last supper before meeting his maker. As he internalized the Eucharist both physically and spiritually, his watchers sang "Amazing Grace" followed by "Our Father." Donald anointed him with holy oil and water as the voices guided Alex into his last sunset. Megory sat vigil all night. In the morning she connected to the congregation at St. Gregory via Donald's cell phone.

"We'll be praying for Alex, and we'll be with Alex, too," Donald said as he presided over the Sunday morning church service. "The cell phone will be the link."

After church, people arrived to pray and sing to Alex. He drifted off into a deep sleep, where he continued on into the unknown. Alex's heart stopped that afternoon.

Megory called on Libby to help her purify and dress Alex's body. The women gathered a basin of warm soapy water and washed his body. Usually a nurse would perform this act at the hospital, and in the time before hospitals, women performed this community service for their dead. Megory picked out the perfect prayer to make this act a sacred one. Together they cleansed his body and blessed him, saying in unison:

> I bless your hair
> that the wind has played with.
> I bless your brow,
> your thoughts.
> I bless your eyes
> that have looked on us with love.
> I bless your ears
> that listened for our voices.
> I bless your nostrils,
> gateway of breath.
> I bless your lips
> that have spoken truth.
> I bless your neck and throat;
> We will remember your voice.
> I bless your shoulders
> that have borne burdens of strength.
> I bless your arms
> that have embraced us.
> I bless your hands
> that have shaped wonders.
> I bless your heart
> that loved us.
> I bless your ribs and lungs
> that sustained your life.
> I bless your belly,
> sacred storehouse of the body.
> I bless your thighs,
> strong foundation.
> I bless your knees
> that knelt at sacred altars.
> I bless your legs
> that carried you.

Megory felt honored to wash and prepare Alex just as she'd promised. Libby found a bottle of Burberry, Alex's favorite scent. Just as they opened the bottle they both were reminded of the hugs they'd received from Alex at church on Sundays. "He always smelled of Burberry Brit," Libby giggled. It was the perfect scent to anoint him with. The last line of the blessing completed the bathing ceremony.

Megory said, "I bless your feet, Alex, that walked your own path through life."

Megory and Libby then dressed him in his white alb and turquoise vestment, which was the one he had worn as a greeter. He looked regal, Megory thought. She wanted the others to visit him, but he wished no one to see him after his last breath, and she honored her promise to him.

Megory sent out an email to the St. Gregory's congregation. She figured now she could be detailed. She would no longer have Alex reading and shouting about every "bloody detail" being shared. And if he did, she more than likely would not hear him.

From: Megory Anderson
Sent: Wednesday, September 21, 2005, 10:57 p.m.
Subject: SGN Pastoral Care: Alex's cremation
Wednesday Evening
Dear All –

Today, St. Gregory's walked further along Alex's journey into death. A small group of us gathered in Novato and witnessed his cremation. It was a very powerful experience. I have never been to a cremation, actually standing at the door of the furnace—like an oven, seeing first-hand what happens, so it was a blessing, albeit a shivering one for me, to be there. That is one thing I think that Alex has given us all—a chance to experience many blessings in dozens of different ways.

Let me tell you about this morning.

Six of us met at Valley Memorial Gardens . . . We met the director of Valley Memorial, and he was very gracious in explaining what the cremation process was, what was going to happen, and to give us an opportunity to be present as Alex's body went into the oven.

He led us into the crematorium room, which was small, quite bare, and mostly cement. It had two ovens side by side. They were both painted green, of all things! It made a wonderful contrast to the gray sterile cement.

Alex's coffin was simple and cardboard. It was on a stretcher at the door of the nearest oven. I thought to myself that it was our Alex inside there, probably just as he had been the day he died. It was Alex, and yet we saw the stark reality of death.

The six of us gathered around the coffin in a circle. I had put together a liturgy for the occasion and we began:

> We are here to commend Alex Cameron's body back to the elements.
> Since the early life of our Alex has come to an end,
> We commit his body to be turned to ashes:
> earth to earth
> ashes to ashes
> dust to dust;
> in the sure and certain hope of the resurrection to eternal life, through Jesus Christ our Lord
> Amen.

We said some prayers, sang the Lord's Prayer, the McFerrin Twenty-third Psalm, blessed him, and said good-bye. Each of us instinctively leaned over and kissed the coffin good-bye, and I saw Linda grin from ear to ear. Alex was going into the oven with lipstick kisses on his top! We laughed and laughed! He was also going into the flames dressed in his familiar blue.

The attendants opened the oven door after our prayers, wheeled the stretcher over, and slid Alex's coffin onto the cement slab. We watched quietly as they centered it and then slowly closed and locked the heavy door behind him.

The director asked us if we would like to "light the fire," as it were, and press the button to begin the flames. Kerry was the one who wanted to do this and she walked over to the side wall where the panel was. As the director showed her what to do, Tracy told us, "Lay hands on her." We reached out and supported Kerry as she began the fire. Tears were in her eyes.

"Alex, go in peace. Thanks be to God."

The six of us then moved to the chapel, a beautiful building on the grounds of the cemetery. The skies were blue, and it felt wonderful to be in that place. We went to a small niche in the chapel and sat in a circle, some of us in chairs, some on the floor. So as the fires began to consume Alex's body, we began,

> Let us keep vigil, reciting the psalms of David, while the body of Alex is being returned to dust.
> All things must end.

In creation, there is destruction,
In beginnings, there are endings,
Yet God's love is forever.

We recited the psalms antiphonally and then sang one of Alex's favorite hymns, "The King of Love My Shepherd Is."

We sat in silence and then prayed . . .

We sang some more—"There Are Angels Hovering Round"—and then it was time to go . . .

I am sitting here, late in the evening, with tears streaming down my face. In all the deaths I have witnessed, this has been the most profound. We have done this together, all of us. We have helped Alex in his fears of being alone by being with him along each step . . .

Love,
Megory

PART TWO

Post-Death and
Memorializing Rituals

NINE Her Twenty-First-Century Memorial Service, His Twentieth-Century Funeral

Around ten o'clock on the morning of February 10, 2002, two men dressed in black suits arrived in a white Ford Expedition from Forest Lawn. They parked their SUV in my garage and carried in a gurney. Before entering the living room, they handed me a stack of stapled papers to sign. My eyes blurred when reading the print. Essentially, I was releasing my mother into their power. I cringed when reading the line "Check the box" indicating if I wanted her cremated with her clothes on or off. Blinded by the sunlight bouncing off the white counters, I looked up and squinted at the two strangers.

"If you take the clothes off," I asked the men, "What will you do with them?"

"Send them back to you in the mail," one said.

Consumed by the images of these men disrobing my mother, I grew increasingly uneasy about handing her over. Swallowing vomit, I checked the clothes-on box. Reluctantly, I directed the intruders, I mean undertakers, into the living room. Without a word, they threw a white sheet over my mother's body, dumped her on a gurney and wheeled her out of the living room. I shuddered with disgust at their disrespectful treatment. Just because she'd stopped breathing didn't mean she'd stopped being Mom. As the wheels of the gurney squeaked across the kitchen tiles and down the pathway where her powerful high heels once clicked, I just wanted to scream, "Wait, don't take her yet." I bit my tongue, but failed to prevent an eruption boiling up from my stomach. I let out shrill, primordial scream and my knees buckled from beneath me. Simon lunged to catch me. He and Beverly carried me to the couch. The trauma had knocked me unconscious.

Within minutes I got back to my feet, I stumbled to the garage where I watched them load my mother into the back of the SUV. They slammed the door to the back so hard that the SUV rocked to and fro. These careless men had no tact, and their actions sent discordant tremors through my feeble body. They treated my mother like debris.

I walked back to the house and fell onto the couch. My eyes fixed on the empty hospital bed sitting in the center of my living room. I listened to the wind rustling through the tree outside and remembered sitting with my mother at her first chemotherapy appointment.

I asked Mom, "What does death mean to you?" Her eyes watered.

"When you were a child, do you remember falling asleep in the car and then you would wake up in your bed?" she asked.

"Yes, I do," I said.

"That's death. You fall asleep in the car and when you awake you are with God or you're in heaven. You don't know how you got there. As a little child, you have no recollection of your dad picking you up out of the car and carrying you to bed. So that's what I think death is, a passing over to another time."

I recalled another death metaphor that followed. Mom recited nearly verbatim the words of Xavier Ries, the pastor who presided over my father's graveside service. She raised her right hand and animated her fingers to demonstrate placing a glove on her hand.

"I loved the way Raul Ries's brother said it. You put the glove on. Your hand gives the glove life. The glove can now pick things up. It can make funny signs and communicate," she said, demonstrating sign language and then lifting up a bottle of raspberry ice tea in the chemo lab. "It turns and opens up a bottle. It feeds the body. It opens doors. But when you die, only the glove is left. It's just this thing that can't do anything on its own. That's death, when the hand leaves the glove."

Her hand lay lifeless and her eyes brimmed with tears.

My eyes blurred from staring at the hospital bed too long without blinking. I guess the men just took away the glove, not the hand. The hand, her spirit, would live on in my memories.

Unfortunately, the uninvited memories of my father's funeral entered my mind. I tried to expel them only to be attacked by flashbacks of yesterday's Forest Lawn experience. The urn and casket showcase room was suffocating as I tried to find an urn for my mother's ashes or as the godmother funeral counselor called them, the "cremated remains." I followed the godmother around a maze of traditional urns illuminated in glass curio cabinets. The creepy casket and urn gallery displayed wall-to-wall open caskets. As we passed the ornate caskets lined with satin pillows, I remembered my father made up like a wax statue resting on a satin pillow in a mahogany casket. The godmother watched me eye the mahogany casket on the wall.

"Would you like to pick out a casket for the funeral?" she asked.

A MODERN FUNERAL REMEMBERED

On the eve of my father's funeral, set for Monday, July 27, 1987, I returned from Kauai. My mother picked me up from LAX airport. On the drive home, she turned to me and said, "Denise, your dad passed away." We had just exited the freeway and snaked our way down the winding San Dimas Avenue. I stared through the windshield at the starry night sky. I couldn't respond. I wanted to tell her I knew. I'd felt it on Wednesday when a three-foot-tall wooden cross washed up on Hanalei Bay Beach, where I was wading in the waves. I believed the mysterious empty cross was a sign from Dad. His pain and suffering ceased.

"He died on Wednesday," she said. "The funeral is tomorrow. I'm so sorry, my love."

"Why didn't you tell me when I called on Wednesday?" I asked.

"We didn't want you to have to fly home on your own," she said.

After lying awake all night in my pink canopy bed, I rose to shower and dress for my father's funeral. I'd never been to a funeral before, so I had no idea what to expect. I decided against wearing makeup because my dad always disapproved of it. As I stared at myself in the mirror, thoughts of a fatherless existence stirred. I felt a chill of emptiness, like I was standing naked at the bottom of a dark well with no way out. My mother called from the bottom of the stairs. "Time to go."

We drove in Mom's Toyota to Bobbitt Memorial Home in San Bernardino, an hour east of Los Angeles. It was a blistering July day. My cousin, Robert Carson, one of the many young Filipino men donning a black suit, emerged from the crowd to direct my mother to park behind the limousine and hearse. As he opened my car door, I saw his sincere brown eyes were bloodshot from crying. I emerged from the air-conditioned car into the suffocating hot wind and a crowd of wailing women rubbing their rosaries and chanting prayers in Tagalog, their native Filipino language. My floral pink and lavender dress stood out as a quiet symbol of my rebellion in the mob of mourners cloaked in black. I couldn't help but think these women were pathetic. None of these people had seen the excruciating pain that my father had suffered in the months leading up to his death, but they couldn't possibly have known. He had isolated himself from his friends and family during the last months of his life. I escaped from the bottomless pool of black garbs, runny noses, and tears staining my dress to enter the grand chapel door.

I hadn't attended the wake, so my mother requested that I get a chance to see my father privately before the mourners were allowed in. I walked down the aisle of the chapel. The chandeliers hanging from the wooden ceiling cast a golden light, crowning my father, who lay in a mahogany casket at the end of the aisle. I yearned to embrace him. I'd been gone a week, the longest period of time I'd spent away from him.

I approached the casket. Immediately I noticed that all the wrinkles in his face had fallen away. He was no longer in pain. The oxygen tubes were gone, his cheeks were rosy and puffed out. His olive complexion was smooth. I giggled to myself because he was wearing makeup, foundation, the type he never allowed me to wear. I touched his face, but it was stone cold. My father was *never* cold. As usual he looked dapper in a gray, double-breasted, Italian tailored suit punctuated by a pale pink tie. I adjusted his tie to center it perfectly with the buttons on his coat. I grabbed hold of his hand but it, too, was ice cold. I'd reached for that hand so many times as a child for safety in a crowd, to cross a busy street, or just to feel his warm presence beside me.

I whispered, "I love you, Dad. I'm sorry I wasn't here for you."

I wanted to cry, but I couldn't. Where were my tears? I had no tears when my mother told me, no tears now that I stood before this lifeless statue that resembled my father. I turned to my mother, and she placed her hand on my shoulder, then escorted me into the private room for the family. I heard the doors open and mourners take their seats on the creaky pews.

Only one lay tribute was allowed at my father's funeral. Ken Trotter, our across-the-street neighbor for the last decade, gave a eulogy that broke through the monotonous funeral service when he read a reflection written by me three months before when I was still in the sixth grade, just shy of my twelfth birthday. The words, my words, my thoughts, resonated with me because it was a drop of reality in a contrived ritual to remember my father. The title was "I ♥ Daddy." He prefaced my words by saying, "I've seen Denise go in and out of our back door with the kids every weekend, but never really thought a twelve-year-old could have so much depth. I think the love for her father shown in these words exemplifies what kind of man Richard really was."

I Love Daddy, by Denise Carson

I want my dad to get better more than anything in the world. I want him to be taken out of his misery and pain. I love him so much that I'd give anything just to wake up one morning and see my dad better and fine. I can't think of a life without that sweet caring and warmth by my side of my wonderful father. He is always there for me. He would never leave me in a hard situation. Always caring for me and protecting me. Now it is my turn to pay it back. I pray for him all the time but it seems it never works. Lord, if this is his time, take him out of his pain and into your safe hands. I don't want to lose my dad because I love him so much. But if it means taking him out of his pain, I guess I have to let him go.

Ken paused to stop his voice from cracking. His deep breath, heavy on the microphone, awakened me from shock. Tears flowed. The numbness fell away. I tuned out his closing as every square inch of my body vibrated with intense pain. The reality of Dad's death crushed my composure. I keeled over as if someone had just dropped a two-ton lead weight on my shoulders. Following the eulogy, the organ resounded with the hymn "Amazing Grace." My mother helped me to my feet so we could sing.

The service and ambiance of that mortuary chapel triggered goose bumps to spread over the back of my neck. The funeral failed to convey my father's spirit with the exception of Ken's tribute and the large crowd of more than 300 relatives, friends, doctors, and nuns touched by his life. Of course, the funeral director presiding over the funeral had never met my father, so his words felt trite. At the closing prayer, we followed the pallbearers carrying my father in his closed casket out the center aisle. They loaded him into the hearse, and the chauffeur opened the door of the limousine for us. The hot sun beating down on me did little to penetrate my inner chill. I climbed inside the limo. I faced the front windshield of the hearse carrying my father in front. I looked out the back of the limousine window to see my mother and Ryan behind in front of a line of cars, a couple hundred at least, which all then turned on their headlights. An orange sticker labeled "Funeral" glowed in their windshields. The procession, followed a police escort on a motorcycle, traveled through the streets of San Bernardino. We crossed through the gates of Mountain View Cemetery and parked on the periphery of manicured lawns studded with headstones. We walked in a line following the pallbearers carrying my father's casket on their shoulders to the gravesite. I turned around to notice the mourners behind us all carrying a single white sheet of paper. I wondered why I hadn't been given one.

The color guard of honor trumpeted as the pallbearers lifted my father's casket onto an elevated metal contraption above the hole in the earth lined with a concrete vault. The dirt mounds masked by green turf served as a background to dozens of flower arrangements.

We sat down on white plastic chairs beneath a canopy in front of the casket set on the mount above the grave. That sorrowful "Taps" played and the color guard folded up the American flag and handed it over to my stepmother. I looked around and my eye caught the sunlight illuminating the white sheet of paper in my friend Jane Daignault's hand. I recognized the handwriting. It was mine. The paper titled "I ♥ Daddy." Everyone at the gravesite, nearly 300 people, held the prayer I'd written for my father. With all that unnecessary pomp and pageantry, it turned out that the mourners related more to the elementary but sincere words of Richard's twelve-year old daughter.

After the service, on the way to the wake, my mother made me promise that I'd make sure she didn't have an open casket like that.

"Just cremate me," she said.

A POST-MODERN DIRECT CREMATION AND MEMORIAL SERVICE

The godmother pointed to the mahogany casket on the wall in the dimly lit gallery at Forest Lawn. I knew my frugal mother was dead against spending such money on her funeral.

"No, my mom just wants to be cremated, no open casket," I said.

My mother reminded me countless times not to spend money on the funeral arrangements. She preached the same philosophy when discussing my future wedding. "I'd rather you place $10,000 or $15,000 on a down payment for a house than spend it on a wedding." I always thought that the funeral expense was the service and wake in the mortuary, but I soon discovered funeral directors learned how to make money out of a direct cremation. I'd taken a death and dying course in college and had some prior knowledge of the funeral industry, but the barrage of questions turned me from an informed consumer into a helpless, needy patient. I was vulnerable and honestly shouldn't have been in that funeral home, not in that condition.

"Where would you like your mother's cremated remains to rest?"

The question hit a nerve. In fact, it was the same guilt nerve keeping me at Forest Lawn for more than an hour instead of making a speedy exit. Visiting my father's grave after he died required a plan since the cemetery sat an hour's drive away from my house. I was only twelve when he was laid to rest. I had to wait four years before becoming a legal age to drive myself. My mother kindly offered to take me when I wished.

Two months after my dad died, we drove out to San Bernardino. I was excited because the headstone had finally been placed. We'd no longer just be visiting a mound of dirt beneath an oak tree. My mother, little brother, and I meandered through the cemetery before nearly tripping upon the newly set headstone adorning his grave. I gasped at the dual headstone. Brenda, my stepmother, had bought a his-and-her headstone designed with an open book with CARSON spread across the top. One page was inscribed "Richard B., August 18, 1949 – July 22, 1987" and the other side read "Brenda K." followed by her birthday and a black square over her death date. A ceramic photograph of my father and Brenda in an eternal loving embrace adorned the headstone. I turned my face upward to look at my mother, wincing at the desecration of his final resting place.

"I'm going to wait for you in the car," she said, with tears welling in her eyes. I plucked blades of grass and covered her face. That's the thing about divorce and broken families—although her picture was on his grave, she wasn't the one who would be leading the pilgrimages with me on Sundays, the anniversary of his death, and his birthday. She was selfish to bury him in San Bernardino when we had Forest Lawn Memorial Park down the street.

After a visit on the first anniversary of his death, I stopped asking my mother to drive me. Instead, we decided to dine out at his favorite neighborhood Italian restaurant on his birthday and the anniversary of his death.

I suppose I believed having my mother's eternal place of rest at Forest Lawn rectified years of never visiting my father. I said to the funeral godmother, "I'd like to have my mother here, but not in the ground."

She suggested the mausoleum or the wall of the chapel.

"Let me just arrange a quick walk around the grounds for you."

"I really do need to get back," I said. "Can we do this another time?"

"It shouldn't take long," she pushed.

The grounds person, yet again another saleslady, showed us around Forest Lawn. We looked at the niches—tiny shoebox-size boxes in the wall of the mausoleum. The side of a shoebox seemed like an unfit memorial. The sales lady suggested a crypt. After an exhaustive hunt, I chose a crypt in the mausoleum adorned with a Life of Christ mosaic measuring 172 feet by 35 feet. After I'd selected the crypt in the Sanctuary of Reverence, the godmother funeral counselor suggested a rite of committal when the urn was placed in the crypt. I declined. Like a black widow, she trapped me, a vulnerable fly in her web, disguised as a supportive blanket spun around me. I'm embarrassed to say, I paid close to $8,000. My mother would've been disappointed in me. A direct cremation costs about $1,800. We didn't even buy the big-ticket items such as the funeral service and a casket, but for some reason I spent $6,000 on an urn and a place to rest my mother's "cremains."

Trying to make decisions in a rushed, distraught state inevitably leads to poor decisions, which is precisely why I was so thankful that my mother asked Pastor Tom and his wife, Patsy, to handle the memorial service. I only had one request, to have an open mic service. I'd attended several funerals since my father's funeral in 1987 and began to notice the shift away from one eulogy. It wasn't until 1997, ten years after my father's death, when I witnessed an open mic eulogy and the celebration of life theme.

Pastor Tom came to the house to interview us in effort to create a personal memorial service that would appropriately commemorate my mother. I appreciated his desire to spend time with us to ensure that he spoke to our hearts in the service. My father's felt like the funeral director just pulled out the canned Catholic funeral liturgy and filled in blank "name of the deceased" spaces with Dad's name.

On Monday, February 11, the first whole day without Mom, we sat in a circle around Tom in the family room as he asked us questions that incited hours of cathartic reminiscence. Instead of being isolated in our grief, the group interview bound us together, Beverly, Ryan, Sharon,

Simon and me, on a remarkable journey of remembrance. Our memories seemed so vivid, detailed, and current, in part because I believe that when someone close dies, as a principal survivor you review your own life shared with that person. Similar to a life review, memories are sensory rich. These memories give some respite from the intense grief. The cognitive dump of reminiscences from subconscious to the weary, grief-stricken conscious is nature's antidote to the initial shock of death. Tom triggered us to move from the cognitive inward journey to a shared outward one. The experience was both healing and binding.

He inspired us to gather pictures for a collage of my mother's life to showcase at the memorial service. We drew on shared memories to arrange a collection of pictures for the montage together with personal effects for a memorial table. We blew up two formal pictures.

I wrote the obituary notice and placed it with the *Los Angeles Times* to run the day before her memorial service, on Thursday, February 14, Valentine's Day. The obituary was telling in its reflection of how I perceived those last seven days of her life:

> Linda Carson, single mother, British expatriate and banker, transcended to her eternal home on February 10, 2002. Our heroine battled cancer for three years and is survived by daughter, Denise Carson, 26, and son, Ryan Carson, 18. We spent seven glorious days sharing Linda's passage between her home in San Dimas to her new home in heaven. Numerous loving family members and friends graced her living funeral. The unconditional love and survival shone joyously through Linda's spirit. Her strength, purity, and peace will remain an inspiration in our hearts forever.

On the eve of Mom's memorial service, my cousins, Aunt Mimi, and Uncle Dennis arrived in town from San Francisco. My mother's friends came over to help finalize plans for the service. That evening our house bustled. We ordered Mexican food, my mother's favorite, and played Andrea Bocelli's CD *Romanza*. I kept replaying "Con Te Partiro."

"What are they saying?" one of my cousins asked.

" 'Time to Say Good-Bye,' " I said.

It was the perfect theme song for our memorial service eve ritual. Together we lay out on the dining room table all the pictures that had been collected over the last five days from all our photo collections. It was like a jigsaw puzzle that we needed to put into chronological order. This new ritual incited the most amazing hours of "show 'n' tell" because everyone found photographs of themselves sharing life moments with Linda. We pasted the photos into an eighteen-by-twenty-inch frame. I even found a newspaper clipping of a profile written about Linda Crook published in the local newspaper in Manchester, England. The story detailed my mother's experiences as an au pair in America. We boxed her bible, photo albums, knitting needles, and quilts she'd knitted for Ryan and me. We continued boxing her QuickBooks software, her Beautiful perfume, her Lennox collectible birds—a humming bird and a blue jay to represent her love for birds and nature—and a figurine of an angel releasing a bird to fly free for the memorial table.

The next morning, we carted everything over to Glenkirk Church. Before the service, in the private choir room at the church, I leaned against a grand piano and gave an impromptu speech to all of the close friends and relatives who'd supported my family throughout the last week and then requested each person share an inspiring memory of my mother for the audience of about 200 people gathering in the sanctuary. At that moment, as I stared at the faces of my mother's and father's closest friends, the young faces of Ryan's and my friends filling about forty seats in that choir room, I knew that my brother and I would survive in the absence of our parents. We were not alone.

Pastor Tom called us out to join the congregation. His comforting introduction of my mother, Linda, spoke about her great faith in Jesus Christ and drew on the Christian story of the resurrection of Jesus, reassuring us that Linda lives eternal. Tom asked us all to stand and sing the hymn "As the Deer." Just as the guitarist hit the first chord, the first tear of the memorial service trickled down my face. I remembered singing next to Mom in our home at her last birthday celebration.

My best friend, Denise, followed the song with a eulogy. She retraced my mother's footsteps from her birthplace following the dark years of World War II in Manchester to her coming of age in America, driving across country with Beverly, meeting Richard, her true love, and becoming a parent. "Her life was about overcoming obstacles," Denise said.

"She was always a mother first. Her decisions always revolved around Denise and Ryan, even if they didn't know it."

Denise added that spending time at our home in the last week, she learned what family really meant. "Family is love. Your family are the people who love you." She said that I often complained that I didn't have a big family like her Mexican/Italian family but she realized that I was wrong—we had a large, thriving family according to her new-found definition.

She spoke about how Linda lived a life devoted to God and even in her last days "instead of praying for healing, she praised him."

"You know what Linda treasured the most?" she asked, a rhetorical question to the audience. "Her memories. She had a safety deposit box, not for her diamonds or jewels, but as a place to store the negatives from a lifetime of photographs."

In closing, she pointed out that "Denise and Ryan are going to be okay. They have an example from a woman who started on a journey by herself and made things happen, and they have each other."

Denise put together a list of words that described Linda—strong, modest, pretty, petite, organized, wise, brave, calm, and down-to-earth. At the end of her tribute she surprised me with words of gratitude that my mother requested she say. My mother had found a creative way to send thank-you notes from heaven at her own memorial service.

Denise said, "Linda has some people she wished to thank and re-member: 'Ron Steinberg and Steve Covey need to know they are my heroes. I would like to thank Dennis and Mimi, Ken and Buffy, Tom and Patsy and . . . Beverly—what can I say? She picked up and left her home in Nevada and came down here to be with me.' "

After Denise sat down, my brother's best friend, Jason Fortelny, just eighteen years old, stood at the microphone in front of the first-row pew where we sat.

"I spent a lot of time with the Carson family. One thing I noticed about Linda was that she would do anything for her children, anything," he said, pausing to collect himself. "As I stand here I see in Ryan his mother's strength and generosity. When I look at Denise, I see her mother's warm heart and smile. Linda was one of those people who always asked me,

'How are you doing?' or 'Would you like something to eat?' She often said I was too skinny. This is how I'll remember her, as a caring person. I'll forever cherish the memories I had with the Carson family, and my heart goes out to everyone here."

My cousin, Robert Carson, stood up barely composed, tears running down his face. I loved the honest display of emotion. It was so refreshing, so authentic. He talked about how one knows a person's style by the way they enter a room, but, he said, "It's not just how you enter, but how you leave, and my Auntie Linda left with style."

I couldn't help but nod my head in approval. "Yes, she did," I thought. "Yes, she did." I raised my thumb at him. The tributes that followed exceeded my expectations. Many spoke not only of my mother but also of my father. I was hearing stories about my father that people probably had wanted to share at his funeral but had never been given the opportunity. For the first handful of tributes, it sounded like a memorial service for both of my parents. Then my mother's boss stood up. He talked of how he'd only known my mother in the last six years of her life, which differed from many of the relationships of the people who'd shared previously.

Ron said, "She stood unique as an example as how to live our lives. If 100,000 people knew her, then 100,000 people would understand compassion and humanity and that there are rights and wrongs. Linda always did the right thing and her heart was always in the right place. Those who didn't know her were unfortunate. Those who knew her well had a role model for life."

Uncle Dennis recalled our visit to the Huntington Library in Pasadena a couple of months before. He described Linda basking in the sun on a bench overlooking the gardens with a look of such contentment in the face of adversity and nearing death. He lifted her to one of the great sages in his life. He concluded by saying, "So I would like to add one more word to Denise's list of words that describe Linda—contentment."

I loved the dynamic of improvisational open mic group eulogy because each person dovetailed with the next. The memorial service was nearly two hours long, filled with about a dozen revelatory tributes. I thought about stepping up to the microphone, but knew that my emotions would strangle my words and make any tribute to her that I would give incomplete. Instead, I listened and learned.

Pat Albert, a silver-haired lady who led the divorce recovery ministry with my mother at church for more than decade, stood up. "Linda used to say how blessed she was to see people so wounded and hurt come from such adversity, change, and grow—but *she* was the true blessing to so many people in the divorce recovery ministry. Her love for the Lord just flowed through her and guided new beginnings for so many people. As for single parenting, she did a wonderful job. She loved to entertain and she had the greatest parties. Those memories will remain in my heart."

Tom stopped the tributes there, but he encouraged the congregation to continue sharing memories at the reception after the service. I noticed Tom even called the festivity after the memorial service a reception rather than a wake. This was truly a celebration.

Dwayne Condon's voice came from behind the piano singing "Amazing Grace." For the first time I didn't keel over. In fact, the song uplifted me. Tom closed with the words of Mom's favorite Psalm, and Dwayne joined in playing on the piano "Search Me Oh God." As I listened to Dwayne sing the hymn I'd sung repeatedly over my mother's lifeless body just four days before, I agreed with my mother—his voice sounded as if it were straight from heaven. Silently I sang along and turned my eyes toward the ceiling of the sanctuary. His ethereal voice rose to a finale, singing "Peace, Peace, Peace."

THE SHIFT FROM MODERN TO POST-MODERN DEATH WAYS

Symbolically, I saw my parents' end of life as the yin and yang of death— his was the black yin and hers the white yang. His funeral emphasized darkness, the mourning of his death, but her memorial service celebrated her life and how the light she shined on us would continue to live on in our memories. Their funerals serve as cultural exemplars of the evolving post-death rites that occurred at the turn of the twenty-first century.

Our modern memory leads us to believe that the "embalm-and-bury regime," a term used by Stephen Prothero in *Purified by the Fire: A His-*

tory of Cremation in America,[1] that honored my father in late July 1987 is the traditional funeral in America. This ritual—characterized by the funeral director swiftly removing the body from the family home or hospital after the death to undergo embalming, cosmetic beautification, and dressing for a viewing in the funeral home followed by burial in a cemetery—describes what historians call the modern funeral. The religious funeral liturgy and the dead body tended to be the central focus of this ritual, and the eulogy is marginal.

Cultural historians of death in America such as Gary Laderman point out that the traditional funeral practiced by pioneers of the New World resembled a simpler family-directed funeral and burial. Before the rise of the professional funeral business in America, the typical funeral began with the family washing and dressing the body in the home.[2] They laid out their dead in the parlor, a front room in the house specially designed to accommodate a wake with a separate entrance and doorway wide enough for a coffin to be carried through. From the home, the mourners followed the casket in a procession through the streets to a graveside service and burial.

During the Civil War, when this country lost more than half a million soldiers on the battlefield, embalming—what Laderman calls the life blood of the modern funeral industry—emerged as a medical science that turned casket carpenters and other funeral services tradesmen into scientists capable of preserving the soldiers' remains to return home for an honorable family wake, funeral, and burial.[3] Medical scientists used embalming to preserve cadavers by draining the blood and flooding the veins with formaldehyde. Laderman says, "Without this procedure, funeral directors would have had a difficult time claiming that they were part of a professional guild, and therefore justified as the primary mediators between the living and the dead from the moment of death to the final disposition."[4] Their increasing authority over the corpse and the simultaneous rise to dominance of the funeral home—a confusing space of business, religious activity, corpse-preparation, and family living—forever changed the social and cultural landscape of death in America.[5]

As funeral homes became a local institution in towns across America, the undertakers took on a new reputation as the funeral "directors" and established a standard set of rituals that came to be known as the

American modern funeral. These rituals were passed down through the "generations of funeral directors" to maintain uniformity to essentially protect their livelihoods. As a professional guild, they preserved these rituals nationwide through their larger professional network known as the National Funeral Directors' Association. These ritual preservationists used embalming as a hygienic technique that "protected" the living from the dead, which consequently further alienates the living from the dead. A familial task of caring for the dead for a millennium gradually transferred to the professionals over the course of the twentieth century. Though embalming is not required by law in any state, most funeral directors refuse to allow a public viewing of the body until it is embalmed.

Anthropologists Peter Metcalf and Richard Huntington, who studied mortuary rituals around the world, found remarkable consistency in American funerary rituals from coast to coast, even though America is a country of immigrants who brought with them many different ways of dealing with death.[6]

I spoke to funeral director John Hogan, a septuagenarian and former president of the National Funeral Directors Association, about his reflections on the early years of the funeral home when his father stopped making house calls and his storefront funeral home, Fogarty Funeral Home, in Queens, New York, became the hub for the visitation and all funerary rituals. Hogan was six years old and lived with his family in an apartment above the funeral home. He recalled families being relieved at turning over their responsibilities for the dead.

When doctors stopped making house calls, more people died in hospitals and, eventually, nursing homes. And it wasn't a far stretch to have yet another institution and set of professionals care for the dead, further diminishing family and clergy involvement in the final stage of life. Laderman goes on to paint the larger picture of the established funeral home in America, saying, "The cultural implications of this environmental shift from death in the home to death in the hospital were profound, and contributed to the literal displacement of the dead from the everyday social worlds of the living."[7]

Funeral directors removed all responsibility for the corpse from the family and the religious services from the clergy. Following a parallel thriving lifeline to the hospitals, the funeral homes and the modern funeral was firmly established in American society by the mid-twentieth century. Laderman concludes in his book *Rest in Peace: A Cultural History of Death and the Funeral Home in Twentieth-Century America* that "combined with the mortality revolution taking place and growing presence of medical institutions that sequestered the dying from the living, new ritual patterns for disposing of the dead founded on the practice of embalming relieved living relations of the traditional duties."[8]

The embalm-and-bury regime rituals remained virtually intact, unscathed with the exception of the sanitation movement during the Gilded Age, which was a period of rapid social and intellectual change in the post–Civil War era.[9] Early advocates and pioneers of cremation introduced returning the body to the elements by the purifying fire as a hygienic solution to the time-honored burial, which cremationists deemed a threat to public health.[10] At the end of the nineteenth century, the early cremation movement shifted to the twentieth-century business agenda. Prothero explains in his book *Purified by Fire: A History of Cremation in America* that "while the movement's pioneers had promoted cremation as a final disposition, these profit-minded crematory operators promoted cremation as a preparation for either inurnment in a columbarium or interment in a cemetery. In 1927 and 1928, in speeches delivered to both crematory and cemetery operators, Walter B. Londelius, the superintendent at Glendale's Forest Lawn, argued for the 'memorial idea,' which he termed a 'sacred obligation which [families] have no right to disregard.'"[11] After a cremation, the postmortem process was only one-third complete; that was because "urn interment" included three "inseparable" features: cremation, niche, urn.[12] The memorial movement succeeded in making a lucrative profit out of an inexpensive, simple, and minimalist approach.

Funeral directors came under fire in 1963 with the *New York Times* best-seller *The American Way of Death*, written by muckraker Jessica Mitford. She lifted the veil covering the funeral industry and opened the general public's eyes to the conniving sales strategies of funeral directors preying on the bereaved by using guilt and up-selling many gratuitous accoutrements. Her book reignited the Gilded Age movement, driving cremation as a final disposition, but not as a hygienic alternative to burial. Instead, Mitford struck a chord that galvanized the consumer movement to choose cremation as a stand against the funeral industry's taking advantage of vulnerable, grieving families. She informed consumers of the astronomical price gouging on funerary items that ultimately cost families then upwards of $5,000 and today upwards of $7,000.

During the 1970s, many people had no rituals at all after cremation and apparently reported back grave results. The Cremation Association now advocates some kind of memorial to complement a cremation. Instead of going back to the established funeral ritual of relying on the funeral director to restore the corpse to appear "natural" or "life-like" thereby giving the living a "therapeutic memory image" and one last opportunity to commune with the dead and facilitate grief at the funeral,[13] families can replace the one-size-fits-all funeral. The counterculture incorporated cremation rather than burial, the memorial service (without the body) rather than the funeral (with the body).[14] Rather than gazing at an embalmed corpse, nonconforming mourners were urged to recall with their hearts and minds the deceased's eternal spirit.[15] The same year that Mitford published her book, the Vatican II approved cremation as an alternative form of body disposal.

Mitford's book led to the Federal Trade Commission hearings and the 1974 Funeral Rule law that states funeral homes must provide families with a price list and forbade misrepresentations of legal requirements for disposition of the human remains. In *Rest in Peace*, Laderman sums up the climate of how that altered the once-sacred American funeral: "The federal investigation of the industry beginning in the 1970s, coupled with the growth and popularity of the death awareness movement during the same period, actively encouraged patrons to take control of the funeral and create ceremonies that suit rather than simply conform to the modern traditions established over the first half of the twentieth century."[16] This cataclysmic shift propagated the post-modern funeral. The post-modern funeral, as described by death and dying sociologist Justin Holcomb, "is not created by isolated, autonomous individuals working in a vacuum but is constructed out of complex negotiations between mourners, funeral experts, and faith communities."[17] In an interview, Holcomb pointed out that in a post-modern funeral, the community is not necessarily bound by a particular faith, but instead by a shared love for the deceased. Therefore it's common to see the personal story of the deceased, such as in an open mic– or shared eulogy–focused memorial, sidelining the religious narrative, such as the resurrection.

My mother's memorial service exemplified the post-modern funeral, characterized by our pastor, family, and community gathering together in a do-it-yourself manner to orchestrate an uplifting personal tribute. Personalized funerals have now existed long enough to begin developing their own tradition in the sense of frequently used elements, like the celebration of life, the shared eulogy, and incorporation of pictures of the deceased.[18]

In the 1970s, John Hogan said he and other funeral directors began training their staff in altering the traditional funeral ritual by speaking to families about how to personally memorialize their deceased loved ones. At that time, he asked families to bring in photos of the person to display at the funeral home during the service. He noted the changing tone of the funeral homes he grew up in, whose ambience resonated morbidly, with dark drapes and sorrowful music. Now, he said, "it's bright in the funeral home, the wallpaper is yellow, the drapes are all a lighter color. The focus is on life lived and life after rather than death." Hogan said the entire funeral industry has turned to this celebration-of-life theme.

He also spoke about how 9/11 shifted older funeral directors into rethinking how to perform a funeral without the body being the central focus. The entire nation was in mourning, and after the deadliest terrorist attack on America soil in U.S. history, nearly 3,000 lost lives were in need of a funeral. The funeral directors were especially driven toward this post-modern funeral as they worked with families to create meaningful memorial services without the bodies.

Funeral directors have changed the score and mood of their services to accommodate the changing demographics of their communities. The personalization of the funeral ritual is not just a shift toward celebrating the individual's life, but may also be an incorporation of religious rituals from the deceased's homeland. It's not unusual these days to have incense burning in the chapel during a funeral or a dual-religion ceremony, much like we've seen in wedding rituals. But Hogan notes the largest segment of the population—and one that is continuing to grow—served in many cities across the nation is "nonchurched," which means the service does not look to religion, but to the family to create a meaningful funeral or memorial service. In a reflection on the changing times, Laderman concludes, "Funeral directors embraced multiculturalism as an unavoidable social and business reality in the late twentieth-century America, although the transformation from a monocultural institution to a multicultural institution took some time."[19]

In the opening years of the twenty-first century, it's difficult to say whether the FTC Funeral Trade Rule has curtailed the funeral industry exploits. The average funeral costs a family between $7,000 and $10,000. Moreover, the $11 billion funeral industry, with the exception of a few bruises on the public relations front, has suffered little decline in their bottom lines as a consequence of making their price lists available.

Recently, I had the courage to reopen the Forest Lawn folder that I filed away after my mother's death. I found inside a bill for my mother's life insurance company in the amount of $7,975.84. I also found a price list within. Maybe I should have just taken the price list home and returned when I was in a clearer frame of mind.

A WALK OF GRIEF

I found a grief counselor a week after my mother's memorial service, but she advised me that she could better serve me in a few months when the grief had sunk in. She didn't want me to waste my money and time. My house felt so empty after my mother died. I bought plants to enliven the staleness and an Asian garden fountain for the living room, but nothing seemed to take off the icy edge. Then we found Moby, a three-pound Yorkshire terrier, who breathed life and a bit of zest back into our home. The stillness continued to harp on me though, so I left the house for Ryan and moved to an oceanfront apartment in Laguna Beach where the sound of lapping waves echoed vigorously morning, noon, and night through my living room. I worked around the clock. All of the grief unexpressed from my father's death piled on my mother's death gradually began to weigh on me until one morning I literally felt pinned to my bed as if a grand piano lay flat over my body. It was six months to the day of my mother's death. That morning, I understood why the grief counselor suggested I wait. I started to spiral downward with crying spells and what would be clinically called complicated grief.

I visited a psychologist. He urged me to hold on to the memories of my mother's last days because they would shine light into the darkest of grief tunnels. I began transcribing the interviews with my mother. I also wrote letters to my mother every week, which helped ease the void left by her parting. I read every book on death and dying at Barnes and Noble, Borders, and the Laguna library. When I finished reading those books, I read the books listed in their bibliographies. I looked to books and their authors for solace. I searched for reflections of my own turmoil within theirs. I educated myself on parent loss, caretaking for a parent, childhood to adulthood grief, death, near-death experiences, and the afterlife. Still, I couldn't find books or rather narratives that directly related to me. I'd come to a realization that my mother and I had carved out a new path into life's final frontier.

I spent time on the beach meditating on how I envisioned moving forward in my life. I wrote down some life goals in a journal. Backpack around the world. Move to Manhattan to study at Columbia University. Since my parents died young, I certainly wasn't going to live my life based on the delayed gratification "when I retire, I'll travel the world" plan. Neither one of them reached retirement. So I began mapping out the route. In late December, my psychologist released me and praised my deep penetrating introspection.

Simon and I left in early January 2003 carrying nothing but North Face backpacks. We planned to travel a year. Our first stop was England. I visited the places Mom talked about in her life review interviews. I walked on the sidewalk where she rode her red tricycle. I saw the home on the corner of Hampden Road that embarrassed her. More important, I spent time in the loving arms of the family that my mother left behind in her decision to make a life in America. Simon and I spent the remainder of our time at his mother's cottage near the Thames just west of London. He guided us on a tour of his birthplace.

A month later, we made an equatorial crossing to Fiji, Australia, and New Zealand. I placed many miles, hours, time zones, and experiences between my mother's death and what I like to call my rebirth. I learned how to breathe, walk, talk, and laugh again without my mother. I felt the heavy, dark cloud of grief begin to lift, especially after I jumped out of a plane 12,000 feet above the ground on a skydive through the clouds. I felt like I'd hit the reset button in my mind's hard drive. Communing with nature while scuba diving in Australia's Great Barrier Reef and swimming with a pod of a hundred wild dolphins in the chilly waters off the coast of New Zealand rejuvenated me.

In India, I began to notice people again. I'd lost a sense of empathy for others in the turmoil of trying to survive my own loss. This wholly different reality placed my loss in perspective. I was in the company of starving children, many probably orphans, and they were fending for themselves at age seven, not twenty-seven like me. There in Deli, I experienced a catharsis, one of many that occurred while trekking around the globe. Death covered the streets. It dwelled in the faces of hungry children and old people in the markets. Even the city smelled rancid. Hundreds of people were dying all over India from the heat, during one of the hottest summers on record. In all the commotion, I felt a peace and calm within.

Eventually, we escaped Deli, Agra, and other Indian cities on a sixteen-hour bus trip with no air conditioning driving up the hairpin turns of the Himalayas to Nepal in the pitch dark. As the rickety bus wobbled around the high mountain cliffs, I felt myself more than once holding my breath and praying we'd survive.

At dawn, we arrived safely.

The burning ghats in Nepal further drew me out of my grief. I sat on the cool concrete witnessing the public cremation of four people, but one family struck me. I saw a son, not too much older than I was, lead the circular procession around his father elevated on the funeral pyre. From what I understood, he and his family had already spent many days at their home in vigil with their father after his death, helping him to be reborn into the next life, and the purifying fire completed this process. After the vigil, they proceeded to the temple where the holy river Bagmati runs below the steps of the ghats. After the son led many mournful, heart-wrenching chants around his father's body, he stopped at his head and lit the purifying cremation fire. Just as he did that, I felt a surge of emotion. I was overwhelmed, even jealous, that he could accompany his father to the flames and never let him out of his sight. He didn't have to turn his father over to strangers. This may seem primitive or arcane to some people, but to me it felt natural, right, especially after I'd suffered from many horrifying nightmares of what could've happened to my mother that day after I closed the garage and they drove away in the white SUV. I wondered then as I witnessed the son watch over his father engulfed by the rising flames why we, as Americans, were so isolated from this experience.

Cremation is an ancient custom imported as a science from the East as a modern improvement to our Western earth burial. In India, the body is burned outdoors on public open pyres, whereas in America the cremation occurs indoors out of the public eye and the flames never touch the body directly. One might think of a firing kiln to envision the difference. At least with earth burial, you accompany the casket to the grave, and if you choose, you can use a shovel to start the dust-to-dust process of returning your loved one's body to the elements. In a cremation, I turned over my mother's body and picked up the ashes later from Forest Lawn.

It didn't help matters when a couple of days after my mother's death, a crematory scandal in Georgia broke. Families had their cremated remains from the Tri-State Crematory analyzed and found out that these remains weren't their loved one's ashes. I thought about them when I held the ashes of my mother for the first time. I wondered how my mother's body was taken care of after she left our home. There had to be a way around this veiled approach. After seeing cremation in its purest form in Asia where the first Westerners witnessed it, I realized we imported the science but left the meaningful family-involved rituals in the dust.

TEN Home Funeral: Eco-Friendly Way Out

The perpetual chill in my closet-sized Manhattan apartment waned as I feverishly typed out an email to Jerrigrace Lyons, a death midwife in Northern California. It was autumn of 2004, yet searing flashes of that morning when those two men from the funeral home whisked away my mother terrorized me. I had tried desperately to prevent consciously tainting the last seven days of her life by erasing her undignified departure from my memory. After learning that Jerrigrace, like a midwife in a home-birth, coached families in preparing the body for a wake and funeral at home followed by a procession from the home to the cemetery, I relived that morning. With Jerrigrace's help, families circumvented the abrupt body removal by caring for their own dead.

Tears flooded my eyes and an epiphany formed. The last time I saw my mother she was beneath a white sheet on a gurney in the back of a white SUV posing as a hearse instead of witnessing her lowering into an earth grave or entering the cremation fire.

As I came to the end of the email, my tears dried and I left that harrowing morning, returning to the present. I stared at the cursor blinking on my screen, highlighted the grim details, and cut them out, but left the essence of my discontent and introduced myself as a student at the Columbia Graduate School of Journalism researching a master's thesis project about the new rituals of dying and death. The journalist in me wanted to know if it was legal to care for our own dead, but the daughter in me finished the email with: "I wish I could have known about you before my mother died."

A few days later I received a compassionate email back from Jerrigrace saying that I wasn't unusual for having such reservations about turning my mother over to the body-removal men. She received many emails and phone calls just like mine every day from across the nation. For nearly a decade, she had been educating, supporting, and guiding families on how to perform home funerals, take care of paperwork, such as filing death certificates, and transport the dead to the crematorium for a "direct cremation" in an effort to return the intimacy and family involvement to this final stage of life.

The home funeral also eliminated the ballooning costs of traditional funeral rituals that had become bereft of meaning. She likened her function to that of the early hospices for families of the dying in hospital. Like hospice, her local operation had spread by way of training other death midwives who brought her methods to their local towns across America. The natural death-care movement struck many of the same chords as the home-birthing/natural-birth movement when women advocated against the over-medicalization and standardization of birthing practices in hospitals that dehumanized elements of the birth process. Although the movement was marginal and 99 percent of births still occur in hospitals, the consumer advocacy did succeed in transforming birthing practices in hospitals to reflect more personalized and individualized services for women, said Markella Rutherford, a sociologist and author of a study entitled "Selling the Ideal Birth: Rationalization and Re-enchantment in the Marketing of Maternity Care."[1]

Although the natural death-care movement is also marginal, the practices are indeed shifting, if not transforming the conventional funeral to better serve those in search of more "hands-on" family involvement approaches to after-death care. Gary Laderman, a cultural historian, explained in his book *Rest in Peace: A Cultural History of Death and the Funeral Home in Twentieth Century America,* that the once set–in-its-own-ways funeral industry has embraced the buzz word "adapt" and consequently is accepting the "unconventional funerals" that represent "a democratization of the consumer marketplace where individuals can, in the words of the ubiquitous contemporary fast-food slogan, 'Have it their way.'"[2]

Yet, the home funeral/death midwife option had remained on the fringes of society until 2004, when green burial, a natural, eco-friendly alternative to the embalm-and-bury regime, mated with a family-directed home funeral in Northern California. The home funeral and green burial of Tommy Odom received nationwide attention because the simplicity and earth-friendly nature of the ceremony spoke to many Americans, discontent with the funerals that had taken place in the second half of the twentieth century. The funeral ritual exemplified many of the "-ism" values we hold dear in America—individualism, environmentalism, multiculturalism, and spiritualism.

In 2004, Tommy Odom had the first green burial in Forever Fernwood, a thirty-two-acre memorial preserve amidst miles of the Golden Gate National Recreational Area along the border of San Francisco. On a hill in the woods, he was buried without embalming fluid in a plain, pine, biodegradable box deposited in an unmarked grave without the standard concrete vault liner. Instead of a headstone, an oak tree was planted as a marker over his grave and later an indigenous rock was engraved. His body would serve as a seed to nourish the land, which is multiuse, with nature hiking, equestrian trails, and picnic areas for the living. Tommy taught Americans that their greatest contribution to the earth could be made at the time of death, because through a land endowment the dead protected the open space for the living. Others who followed Tommy at Fernwood would also have camouflaged or unmarked graves so the land could be left natural instead of cluttered by rows of headstones placed in manicured lawns.

His green burial reminded me of the first cremation in America. In *Purified by Fire: A History of Cremation in America*, Stephen Prothero writes that on December 6, 1876, in the small town of Washington, Pennsylvania, "the corpse of Baron Joseph Henry Louis Charles De Palm went up in flames in an event billed as the first cremation in modern America. Supporters hailed the event as a harbinger of a new age of scientific progress and ritual simplicity. The cremation as a modern alternative to burial debate was covered in every major newspaper across America and Europe."[3] Persifor Frazer Jr., a sanitarian, and the Reverend Octavius B. Frothingham, a preacher, set out to overturn the time-honored tradition of burial.[4] Today, at the height of a new millennial age, the eco-friendly-death movement gave birth to a similar cast of characters to shift American perceptions, including Jerrigrace Lyons, a fifty-seven-year-old death midwife who is Mother Nature incarnate; Dr. Billy Campbell, the forty-something environmentalist founder of the first green burial cemetery in America; Tyler Cassity, a thirty-five-year-old innovator and part of a second generation of a family renowned in the funeral business and Tyler's right-hand man, Joe Sehee, a forty-four –year-old evangelist.

I shall share in greater detail the story of the first green burial in California because it was a flashpoint in Americans' choosing to personalize the rote funeral rituals of their parents and grandparents. Although this story appeared in abbreviated form in many major newspapers and magazines, the adaptation of ancient cultural rituals was glazed over in lieu of reporting about the business of green burials. After this green burial, America saw the do-it-yourself funeral movement spill beyond the borders of Northern California (which I talk about in chapter 11). Since the 1970s, Northern California, has been a breeding ground of avant-garde death ways due in part because it's Mitford Territory, where Jessica Mitford author of the scathing *American Way of Death* and her alternative-death movement was born. Laderman, writes, "Without a doubt Californians were exposed to progressive alteration in funeral traditions earlier than most of the country's alterations according to one industry trade article in 1974 'unconventional funerals' growing in popularity. California's do-it-yourself ceremonies seek what they consider a more personal approach one they believe that gives greater meaning to funerals.[5] . . . Surprisingly, this 'spirit of change' among Californians, the article reports, is not limited to young people, but includes older, even more conservative individuals. Funeral men and women did not know if this regional trend anticipated larger national fashions, but clearly understood that pervasive changes were afoot."[6]

Laderman goes on to say, "After Mitford's book, and certainly over the course of the FTC investigations (that lasted into the 1990s), funeral directors sensed a shift in American funerary sensibilities and an increased willingness to defy the institutionalized prescriptions that ritually removed the dead from the living community."[7] Until the news of green burial and home funerals spread, most Americans were unaware that in all but seven states,[8] it's legal to care for your own dead, without the aid of an undertaker/funeral director.[9]

Like many Americans, fifty-year-old Rebecca Love, Tommy's best friend, read about the green cemetery, Forever Fernwood, in the July/August 2004 edition of the AARP Bulletin in an airplane on the way to her mother's funeral in Louisiana. After the article appeared in the AARP Bulletin, the AARP website polled readers, asking: "Which type of burial is most appealing?" The Los Angeles Times reported the results: only 8.1 percent wanted a traditional cemetery burial; 18.6 percent picked cremation; 2.9 percent went for an "exotic burial," such as being shot into space; and the rest—70.4 percent—chose a green burial.[10]

When Rebecca arrived at the Louisiana funeral home, she asked the funeral director if she could join him in the preparation room to apply her mother's makeup, comb her hair, and dress her. The request was unusual, but the funeral director warmly invited her in. Together they prepared her mother and placed her in the casket. Rebecca couldn't help but wonder why we call on professionals, essentially strangers, to perform such an intimate last act, which we could give to our loved one at a time when we feel most helpless.

Shortly after her return, Rebecca received a call in the early hours of Sunday morning before Labor Day 2004. Her friend, Tommy Odom, had been in a serious car accident. She pulled off the side of a hairpin curve in the road just a mile from their home in Occidental, California. Red, blue, and white flashing lights illuminated the darkness. The passenger in Tommy's car, Laura, couldn't answer Rebecca's question. "Where's Tommy?" A member of the ambulance crew shook his head.

"Nooo," she screamed.

Tommy knew those roads like the back of his hand, but she knew he'd had one too many at the bar downtown, where she had seen him just a few hours earlier. She tried to go down the ravine to find Tommy, but two chaplains clutched her arms.

"I just need to get to Tommy," she yelled. "Please let me touch him. Just one more time, please let me touch his body."

When the stretcher rose from the ravine, she broke loose of the chaplains holding her back and raced toward Tommy, but two police officers surrounded her just before she reached him.

"Please," she begged. "Let me just—"

She was pulled away and returned to the chaplains' arms. The pastor from her church intervened on her behalf to speak to the police about allowing Rebecca to touch her beloved best friend before they took him to the morgue. Once the white sheet was draped over his body, they allowed Rebecca to kneel down to the stretcher resting on the asphalt. She pawed his chest and legs, taking in the familiar warmth one last time from his lifeless body.

"I'm here, Tommy," she cried. "You're not alone."

She reached for his bare feet sticking out from the sheet. She wanted to touch his skin. But the police officer blocked her hands with his knee. The police officer gave the cue to the chaplains to take her away. She watched in terrified shock as they loaded him into an ambulance headed for the Santa Rosa morgue.

It was two o'clock in the morning. She learned that Tommy had taken the curve too fast. His truck had skidded to the edge of the ravine, teetered on the ledge, and then tumbled down. Rebecca watched as a crane pulled his red Ford truck up the cliff and dropped it on the road. As she quietly prayed for Tommy, she saw letters scrawled in the dust of his windshield illuminated by the police car's headlights. The message read "JESUS."

At dawn, she finally returned alone to her farmhouse. It was still too early to call anyone. She sat on the couch reflecting on Tommy. They'd met nearly a decade earlier at the Renaissance Faire. Tommy's knightly nature and old English accent charmed women, children, and even men. He most certainly captivated Rebecca. He was a former marine from Texas with long blond hair and a muscular, martial-arts body. More recently, Tommy had become the iconic court jester at the fair. His free spirit couldn't be captured, but they stayed intimately connected as close friends. Over the years, he lived with her on and off in a small trailer on her farm acreage. They shared twin fair booths next to one another. At her booth, she sold her clay and bronze sculptures, such as facemasks and full body casts adorned in forest backgrounds. He had a booth for children to paint on clay ornaments. He was still a big kid, even at forty-one years old.

She began to call their friends and his family. A friend suggested she call Jerrigrace, the local death midwife. Rebecca then remembered attending a few home funerals that ended in cremations. She knew Tommy didn't want to be cremated. She called Jerrigrace and received instruction on how to get Tommy's body discharged from the morgue. Jerrigrace reassured Rebecca that Tommy could be buried after a home funeral. Rebecca then called his brother and sister in Texas. They suggested a cremation because Tommy had died without a penny in his pocket. Rebecca assured them that she would find a way to bury Tommy.

She called Tyler Cassity at Forever Fernwood and spent some time amid the forest picking out a plot. The total cost was about $4,500, which included a pine box that a friend made for $400 and the home funeral. All together she spent a little more than a cremation, but far less than a formal burial with embalming, the burial plot, the vault to hold the casket in place beneath the ground, and the funeral home rental for the wake and funeral.

A CEREMONIAL WASHING OF THE BODY

A couple days later, Jerrigrace suggested Rebecca think about how she wanted to direct Tommy's funeral and burial. Rebecca envisioned giving him the burial of the "King of Kings"—Jesus. Both she and Tommy were born-again Christians. Rebecca looked through the Holy Scriptures to find ritual practices for preparing Tommy's body. In Mark 14:3–9 she read about a woman anointing Jesus with the precious oil spikenard to prepare him for burial. In the books of John and Matthew, she found similar references as well as the story of how Mary Magdalene cared for Jesus.

On Wednesday, the third day without Tommy, Rebecca prepared her barn art studio for his homecoming. Hundreds of lifelike faces stared at her while she moved her art tables to the edges of the studio. She stopped for a moment to catch her breath. Through her tears, she scanned all of the life and death masks she had sculpted of friends, family, and children. One was missing.

The following afternoon, Jerrigrace accompanied Rebecca to pick up Tommy from the morgue. When they returned to her farmhouse, Rebecca chose to put up a massage table under the majestic canopy of oak trees near the barn. Tommy had loved to sit in the shade of the oak trees, she thought to herself. Rebecca called on a friend of Tommy's to help transfer Tommy from the van to the table using a simple backboard. Jerrigrace followed behind with her death midwife kit.

Jerrigrace's techniques had evolved from studying how other cultures prepare their dead and a personal experience of caring for her friend, Carolyn Whiting, who died suddenly in 1994. Carolyn was a nurse and had thoughtfully left a list of last wishes with her will. She requested that her friends take care of her body and avoid turning her over to a coroner for autopsy or mortician to be embalmed. Carolyn detailed that she wanted a three-day wake in her home and to be cremated. Fulfilling these wishes was certainly not as easy as writing them down. Jerrigrace and her friends reawakened the ancient work of midwives to care for their friend. They relied on a mortuary to draw up the paperwork to bring her body home. They prepared, dressed, and honored her body for a ceremonial wake and then transported her to the crematorium. This transforming experience inspired Jerrigrace to educate and empower families and/or individuals like Rebecca to do the same for their loved ones.

Rebecca went inside the yellow farmhouse to prepare a rosemary infusion. When she returned to the oak trees, Tommy lay on the table wrapped in plastic.

"Oh, Tommy," she said. Tears slid out of her eyes.

Rebecca tied her strawberry-blond locks into a ponytail, wrapped an apron around herself, and stretched on latex gloves. Jerrigrace supported Rebecca as she carefully peeled back the plastic from Tommy's body. His body had not only suffered trauma from the car accident, but also an invasive autopsy performed by the coroner. The large Y-shaped incision that sliced open his chest was merely sutured back together. Rebecca thought about how Mary Magdalene prepared Jesus' beaten body for interment after the crucifixion. Rebecca hosed down Tommy's body, then rinsed him in a fresh rosemary-water infusion underneath the shade of the oak trees, out in nature with the warm summer sun shining down on them. She gently dried Tommy with towels. His body was still cold from the morgue.

"Is it bad to touch him with my hands?" Rebecca asked Jerrigrace.

"No, it was just better you wore them before we cleaned him up," Jerrigrace said in a gentle, motherly tone. She had often heard these questions when guiding families through this ritual. Although Rebecca rinsed his body of residue from the autopsy, the intimate task of sponge bathing him still lay ahead. She removed the latex gloves.

Rebecca had been in shock since returning with Tommy, but touching his body, holding his hand, and caressing his face in the familiar comforts of home made it real. She mixed clay and made an impression of his face.

"His face is very serene," Jerrigrace said. "He's looking like he went home."

"I wish this could have been a life mask," Rebecca said.

Rebecca pointed out slashes and bruises on his body, then tried to reconstruct how the wounds were inflicted during the fatal car accident.

"This is not as hard as I thought it would be," Rebecca said.

"It's usually more comforting to have the person here and reconnect to them," Jerrigrace said. "It helps the grieving process."

After twenty minutes, Rebecca pulled the mask off his face. She gently washed and caressed his face. "You know, he doesn't have a smell at all," Rebecca said. "I thought there would be a really heavy stench."

Rebecca washed and combed his hair. She sponged down his body with warm soapy water from a large ceramic bowl. The funeral director usually performs this restorative care. Rebecca kept Tommy's body respectfully covered with towels as she bathed him in front of the old-fashioned farmhouse on her lush acreage. It was a scene from early America, when women cared for the dead at home and buried them on the farmland.

Ever since Jerrigrace had become a death midwife, it saddened her that people don't spend this intimate time with their departed loved ones. It's often difficult to share an intimate moment with a loved one in a funeral home when time is limited because of other scheduled funerals. The unnatural setting can make you feel like you must grieve on cue in the short period allotted, and it can feel uncomfortable reaching into the casket to hold the hand of the loved one. But as Jerrigrace often tells the families she helps, there is no right way, just your way. She witnessed many families, allowed to care for their own in the familiar, intimate comforts of home, engage the realities of their physical loss and release the often primal set of emotions of grief.

Jerrigrace stood back as Rebecca anointed Tommy's head, arms, and feet with spikenard. She also used frankincense on his back. Rebecca set up the simple pine box on a table in the barn studio. She lined the pine box with plastic and then placed three slices of dry ice wrapped in brown grocery bags on the bottom. She and Tommy's friend laid him inside the pine casket atop the dry ice carefully positioned beneath his body to preserve him and freeze all the organs and internal fluids during his three-day wake. The dry ice method was a natural alternative to embalming the body. A chuck made out of cotton pads was used to protect his incisions. Rebecca shrouded him in a white muslin cloth. She pulled out a makeup bag and gently painted his bruised, purple face with liquid foundation.

"Tommy T," she said. "You're such a knucklehead. What did you do this for?"

She paused and stared at her dear friend.

"Why did you have to leave me?" Rebecca asked aloud.

A HOME FUNERAL

After she finished preparing Tommy, Rebecca decorated the trees in the yard with multicolored ribbon and streamers, which transformed the entrance of her barn studio into a luminescent, festival-like atmosphere.

She invited friends and family to stay for the weekend and camp. That evening they began to arrive with their tents and instruments in tow. A drum circle formed with guitarists jamming outside the barn. They flowed in and out of the barn studio to view Tommy's body.

Rebecca set out the clay ornaments from Tommy's painting booth. Friends sat around art tables, painting the ornaments. One by one they approached the casket, said their farewells and placed the ornament inside. Jerrigrace assisted Rebecca in laying out palettes of paint and stencils for people to decorate Tommy's plain pine casket. Some wrote poems of farewell, and others painted scenes of memories they had shared with Tommy. On the front panel, Rebecca painted a cross with the words of Jesus that Tommy always used to say: "I am the way, the truth, and the light." She also made an altar for Tommy. At the head of his casket, she flew the American flag, representing his service in the U.S. Marine Corps. She lit candles and hung a collage of photos arranged in a timeline of his life from youth to the most recent photos of him dressed in gold, green, and red as a jester at the Renaissance Faire.

The three-day wake culminated with his home funeral on Saturday. Tommy rested in the barn to the tunes of country and rock music. Harley Davidson motorcycle riders, born-again Christians, long-haired hippies, and children hovered over his casket. Around two o'clock in the afternoon, the pallbearers lifted the casket out of the barn studio and carried him out to lie under the shade of the leafy oaks. About fifty friends and relatives sat in white plastic patio chairs among the lush vegetation and white wedding canopies. Everyone was dressed in light summer clothing. Beside his casket, Rebecca sat on a barstool. In her long flowing pine green dress, she blended in with the foliage. She presided over the ceremony and began with a eulogy.

"We are gathered here today to honor . . . a special friend. And each one of us has not one story of Tommy, but, I am sure, many."

Chuckles resounded in the audience. His brother, Mitch Odom, stood up and thanked Rebecca for preparing his brother's body. He shed tears when speaking about her absolute love for him.

"Tommy was the pied piper of children, and I know many will carry the fond memories of him always, just as I will," Mitch said. "He was always quick to laugh and slow to judge."

THE GREEN BURIAL

At the conclusion, Rebecca rounded up the mourners into a funeral procession. She then hopped in the back of the minivan and clutched onto the casket for the hour-long trip to Forever Fernwood. The caravan traveled south toward Marin County. The procession snaked up the hill of the newly opened Forever Fernwood, and Tyler Cassity met them at the burial gravesite. Tyler donated a young oak tree to Tommy to commemorate the occasion. He approached the green minivan leading the caravan. He greeted Rebecca to make sure she had everything in order. She followed Tyler to the edge of the hill. Below was a freshly dug grave. Rebecca introduced Tyler and Jerrigrace.

"Oh, hi, Tyler," Jerrigrace said as she held down her violet sundress billowing in the wind.

"Jerri?" Tyler asked with a quizzical look on his face, realizing this was the death midwife, Jerrigrace Lyons.

"Yes I'm Jerri," she said.

"It's great to finally meet you," Tyler said with a smile. Together they were on the forefront of the natural death care movement in California. Together they were driving change in the funeral industry. Tyler stood underneath the hood of the minivan and looked at the pine casket painted with modern hieroglyphics. The pallbearers gathered around him. He gave them directions as to how they should carry the casket to the gravesite. With his spiky blond hair and slick designer clothes, he stood out in the crowd of casually dressed mourners. He led the pallbearers as they zigzagged down the golden hillside on a pathway designed in natural woodchips. Native amber and lilac grasses swayed at the trunks of oak trees and shrubs. The camouflaged burial grounds were tucked into Mill Valley that stretched to the horizon. To the left was the peak of Mount Tamalpais and to the right was the Golden Gate Bridge. At the foot of the hillside was an elementary school.

As they approached the mound, Tyler hopped up on the wood panels above the grave and guided the men to slide the pine box carefully on. Four-foot mounds of golden dirt and half a dozen shovels surrounded the grave. There was no Astroturf. There was no mechanical device to lower the casket into a concrete-lined grave at the touch of a button.

Rebecca stepped up on the wood planks in front of the piles of broken earth. She held a bible in one hand as her chiffon skirt and long red locks flapped in the wind. The pallbearers sat on the gravel in front of the casket. Most of the friends and family moved out of the chairs and sat on the ground so they could be closer to Tommy.

"Tommy is going to be able to listen to children all day," Rebecca said. "Thank you, Tyler, for providing the oak tree."

Tyler nodded and smiled at Rebecca. This was a big day for both of them. It was Rebecca's first time presiding over a funeral and burial service. After months of preparing and restoring the land, people were gracing the grounds of Forever Fernwood.

"This is the first natural burial, and Tommy is number one," she said as she pushed up her index finger. Everyone clapped. She recited the Twenty-third Psalm, and the mourners joined in unison. She then cast her eyes down at the casket mounted on the wood panels above the grave.

"So, Tommy, we're going to come hang with you and picnic with you and laugh with you," she said, turning her eyes to Tyler. "And they're going to plant an oak tree right here to shade the area, and you'll have a great view."

The pallbearers stepped up on the wood mount. Four men clutched a rope belted around the casket. On cue, Tyler pulled the planks of wood holding up the casket. The full weight of the casket dropped onto the ropes. The men holding the ropes slowly lowered him into the grave. The women began singing "Amazing Grace." The wind carried wails across the valley. Once the casket hit the floor of the grave, friends and family kneeled down and dropped flowers in. As the women were singing the second verse, flowers were floating down to the lid of the pine box. Six pallbearers picked up shovels and began filling the hole in the earth. Dull sounds of gravel hitting the pine casket echoed above the grave. The men and women handed off the shovel to each other, coupled with long embraces. They shouted out, "This is for you, Tommy." It was as if they were channeling their anger and grief into each dig on the mound and dumping it into the grave. The dull echoes of gravel spattering on the pine box was interrupted by the bellowing of bagpipes playing an ancient funeral song atop the hillside.

The mourners stopped, placing their shovels at their sides, and turned to acknowledge the Scottish bagpipe player dressed in full green and navy tartan regalia. Amid the trees, the piper looked like an apparition with his long, curly, gray hair and matching beard. It was as if he was resurrected from another century, much like the green burial.

ROOTS OF THE GREEN BURIAL

Describing the traditional funeral practiced by the Puritans in early America that mirror the home funeral and green burial, Laderman reports that "preparing the corpse was understood as a component of domestic life, and therefore within the purview of women's activities."[11] They ritually washed, shaved, and dressed or shrouded the body in muslin, wool, or cashmere.[12]

"The intimacy that survivors maintained with the corpse preserved it, at least until the actual interment, as evidence of a valuable and vital social relation. Although the body had lost the spark that animated it, deeply rooted social conventions demanded that it be given proper respect and care from the living."[13]

The wake was essentially the "constant surveillance," vigil, or "watching" over the body of the deceased for one to three days in the home before burial to prevent "live burial."[14] The family placed a block of ice in a tub beneath the coffin and smaller slices of ice around the body for preservation. Visitors to the recently deceased "engaged in a variety of activities, including somber reflection, scripture reading, and socializing, which usually involved some eating and alcoholic drinking."[15] The wake was followed by a procession behind the pallbearers carrying the coffin to the burial site. Laderman writes, "The last act of throwing into the grave a branch, straw, or commonly dirt from the earth before leaving the place of interment was a frequent gesture recognizing the finality of the journey."[16] Family members tended to stay and fill the grave with dirt or watch on as other community members completed the task.[17]

In fast-forwarding through the eighteenth and nineteenth centuries to today, I'd like to point out that some cultures in America and around the world have preserved and continued death rituals that circumvent the modern-day embalm-and-bury regime. The Jewish way of death has held onto traditions practiced for centuries in Israel and continued here in America. Many non-Jews find the simplicity of the Jewish funeral and burial refreshing and meaningful. The green burial is an adaptation of a Jewish burial. A governing tenet in Jewish burial is "blood which flows at the time of death may not be washed away."[18] Essentially, this forbids embalming. Embalming and beautifying for the living contradicts the purpose of Jewish burial.

Taharah, known as the body-washing and purification ritual for burial, is similar to that adopted in the home funeral, but is practiced by the *hevra kadisha,* the Jewish burial society, a sacred society of anonymous volunteers. Orthodox men perform the *taharah* for the deceased Jewish men and Orthodox women for the women. Family, or those intimate with the deceased, are advised against engaging in this duty. Jews believe the highest act of kindness, or good deed known as a *mitzvah,* is the *taharah* because the deceased cannot repay the deed. Rochel Berman, author of *Dignity Beyond Death: The Jewish Preparation for Burial* and a member of a *hevra kadisha* in Westchester, New York, said, "The overriding principle of Jewish burial custom is *kavod haeit,* respect for the body of the deceased. From the moment of death until burial, the deceased is provided with a *shomer,* a round-the-clock honor guard who prays for the soul by reciting Psalms."[19]

Judaism teaches that the soul hovers near the body and that the totality of the person who died continues to exist.[20] It's believed the soul retains consciousness, so volunteers from the *hevra kadisha* attempt to comfort the soul through lyrical prayers and reciting passages from the Torah.[21] They address the soul directly by name. After the meticulous and careful washing of the body, which starts with the face and then moves to the right side of the body and then the left, twenty-four quarts of continuous cascading water are poured over the body for purification. Prayers and songs sounding like lullabies accompany the purification. The body is dressed in white linen shrouds, placed in a simple unfurnished wood casket lined with earth from Israel, and returned to the earth.

Modern green burial cemeteries have roots in the island nation of Britain where space constraints created a need for alternative burial methods. But it was 1998 when Dr. Billy Campbell opened America's first natural memorial grounds, called Ramsey Creek Preserve, on thirty-three acres in South Carolina. Inklings of green burial started for Dr. Campbell as a student at Westminster High School when something his teacher said resonated with him. "I want to be buried in a potato sack under a tree when I die, so I can become a part of the tree" underlined Dr. Campbell's belief in the life cycle ending with the natural decomposition of the corpse. After high school, he pursued medicine and became the only doctor serving his hometown of Westminster, population nearly 3,000. In the late 1980s, after reading in the book *Kuru Sorcery* about how people in New Guinea preserved sacred groves for the dead, he envisioned spirit forests where the dead protect and conserve the land for the living. He wrote an article for a local environmental magazine that postulated the concept of sacred groves. When his father, George Campbell, died at aged fifty-four of complications from lung surgery in 1985, he had an alienating experience in dealing with a funeral home. In his state of shock and grief, Dr. Campbell felt pressured into purchasing a small plot of cemetery land, signing a deed and turning over $5,000 to memorialize his father. When he requested a simple wooden box, only an ornate oak casket was in stock.

Disconcerted by the waste of money and land, Dr. Campbell calculated that he could have purchased five acres of woodland with the $5,000, and he thought five acres would be a better memorial for his father than an underground concrete vault and oak casket. He began buying land surrounding the river that he and his father fished in for Ramsey Creek Preserve. Dr. Campbell dug the graves himself and studied how the body could best nourish the eco-system. The concept of spreading memorial-ecosystems across the planet remained in incubation.

Five years and twenty interments later, Dr. Campbell received a call from Tyler Cassity, a renowned visionary in the funeral industry, and Tyler's right-hand man, Joe Sehee. The Cassity family owned multiple funeral homes and cemetery properties in the Midwest and one in Hollywood. Dr. Campbell knew of Tyler because of his fame for purchasing the dilapidated, bankrupt Hollywood Memorial Cemetery for $375,000 and restoring the grounds to their former glitterati glory. Tyler had invested a couple of million dollars into restoring the cracking mausoleum and sinking graves and then renamed the grounds Hollywood Forever. Many have named Hollywood Forever, Cemetery of the Immortals, because it's known as the resting place of silver screen legends.

At Hollywood Forever, Tyler incubated his idea of turning the cemetery, which he called "card catalogs for the dead," into a "library of lives." He opened Forever Studios on the grounds that housed biographers, historians, and filmmakers to produce A&E-style biographies for those interred. He wired the entire 140-acre cemetery with video kiosks so visitors could watch the biographies and learn more about those interred.

With his classic James Dean looks, Tyler became the Hollywood Forever poster boy. In 2000, he starred in the documentary *The Young in the Dead*, about the Hollywood Forever Cemetery. And it's not hard to recognize Tyler and his brother, Brent Cassity, in the characters Nathaniel and David Fisher, second-generation sons in a funeral business family in the HBO series *Six Feet Under*, a series that brought death, grief, and its rituals into the living rooms and conversations of many Americans for the first five years of the twenty-first century. Alan Ball, the Academy Award–winning writer and director of the series, had worked in Hollywood in the late 1990s into 2000 and had no doubt heard of the Cassity brothers. Though Tyler served as a consultant on the show and Tyler's family story in many ways resembles the fictional Fisher family, the series is not a biographical sketch. And it was Tyler who inspired the writers of the final season to feature the eco-friendly burial after he opened the first green cemetery in California.

In 2004, Tyler, Joe Sehee, and Dr. Campbell set out on a mission to merge the totally natural with the totally virtual cemetery to design multiuse land for the living and the dead. Tyler found an ancient graveyard, Daphne Fernwood Cemetery in Mill Valley, cradled in the majestic Golden Gate National Recreational Area. The cemetery had nearly a hundred broken and weathered headstones from the late nineteenth century scattered on the hillsides of the forest. Tyler bought the land for a mere $495,000. In the midst of preparing the land to design a memorial eco-system similar to Ramsey Creek in South Carolina, Tyler and Dr. Campbell went their separate ways. Dr. Campbell, a purist environmentalist, was headstrong about land conservation and his goal to preserve a million acres of land through the spread of memorial eco-systems. Tyler, an entrepreneur, respected the importance of land conservation, but also needed to turn a profit. They butted heads on how to achieve these goals. But even though they parted ways, their vision led the way for many funeral director–types like Tyler and environmentalists like Dr. Campbell to find common ground and meet the needs of environmentally conscious Americans.

Today more and more green burial grounds are sprouting up across America—New York, Florida, Georgia, New Mexico. Some are hybrid cemeteries similar to Fernwood, where some plots of land are for green burial and other plots are for the embalm-and-bury method. Joe Sehee also parted with Tyler and now runs the Green Burial Council, an organization that established standards for green burial grounds and educates consumers on eco-friendly funeral/cemetery options.

THE GREEN BURIAL GROUNDS

I visited Forever Fernwood with Rebecca after the one-year memorial celebration of Tommy's life at the Northern California Renaissance Faire in Hollister. During the fair, his clay facemask decorated by Rebecca hung at the entrance of his painting booth, which she continued to run. At the memorial party, Rebecca gave some dirt from Tommy's grave to all of his close friends as they toasted his life. She announced the soil held some of Tommy because his body had now blended with the earth.

On Monday afternoon following the weekend festivities, Rebecca ran her fingers through the dirt above Tommy on the hill overlooking the children's playground. She still missed Tommy dearly, but coming out to Fernwood to spend time with him comforted her. She told me she had no nightmares about the body washing and burial preparation ritual for Tommy's body; in fact, she felt that the process helped her to physically internalize the sudden shock of his death and part with his life in a natural way. While we sat on the hill listening to and watching the children play below, I noticed hikers and cyclists on the pathway above us. Tyler had achieved his goal of making Forever Fernwood a forest for the living and the dead.

We visited the Fernwood office and I got a better idea of how they identify the location of the unmarked graves with Global Positioning System markers. Each grave has a GPS number. Eventually, Tyler intends to have life bio videos play on the GPS handset, so when a visitor walks near a grave the GPS locates, instead of seeing a headstone with the name, date of birth, and date of death, a video will play the life story. The layout of the cemetery was different and not as dense as a traditional cemetery. As I looked at the layout, I saw that the burial plots were octagonal rather than rectangular and spaced out so that the body could truly fertilize the land. I wondered if green burial was just a trend or would eventually become a mainstream alternative form of interment, like cremation.

In 2004, when green burial hit the mainstream media, Laderman said to a *USA Today* reporter, "The soil is right for experimentation. There is an environmental movement that didn't exist decades ago, as well as an interest in customization and customer empowerment."[22]

THE SPREAD OF DEATH MIDWIFERY

The soil is equally ripe for death midwives seeding, growing, and serving in Southern California, Oregon, Utah, Washington, Texas, Colorado, Iowa, Hawaii, and Maryland. It is Maryland where Elizabeth Knox, a woman who lost her seven-year-old daughter and held a home funeral, teaches families about their legal right to have a home funeral for their deceased loved ones. There is a home funeral directory guide online to find these local resources.

Jerrigrace wrote a guidebook for death midwives and families entitled *Final Passages: A Complete Home Funeral Guide* that provides in-depth instructions on how to wash, prepare, dress, and preserve a body for a home funeral. She gives tips on how to keep the mouth closed by using a scarf to tie it shut shortly after death. Before the wake, the scarf can be removed. To shut the eyes, she suggests coins or small bags of rice or sand over the lids for a few hours after the death. Jerrigrace also includes narratives drawn from more than 300 home funerals and provides information on how cultures from around the world care for their dead. For example, in Iran, the body is washed three times, first with lotus water, then with camphor water, and finally with pure water.[23]

Jerrigrace developed the manual for her death midwifery workshops. Originally, there were two levels of midwifery workshops, but more recently, Jerrigrace has added a third level while also increasing the frequency of workshops to meet the high demand.

I followed the path of a local death midwife trained under Jerrigrace to report on the burgeoning death midwifery. Barbara Kernan, a registered school nurse for San Diego Unified School District, attended Jerrigrace's death midwifery weekend retreat in the spring of 2000. She'd been an elementary school nurse for nearly a decade when in late 1999, she charted a new course in health care to become an herbalist and acupuncturist. While taking a college course, she worked in a wellness workbook. She got to the question "Are you prepared for your own death," and a siren sounded off in her head. She rated herself a "zero." Her quest online to discover how to create your own memorial service led her to Jerrigrace's manual and then a weekend midwifery retreat.

The first retreat delves into the basics of death care, ancient customs, and multicultural perspectives of the funeral industry today. The second workshop introduces Jerrigrace's midwifery method, from body care to her midwifery kit. The following spring, Barbara started her own death midwifery business and called Crepak, a San Diego company, where Jerrigrace bought the cremation caskets. Owner Eric Putt intercepted this call. He asked what she intended to use the boxes for. Barbara explained Thresholds, a new family-directed, in-home funeral service in San Diego. Eric was intrigued. Aside from owning Crepak, he was a licensed funeral director and first-responder body removal service for funeral homes in San Diego County. He invited Barbara to apprentice. During her apprenticeship, Barbara noticed that about eight out of every ten families were often not ready to part with the body.

Simultaneously, Barbara drew up brochures and began to call hospices, but received an icy response. One hospice nurse said, "We just can't have families picking up the bodies from here and driving them all over San Diego." Barbara realized just how naïve she'd been. Jerrigrace's crusade is for having an alternative to the funeral home and so never obtained her funeral director license in Sonoma County, where the clock still ticks to the same rhythm of the 1960s. Jerrigrace carries the standard philosophy of birth midwives, which is "you're able to do this yourself; the midwife empowers and assists the family" to perform all the tasks of a home funeral, and a licensed professional—in this case a funeral director—is the establishment not needed because this is a "normal, natural family-centered event."[24]

In conservative San Diego, Barbara needed more than a few courses of midwifery training. She obtained her funeral director and funeral home license. She called Thresholds the first licensed holistic funeral establishment in California.

Similar to birth midwives getting certified to practice in hospitals so that hospitals could offer the choice of a family-centered, natural birth, we're seeing the service of a natural, family-centered home funeral service provided by a funeral home.[25]

Thresholds is just one of many examples of how the fringe home funeral movement is mixing with the established funeral industry. At Thresholds, Barbara is death midwife and an established funeral director. Some of the advocates in the green funeral movement, including Joe Sehee, director of the Green Burial Council, see in the future death midwives actually licensed and working with established funeral homes.[26] The home funeral is a do-it-yourself, or better, a design-it-yourself experience that funeral homes could potentially provide to families.

Markella Rutherford, a sociologist studying the sacralization of the individual in American culture through a study of the natural birth movement, pointed out in an interview that the language hospitals use in advertising directed toward mothers-to-be exemplifies individualizing the birth experience, for example, "this is your special day," "this is a special event for your family," "we want to honor your wishes and make you a player on our team in designing this experience," and so on. She also points out this language in wedding planning—and now we see this language in funeral planning.

This do-it-yourself, holistic, or home funeral approach is not the pana-
cea for the pitfalls that families wrestle with in dealing with funeral directors and funeral homes. The home funeral as I have described requires
heavy lifting from the family and community, which I further explore in
Chapter 11. The home funeral requires an appropriate physical location
to accommodate guests, a strong support system, and access to resources/
contacts necessary to create this kind of experience. For example, a small
apartment may not be able to house this kind of funeral experience.
Also, the family essentially assumes the duties of a funeral director, and
some may not be comfortable in caring for the body or handling hospi-
tality duties when they've just endured a death.

The home funeral is not for everyone. In fact, third-generation funeral
directors that served families in the transition from home wakes to funeral home wakes in the 1930s tell me that families desired a more hands-
off approach.[27] Families were happy to turn over the body preparation
and wake to the professionals.

The home birthing/natural birth movement did not return births
back to the home in large numbers, but natural birth advocates did succeed in providing families with a menu of options for birthing.[28] Rutherford makes the argument that it is individuals' having this menu of options that is sacred and as such, supersedes any institution's once-inviolable
practices or traditions. On the other side of life, the traditional American
funeral is no less sacred, but rather just one of the funeral options available in the twenty-first century. This menu of options has liberated and
re-enchanted families in their quest to meaningfully engage death in
life and life in death.

ELEVEN

Holistic Approach: Design-It-Yourself
Funeral and Cremation Witnessing

In the still heat of July 2004, Barbara Kernan, a death midwife, and her
funeral director partner, Eric Putt, responded to a house call in an ex-
clusive neighborhood known as Floral Park in conservative Orange
County, California. Barbara eyed the street lined with double-headed
vintage gas lamps, wide front lawns, and driveways leading to two-
and three-car garages. She was a long way from tree-hugging Northern
California, yet she exuded the air of Mother Nature's daughter with
loose chestnut tresses, olive eyes, and a saunter that swept the floor with
her long flowing skirt.

They climbed the stairs of the bricked front porch illuminated by a
summer blossoming rose garden. Carol Ann Wikstrom, a radiant woman
with emerald eyes and curly mocha locks, opened her door to welcome
them into her home. Carol Ann's husband, Ron Wikstrom, and Jill Cross,

her best friend, were gathered in the living room to discuss after-death care plans.

In spring 2004, shortly after her forty-eighth birthday, Carol Ann received the news that her cancer had awakened from an eight-year remission. She joined St. Joseph Hospice and shared with both Ron and Jill her wish to die at home, but afterward was not so clear. Carol Ann remembered talking to Jill several months prior about Thresholds. Jill was a former nurse and now office manager at LivHome, an at-home care service for seniors. Thresholds had given a presentation at her office.

Over iced tea, Barbara explained to Carol Ann how she could have the funeral in her home without any intervention from a conventional funeral home.

"Wow, we could do all that?" Carol Ann asked, surprised but also skeptical.

Although interested, Carol Ann worried about the home funeral becoming too labor intensive for Jill and Ron. She suggested a direct cremation would be best without a ceremony and fuss. She didn't want to be a burden.

Jill's eyes met Carol Ann's. Their friendship matured through junior high, high school, living together as roommates in college, their first marriages, the births of their sons, and their divorces and now they'd embarked on a journey to Carol Ann's final rite of passage.

"Carol, I'll take care of you," Jill said.

Carol Ann looked at Ron. He shrugged his shoulders.

"Whatever you want," he said with a half smile.

"Are you sure you can do this?" Carol Ann asked Barbara again.

Carol Ann knew her fair share about death care, but she'd never heard of a family orchestrating a funeral at home. She had worked as a pre-need and at-need funeral-planning counselor at a few funeral homes throughout the 1990s. In an odd way, she felt liberated by these progressive death choices. Barbara went on to discuss how she cordoned off a sacred space in the house for the bathing ritual and wake.

"I think this home is already sacred," Barbara said, as she looked around the ornate living room and then up at the chandelier dropping from a dome in the ceiling, which was painted al fresco style with cherub angels in a heavenly setting.

She was right. Carol Ann had spun her spirit into every detail of the home, and Ron had drawn on his talents as a residential designer, and together, they'd re-envisioned their 1929 vintage home from the bottom up. Carol Ann and Ron had been together for fifteen years and were inseparable. Their house was a reflection of their intense love for travel, art, and each other.

DESIGNING HER OWN WAKE AND MEMORIAL SERVICE

Carol Ann guided Barbara on a tour of the house and brainstormed out loud about possibly lying in the guest bedroom for the wake beneath the four-poster bed. She imagined the memorial service held outside in the Japanese gardens beneath the shade of the bamboo, beside the koi pond and waterfalls. Carol Ann had also, just the year before, envisioned marrying Ron in the same spot that she pointed out to Barbara, but the cancer had spoiled their plans. As she stared at the spot where she'd intended they exchanged their vows, it dawned on her what she would wear for the wake.

While vacationing in Canada the previous summer, Carol Ann fell in love with a hand-beaded ceremonial sari that she found in Little India. She intended to wear the sari for the wedding. It hung in her closet with no occasion fit for its magnificence. She buzzed with excitement about wearing the dress for her final rite of passage. Preparing for her wake gave her a sense of purpose in approaching the final days of her life. Like a bride preparing her wedding, she made a guest list, designed the announcements, and selected a local printer.

Similar to a bride choosing and asking her bridesmaids, Carol Ann called upon her closest girlfriends for their commitment in supporting her through the transitional period and rite of passage. Carol Ann had known these four great women since childhood. She invited them to her home for dinner. She bestowed a special mission on each one. As already agreed, Jill, like the maid of honor, committed to bathing, dressing, and preparing Carol Ann for the ceremonial wake. Sue Compton, a close friend since elementary school, would take care of the toast at the wake and orate a tribute at the service. Karen McIntyre, a friend since kindergarten, would create a slideshow of Carol's life. Barbara Smith, her closest confidante for the last ten years, was elected to fine-tune the wake and memorial to reflect Carol's personality and tastes. Carol Ann wanted to ask Barbara to fulfill a more intimate wish, but couldn't.

Instead she said to Barbara, "You'd better raid my wine cellar and find a really fine bottle of wine. Don't allow them to use paper plates and cups in my home. I don't want it to be some hootenanny with ribs, casseroles, and boxed wine. I want it to be classy, catered, with excellent wine, nice food and hors d'oeuvres. You know I want everyone to have fun, drink too much, and laugh a lot."

With the memorial plans firmed up, she invited her friends for one last wine-tasting tour in a limousine around the Temecula wine region. Although Carol Ann's appetite and strength diminished in the last days, she never lost her sense of humor.

"The next time you'll see me will probably be at my memorial," she said, chuckling, as her friends departed that evening.

CHOOSING HER OWN URN AND CASKET

In late October, Barbara Kernan returned to Carol Ann's home to discuss the final arrangements. Carol Ann had set up the guest bedroom like a new mother tenderly preparing a nursery, with a new scallop-patterned champagne comforter punctuated by shimmer-gold pillows. She had dressed the four-poster canopy bed with sheer white netting similar to mosquito nets. She'd found it all on eBay, including the white marble urn.

Carol Ann planned to rest in the guest bedroom when death neared so she wouldn't have to be moved for the wake. Just as that moment became a spoken reality, both she and Ron were overcome with emotion. Their pain was intensely palpable. Barbara had to pause before raising an even more difficult subject—the casket. They discussed a cremation casket, which was cardboard and cost $20, or a plain pine casket. Carol Ann chose the pine over cardboard. Barbara ordered a biodegradable pine box from ABC Caskets for $550 and had it delivered to their home. Carol Ann asked Barbara to officiate the memorial service. They'd forged a relationship over the past four months and shared similar beliefs in Buddhism. Barbara asked about some of the poems that she might like read.

"Oh, I can do that?" she asked, again surprised, but also utterly delighted.

With Jill's help, Barbara created what she called a "soul-sketch" of Carol Ann. They showed it to Carol Ann for her suggestions and edits. Carol Ann selected the poem "Today."

When the casket arrived, Ron had the delivery men take it to the garage. This was one delivery he didn't want his wife to sign for. The time had come for Carol Ann to bestow a special mission on her husband. She asked him to decorate the casket.

"Just do what you think is right, Ron," she said, trusting his judgment. Ron wasn't just a designer, he was also an artist. Ron adorned the casket in birds, butterflies, and a birdhouse—all symbols of freedom.

In mid-autumn, Carol Ann brought out the sari to show her close friend, Barbara Smith. They shared similar tastes in makeup, clothes, and hairstyles. Carol Ann asked her opinion on the kind of makeup she should choose to complement it. At that moment, Barbara intuitively realized what Carol Ann wished for.

"Carol, do you want me to do your makeup?" Barbara asked.

"Would you really?" Carol Ann said.

So they made a special trip, one last shopping escapade. Carol Ann sat in her wheelchair and Barbara pushed her through Nordstrom and stopped at the makeup counter.

"My eyes have to look good because they're going to be closed," Carol Ann said. They chose a shimmering gold shadow and crimson red lipstick and nail polish to match. When they returned home, they discussed the makeover. Carol Ann gave Barbara a few tips warning that her teeth should be covered, but her mouth open a bit as if she were smiling. They set a place for Barbara to find the sari and the makeup bag when the time came.

Carol Ann had wrapped up the final details for the wake and memorial. Her thoughts turned toward Ron. The time had come to marry the man she loved. On a bright November afternoon, she and Ron married at the historic 1920s courthouse in Santa Ana and celebrated with her son at a chic restaurant in the Bowers Museum. Ron smiled as he watched his beautiful bride toast the two men she loved and shared her life with.

Soon after, the winter chill fell outside and with it came Carol Ann's darkening days. Jill stayed at the Wikstrom home in the dimming months of December. Carol Ann suffered from unmanaged pain day and night. She managed to control every step of the plan, except the final transition. She just couldn't let go.

The pain increased and Carol Ann had to go into the hospital. Carol Ann's family, including Jill, held around-the-clock vigil at her bedside. Jill had the nightshift to early morning. As the morning sun shone into the window, the nurse noticed Carol Ann was awake and alert. "Who's this?" the nurse asked, gesturing at Jill sleeping on the lounge chair beside her bed.

"This," Carol Ann smiled at Jill, "is my sister."

Jill glowed. That morning, the pain escalated. And the physicians placed Carol Ann on controlled sedation. For three days she slipped in and out of a deep coma-like sleep. On Friday morning, Ron and Carol Ann's son, Joel, came to relieve Jill. Within a few moments after Ron's arrival, Carol Ann took her last breath.

She'd waited for Ron and her son.

After her last breath the hospital asked the family to leave. Barbara called the hospital to ask if Carol Ann could remain in the room for a couple of hours with her family. The nurse agreed to one hour. After the hour, against the family's wishes, they rolled Carol Ann down to the morgue. Barbara arrived a half an hour later to rescue Carol Ann from the hospital morgue, the most undignified chamber of the hospital. Tears of frustration welled in her eyes. She looked upon Carol Ann's face. "Such grace and beauty shouldn't be stored like debris," Barbara thought. She shrouded Carol Ann in a sheet and prepared her to go home, where she belonged with her family and friends.

HER LAST WISH: A HOME WAKE

Eric and Barbara carried Carol Ann into her living room. The journey was tough and conditions harsher than everyone involved expected. The plan from the beginning was for Carol Ann to die at home. An overwhelming sense of a relief came over Jill upon Carol Ann's homecoming. "She's ours again," Jill thought. Now they could carry out Carol Ann's last wishes on their own terms.

As Carol Ann had planned, Jill guided them into the guest bedroom. She helped Barbara lift the sheet from Carol Ann's face. She died with a sweet smile on her face and her eyes set dreamily at half-mast. Barbara set out her midwifery bags on the dresser near the bed canopied by sheer, gleaming white mosquito nets. Barbara filled a couple of basins with warm soapy water and set them on the marble surface of the dresser. She infused the water with lavender oils. Jill waited for Barbara's lead and watched over Carol Ann resting on a gurney beside the bed.

"Some candlelight might be nice," she said to Jill. As Jill lit the candles that Carol Ann had already set out in the room, her son, Joel, a twenty-three-year-old with a military-man physique, entered with a CD player and some James Taylor. He set up the music and hit the Play button.

"Don't forget to paint my mom's nails," he said on his way out. "She wanted me to remind you."

James Taylor's soothing, melodic voice and comforting acoustic guitar blanketed the room. Barbara Smith arrived shortly after, but she struggled seeing her lifeless best friend. She left the bedroom to catch her breath and find the makeup bag and sari Carol Ann had left in her bedroom. When she returned, Barbara, the midwife, noticed Barbara Smith's apprehension.

"Look at how beautiful Carol Ann is," the midwife said.

Barbara Smith and Jill cast tearful gazes onto her face.

"She looks like she's smiling," Barbara Smith said.

"Why don't you wash her hair," Barbara, the midwife, suggested.

She led the women gently through the sacred ritual of washing and restoring her body. She reminded Jill that the process was just like giving her a sponge bath in bed. Jill began washing Carol Ann's face and then moved down to her arms and hands. Lavender aromas filled the room as the women sang along with James. Every touch brought Jill closer to internalizing Carol Ann's death. Barbara Kernan spread plastic on the bed and pulled dry ice from an ice chest. She covered the vapors of ice with paper and placed it on the plastic. She shrouded Carol Ann in a clean sheet and then Eric came in to help the women move her to rest on the dry ice.

They dressed her in the crimson and gold beaded sari. Barbara Smith brushed Carol Ann's lips with red lipstick, blushed her cheeks rouge and shadowed her eyes in gold. Then she painted her fingernails red. The women reminisced, cried, and even joked.

At the end of the ritual, they draped the scarf of the sari around her head like a veil and pulled down the sheer mosquito nets and left the room. She looked like the Greek princess Andromeda.

Jill gave Ron the okay sign for him to go on in and see his wife. He cast his eyes down and tears streamed down his face. For the first time in months, Ron recognized his beautiful wife was no longer ravaged by pain.

"I have my beautiful Carol Ann back," he said with a huge sigh of relief.

Carol Ann's brother, her son, neighbors, relatives, and friends entered the guest room one by one and shut the door to say good-bye in private. Ron set out a feast and uncorked many bottles of wine. Sue Compton brought shot glasses and a bottle of tequila.

"All right, ladies, let's have a toast to Carol Ann," Sue said. They filed in the room, some double-fisted with wine and tequila. Each of Carol Ann's "bridesmaids" shared their gratitude for having such a true, irreplaceable friend.

"To Carol Ann," the women cheered in unison, clinked their glasses, and downed the tequila. Their eyes fell on Carol Ann. She looked like a China doll.

The following day, the house buzzed with visitors celebrating and commiserating in the Wikstrom home. For hours, they entered the guest room to reminisce, hold her hand, laugh with her, toast her, and mourn her passing. After everyone had left, Ron walked into the bedroom and sat with Carol Ann. He lifted up the sheer netting that draped his beautiful wife and placed his hand atop hers. In that sacred space, in his own home, he had some private time to really say good-bye. As he looked upon her dreamy eyes, her scarlet lips, and her glimmering gown, she took his breath away.

He quietly said, "I love you."

Barbara Kernan arrived in the morning to transport Carol Ann to the crematorium. Ron helped Barbara and Eric lift her into the casket, then he cut some roses, her favorite flower, from their garden and placed them around her. He collected a little pillow she always slept with and tucked it beneath her head. Just before they were about to close the casket, he stopped them and remembered to place her prayer beads in with her. He exercised much restraint when reluctantly placing the lid on the pine box. The gravity of being alone in that home without Carol Ann's laugh, love, sweet kisses, and warm cuddles at night walloped him.

WITNESSING THE CREMATION AND RITE OF COMMITTAL

Two days later, he and his parents met Barbara and Eric at a crematorium in San Diego. Ron lifted the lid off the casket and said his final farewell. Barbara gave a brief prayer of committal to the fire and then Ron closed the lid. The casket moved on a conveyor belt, and the door to the retort opened. She entered. With the push of a button, the cremation fire ignited. A few days later, Ron made the journey with Carol Ann's ashes at his side and brought her back where she belonged, to the home she had created.

A couple of weeks later, Jill returned to Carol Ann's home for the memorial service. She set up an altar for the urn next to a large statue of Buddha on the edge of the koi pond in the backyard. Ron displayed a collage of photos telling Carol Ann's life story. All sixty guests received a slender white candle as they entered the backyard. At the opening of the ceremony, Barbara Kernan lit a large white candle, which symbolized the light of Carol Ann's life. At the end of the service, Barbara guided Ron to light his candle from "Carol Ann's light and pass it on for everyone to carry on." The song "Morning Has Broken" by Cat Stevens reverberated as Ron lit Jill's candle and the flame of Carol Ann's life passed around.

A year later, Jill returned to the house for a Christmas and one-year memorial celebration of Carol Ann's life. All four women were there to go into the guest bedroom and toast Carol Ann. As Jill reflected on the one-year anniversary of Carol Ann's death, she said, "I couldn't have imagined it any other way. Through letting me be with her when she died and take care of her after, I'm not afraid of my own death. It was a life-changing experience. That's a pretty big gift."

KEEPING COMPANY WITH THE DEAD

At Christmastime 2006, I visited Barbara and Eric at the first holistic funeral home in Southern California. She lived in a peaceful ranch home ornately dressed in colorful Bohemian décor. Families never visited Barbara here because she, like all death midwives, made house calls. Our intimate interview ended with Barbara and Eric, like most of my sources, asking what drove my interest in death midwifery.

I paused.

Before launching into the story about how my parents' total opposite approaches to death evoked an insatiable curiosity to find new ways to celebrate the end of life in America, I stopped short and changed course. Knowing they spent time working for the funeral homes in body removal, I shared the one thing about my mother's death that I was ashamed of.

I told them about her amazing last week that ended horribly when two men from Forest Home came to remove her body and I relinquished my duty to care for my mother until the end. I knew now from witnessing home funerals that the last breath didn't necessarily mark the end.

Eric winced and tears welled in Barbara's eyes. Their reactions silently showed me they understood. Eric explained that I had obviously encountered two inexperienced young men. Out of respect, he always asked the family for their permission before shrouding the body and face. I reluctantly spat out that I had no idea what happened to my mother's body after she left my home that morning.

Eric asked if I would like him to call and find out at least the general procedures of cremation for Forest Lawn. I declined his offer. When I returned home, I followed his instructions to find the cremation papers to uncover for myself what had happened to her. I found the file marked Forest Lawn in my cabinet and in it I found a signed document approving a ten-day wait period for her cremation. It was dated February 14, 2002. A flashback formed. The funeral director came to the church just before the memorial service with an empty urn, this letter, and an excuse that the crematorium was booked up until February 20. I remembered the empty urn sitting on the altar at my mother's memorial service. As I read through the papers, I envied Ron Wikstrom, who went to the crematorium and saw Carol Ann enter the fire. Eric and Barbara said that witnessing at crematoriums was becoming more prevalent.

I recalled that Stephen Prothero wrote in his book *Purified by Fire* that the first cremation of Baron De Palm in America had many witnesses like a burial. Family and friends could view the cremation through a peephole in the side of the furnace in 1876. For the first half-century of cremation in America, peepholes were standard and families witnessing the casket enter the cremation chamber was the norm.[1]

Prothero added that for decades the rites of committal for cremation were modeled on the gravesite service and the emotional moment when the casket entered the grave in the earth was just as poignant as when the casket entered the fiery furnace.[2] It wasn't until 1912 that the first peephole in front of the cremation furnace was covered at California Crematorium in Oakland.[3] The rite of committal instead happened at the columbarium after the body had already been transformed to ashes. Over time the family and friends were banished from the furnace rooms of the crematorium, and by the 1990s most cremations occurred without family members present.[4]

This began to change at the turn of the twenty-first century; as cremation increased, so too did the need for transparency and a revived witnessing committal ritual. Many crematoriums were set up to handle the Hindu cremation ritual that I witnessed at the burning ghats in Nepal, where the son must light the cremation fire. But for some the witnessing is more than just a ritual of ashes to ashes. The *New York Times* reported in October of 2000 that families had heard horror stories about crematoriums where the wrong corpse would be cremated or where people would be cremated alongside animals.[5] Witnessing gave the family watchdog or guardian rights to ensure their loved one was treated properly and no mistakes were made.

Rabbi Regina Sandler-Phillips, the founder of a seventy-member Chevra Kadisha and Sh'mirah sacred society at Park Slope Jewish Center in Brooklyn, has intimate knowledge of keeping watch over the dead. Rabbi Regina shared with me the story of how she engaged in Sh'mirah, a ritual of holding vigil with her deceased father. The ancient Jewish vigil led her into the unfurnished basement of a funeral home where she sat in front of her father's body tucked inside a large refrigerator. Her physical presence lessened the ugliness of the place her father awaited burial. Since 1995, she has mobilized volunteers in pairs scheduled for two-hour shifts around the clock to sit with the recently deceased at the hospital morgue or the funeral home refrigeration unit. In this passage taken from the manuscript of her forthcoming book *Sacred Undertaking: Jewish Acts of Kindness with the Living and the Dead*, she reflected on the need for Sh'mirah most especially today when end of life has moved out of the home into the public, impersonal institutions.

> Have you ever accompanied someone's body down a freight elevator marked "TRASH"? I have—and was thankful that my presence could mitigate against the indignities of the moment. Our modern technological facilities are simply not designed to be a sacred space for the end of life. I believe that an essential part of vigil-keeping is to create a spiritual buffer, through our spiritual presence, for those in our care, against any and all ugliness and dishonor that they and we may encounter in the external environment.

Rabbi Regina said, "In previous generations, sh'mirah served the practical function of protecting the dead body from the elements, as well as from desecration by animals or human vandals."[6] Today, she noted families feel comforted in knowing vigil-keepers watching over their loved ones before burial. On 9/11 and the days following the terrorist attacks on the World Trade Center in 2001, Rabbi Regina and many other Jews sat at the New York City's morgues around-the-clock to hold Sh'mirah for the recently deceased until the recovery effort came to a close. I asked Rabbi Regina why Sh'mirah and Taharah, ancient traditions survived in modern day.

She said, "I see traditional ritual as a form of swaddling parallel to the beginning of life when we swaddle a baby to be held close and tight. Turning to traditional ritual at the end of life for survivors is a form of swaddling, taking this huge hole that's been blown in your universe and create a smaller, safer space. It allows us to contain the enormity of the experience, that's why people turn to tradition."

The traditions of our forefathers have been modified and abbreviated to fit into modern day. Once we held vigil with the dead in the home, now we must go to a morgue or funeral home. The time-honored tradition of accompanying the body to witness the committal to the elements of the earth has also changed.

CREMATION WITNESSING

I called on a spokesperson at the National Funeral Director's Association, Kurt L. Soffe, CFSP, to discuss the revival of cremation witnessing. He is the co-owner of Jenkins-Soffe Funeral Homes and Cremation Center located in Salt Lake City, Utah. He's a fourth generation funeral director in a family-owned and operated business since 1915. He confirmed that many funeral homes and crematoriums are investing in witnessing rooms or platforms in front of the furnace and allow the family to start the fire. He pointed out that many families not able to witness the cremation of their loved one may not be affected immediately, not for six months or year, but almost invariably he had people return to him and ask, "Was my Mom okay? What did she look like? Was she dressed? Did you do her hair or did you just toss her in the casket and put her in the cremation unit? What happened? Explain it to me."

Now Kurt encourages every family to come and identify. He said most families requesting "direct cremation" don't want a viewing, so he calls the process "identification." He added, "We just want the families to know their loved one is safe, treated with dignity, is in a very respectable container and not just laying out on a slab somewhere because that's what they hear."[7] His voice grew more impassioned as he said, "That's what people think, that after someone dies we treat them with disrespect."

I knew exactly what he meant.

Kurt continued, "That's why I say to the families in our meeting, 'If we were going to bury your mom would you accompany us to the cemetery?' and they say, 'Sure we would.' Then I say, 'Well, we're not, we're going to cremate your mom, please accompany us to the cremation center.'"

The increasing return of families pained by the unwitnessed cremation and the bad media of a few corrupt crematorium operators' practices prompted him to build a witness room in his cremation center in 2002. He built a four and a half foot by six foot window in front of the furnace that allows families to see the cardboard box cradling their loved one move up the conveyor belt and enter the fiery chamber. They can see nearly three feet inside to ensure that the chamber is clean and nothing else will be cremated alongside their loved one. He also gives the family the opportunity to start the cremation with a remote. Ninety-nine percent of the time, they choose to ignite the fire. He said pushing the button empowers many families. Before the cremation, he explains to the family the identification process. Their loved one is given a stainless steel disc with a unique number stamped on and logged into a book with their name. The disc enters the crematorium and stays with the body. The family is presented with the cremated remains and the disc.

Kurt said this identification assures the family that "their loved one is taken care of before, during, and after, and they know who they have."

After I spoke to Kurt, I reached a director of cremation in the Forest Lawn Glendale Crematorium. He had a warm, amiable telephone voice. When I told him about my mother and asked about the identification process, he instantly understood my concerns. I could tell he'd done this before. He gently guided me through the entire journey of cremation that Mom embarked on once she departed from my home. She was dropped off at Forest Lawn Covina Hills where she was paired with a metal disc stamped with an identification number, kind of like a social security number for the dead. This disc was attached to her lower left leg with a plastic band. She entered a refrigeration unit at the funeral home. When her cremation was scheduled she was transported to Glendale. On February 20, two cremation directors, assigned to oversee her cremation, placed her in a cardboard box. All bodies are placed in a cardboard box, the standard cremation casket, unless they arrive in a casket. At this stage, I could have spent 15 minutes with my mother to pay last respects, identify her body in the cremation casket, and light the cremation fire.

The disc was removed from her leg and placed in the metal pan that collects the ashes before she entered the fire. She remained in the retort for two and half hours. Afterward, her cremated remains along with the disc in the pan enter a cooler for a half hour. The disc accompanies the body in whatever form throughout the entire journey. Her bone fragments were placed in a processor for 50 seconds and pulverized into sand, or what most people call ashes. Her ashes were poured in a bag with the disc and inserted into the urn. The bag and urn have an identification card with her name, date of cremation, mortuary and disc number. I thanked the gentleman on the other end of the line for leading me through my mother's transformation into ashes.

HOSPICE TO HOME WAKE: A HOLISTIC APPROACH

Shortly after my visit with Eric and Barbara, they invited me to meet a family taking the whole journey to the threshold where boundaries, lines, and definitions between life and death blur. Juanita Marquez Kelley's miracle of death exemplifies how a domestic, family-centered approach to dying and death utilizing hospice and a home- and family-directed funeral service inspired a family and a community to birth individualized rituals.

On the shortest day of sunlight and longest night of darkness in 2006, Juanita Marquez Kelley and her fiancé, David LaVine, arrived in an ambulance at the doors of San Diego Hospice on a mesa overlooking the Pacific Ocean in Southern California. Linda Marquez stepped from her car behind the ambulance and watched the crew unload her semiconscious twenty-eight-year-old daughter onto a gurney. Juanita had just come out of major brain surgery, and the doctors didn't expect her to make it to Christmas, just four days away. The doctors transferred her from the surgery recovery room to hospice, a home away from home for the dying. Linda felt as though they'd boarded a runaway train racing along the edge of a sheer cliff with no tracks ahead, no way to stop it, no way to get off. Just days ago, she had been sitting beside Juanita at a long dinner table at a Mexican restaurant with the entire family after watching a performance of *The Nutcracker*. Juanita was laughing, carrying on . . .

It was her last supper. Juanita had an intense headache that night, visited the doctor the next morning, entered surgery the following afternoon, stayed in recovery the day after, and was now here.

The sea air blew through her curly golden locks and she squinted her almond eyes to watch David eyeing every move of the ambulance crew. At age forty-eight, Linda never thought she'd live to see this day. David swept his long sandy-blond dreadlocks from his face and held Juanita's hand to assure her she wasn't alone. They crossed the threshold into the front doors of the hospice. Even after the brain surgery, her beauty radiated in the sun's rays overhead. She continued to captivate him. Juanita resembled a young Michelle Pfeiffer. David had first laid eyes on Juanita four years ago, near the Oceanside Pier, a few months after the brain cancer announced itself with a grand mal seizure. She was twenty-four, he was twenty-six.

Linda and David followed the ambulance crew carrying Juanita into a room about the size of a master bedroom with cozy couches, carpeting, and a sliding glass door leading to a garden terrace. Just beyond the terrace, Linda spied a sunlit valley dotted by eucalyptus trees and nature trails zigzagging to the waves crashing on the rocky shore below. She was relieved the room felt more like a sanctuary than a sterile hospital room.

Linda watched Juanita's chest slowly rise and fall beneath the blankets on the hospital bed. For the past four years, the cancer was like a big trunk encasing a scary thing in her living room that she could only open now and then. Sometimes she could open it wider than others, but never could she open it all the way. Now, though, she felt the lid of the trunk swung wide open. Its force suffocated her.

She followed David into the hallway and slung her arm over his shoulder. The nurse unfolded the house rules.

"The rules here are there are no rules: children, pets, and any guests can visit at any hour of the day for as long as they desire." David's anxiety lessened when he realized that J.T., their Dalmatian, could be there with them. Linda looked at the nurse.

"What am I supposed to do, sit here and watch my child die?" Linda asked. She might have been out of order, but witnessing and surviving this was out of nature's order.

The nurse stared directly into Linda's weary eyes and said, "No, you take the journey with her."

Linda didn't quite understand what that meant. "Take the journey with her." Juanita's quiet room soon hummed with the arrival of her father, Howard, her Aunt Sandy, and a dozen cousins, all in their late twenties. David joined them at the bedside. He pulled Juanita's engagement ring from his pocket. He'd been protecting it since the surgery. He looked at the diamond-encrusted ring and held it up above Juanita.

"Juanita, would you like me to put your ring on?" he asked her.

Juanita's jade eyes opened just slightly for the first time since she arrived at the hospice. She summoned every last bit of energy from the depths of her soul to mumble an affirmative "yes."

"I love you, Juanita," he said as he lifted her hand and slipped on the ring. The hospital room receded as he remembered giving her the ring on a moonlit rocky beach near Santa Barbara in August. He kneeled down on the cold sand in front of her. The starry night sky cast a halo over her. He watched her soft blonde locks billowing in the gentle sea breeze. He'd had the words "Love heals all" engraved on the inside of the ring. He held her hand and slipped the ring on her finger.

"Juanita, I promise that I'll always be by your side and I'll always take care of you," he said. He kept his promise. He ran his own carpentry business and could always arrange to be there when she needed him.

As the sun began to dip toward the sea, Rosaria Cabrera, Juanita's older sister by two years, arrived like a whirlwind in the room. She carried Juanita's year-old niece Satya on her hip and bags of decorations. Her husband, Joey, and his parents followed closely behind. They carried in a four-foot potted Christmas tree.

"Juanita, we're here and we're going to decorate your room. It's the Yule, the Winter Solstice, and we were going to do the Solstice later on," she said. Rosaria swept her spiral locks from her face and lent down to kiss Juanita and also let Satya kiss her Tia Nita. Rosaria was an R.N. at Stanford's Pediatrics Hospital in Palo Alto and so on familiar turf. She turned on some Celtic seasonal music and invited everyone to decorate the room.

"Juanita, we're placing a tree with twinkling white lights on the left side of your bed," Rosaria said. She led the cousins in stringing twinkling blue fairy lights around the door and in a dipping fashion over the sliding glass door. They'd all grown up together and so reminisced about Christmases past with Juanita.

"Juanita, we're hanging crystal cherub angels on a string of blue lights behind your bed and on your IV pole," Rosaria said describing her actions because Juanita's eyes were closed.

By sunset, they'd transformed the clinical room into a winter wonderland permeated with the scent of fresh pine needles and wafting aromas of cinnamon apple cider. David returned with J.T., Juanita's Dalmatian. J.T. curled up beneath the Christmas tree by Juanita's bedside.

Serendipitously, Christmas carolers arrived as Rosaria turned off the fluorescent lights overhead, leaving just a peaceful, blue glow in the room. Everyone relaxed, sipping hot cider and listening to carols. The hospice nurse walked in and her eyes misted upon seeing Juanita steeped in affection overflowing from friends and family members' arms and legs enmeshed around the bed.

"Wow, the love is palpable in this room," the nurse remarked.

In the midst of the festivities, David's younger brother brought a feast and set a buffet table prepared by Juanita and David's neighbors. David's parents arrived from Sacramento and his other brothers arrived from Wisconsin.

David and Linda felt cradled in everyone's love for Juanita. At the peak of the evening, more than fifty people surrounded Juanita. They showered her in kisses, hugs, foot rubs, back rubs, and all kinds of physical affection since her eyes remained closed.

When the feast cleared, Rosaria said to Juanita, "We are now going to prepare for the winter solstice, Juanita."

She narrated her every step in the preparation for the Yule, which stems from *Yula,* an Anglo-Saxon word that means "wheel." Solstice literally means to "stand-still" or "stop." The Celtics for millennia celebrated the winter solstice by making Yule logs, wreaths, and mistletoe to burn in a Yule fire. Everyone watched as Rosaria spread a red quilt on the floor and grouped separate piles of foxtails, berries, sycamore leaves, pinecones, pine needles, tree bark, bright orange wildflowers, and ribbons.

"Okay," she said. "Everyone gather around."

The family and friends made a circle around Juanita's bed and linked hands. David held Juanita's hand on one side and Rosaria's on the other. Rosaria recited these words:

"We are about to begin the Yule ceremony. This is a ritual and celebration that has been happening since ancient times. This celebration of the Yule is usually performed on the longest night of the year . . . It is a ceremony to call back the sun, to bring us light, new life, vibrant hope, and joy. It marks the end of one cycle and the beginning of another.

"This night of the Yule, the veil between the world of the physical and the world of the spirit grows thin . . . Healing comes in many forms— physical, mental, emotional, and spiritual. On this night we all will be guided to receive the healing we are in need of. We call upon beings of light, guardian angels . . . as well as our loved ones who have passed before us."

Everyone around the circle called out the names of their loved ones who had passed on. For ten minutes the names of grandparents, parents, uncles, aunts, brothers, and sisters emerged from the lips of those bound together in the circle. Rosaria then asked for a moment of silence, which felt so powerful, so reverent. She went on.

"There are many things in the physical world that we cannot explain, many things that just don't seem right. This has been a time for great challenges for all of us. Everyone in this room is in need of healing in one form or another. We have invoked the presence of our spiritual force to ease our burdens, give us guidance, and help us bring back the light, love, and healing force into our hearts, minds, bodies, and souls . . .

"Just as our ancients have done, so we do today. Laid before us are pieces of nature to evoke the power and beauty within us. Each one has a unique quality. Some represent never-ending life, that's the evergreen; while others call to the sun, they are the brightly colored orange items. We now ask them to speak to us as we each create our own bundle."

Rosaria handed everyone pads of paper and pencils to write a prayer, blessing, or wish and then invited each person to come forward to create a special Yule bouquet. Traditionally, each person places the Yule into the flames, but instead she improvised the Yule fire with a dozen votive candles lit on the table like an altar beside Juanita's bed. Everyone fanned out around the room to transfer the farewells and prayers floating in their minds into ink on paper. The healing ritual really helped each person still their racing thoughts about losing Juanita and instead focus on messages of love. Since Juanita hadn't opened her eyes, each person described the bouquet and read their blessing or farewell to her before placing it on the altar. Rosaria knitted a circle out of foxtails and placed three little flowers in it. She sat beside Juanita's bed to explain it was the never-ending circle of life that bound Juanita, Rosaria, and Satya. She placed her hand on Juanita's chest.

"We will never be apart ever, and we will always be together," she wept.

Juanita let out a big sigh reassuring Rosaria that though she could no longer communicate, she could feel and hear her.

David collected a beautiful bouquet and wrote how he loved her spirit and admired her courage and reminded her she would always be his world. Linda wrote words of love to her daughter, a wish for the pain to cease and peace to fill her. She found herself in the midst of the ceremony reflecting on her daughter's short life. As her last breath drew near, she remembered Juanita's first breath in the hospital room in Tucson, Arizona. Linda chose natural childbirth, and she recalled with sharpened clarity the visceral experience of her body splitting open as her daughter moved through the birth canal and landed in her husband's arms.

As she fondled the bouquet, she returned to the campground on the Black River where they had spent summers camping in a tent. The river and the trees became Juanita's second home, her playground. They cooked and dined around the fire at night, which ignited Juanita's love for the warmth and conversation spawned around a fire pit. Juanita was a natural beauty masked by a tomboy's love for insects. Her bedroom buzzed like a science lab with jars housing live bugs collected on her hunts through the backyard and hikes around the neighborhood. As she grew older, she evolved into a chameleon, always changing the color and style of her hair, from bleached spikes to long crimson tresses. She was a true artist with a multidimensional personality that she relished exhibiting through outlandish outfits, patterns, and materials plucked from thrift stores.

She strayed from order and lived by a philosophy of always trying something once. Her zany demeanor manifested the kookiest faces that sent her audience into bellyaching laughter. Though a striking beauty, Juanita never took herself too seriously or showed shame in pointing out her idiosyncrasies. She was always the first to pass gas and make note of it. Often her verve disguised her softer side. Juanita possessed a deep reservoir of compassion for people that led her to midwifery. She trained as a birth midwife in Virginia, but the cancer struck and ultimately aborted her apprenticeship. In the absence of fulfilling a dream, she found love on a trip to San Diego to visit her cousins. She met David, a modern-day carpenter who instantly fell in love with her. She tried to maintain a normal life in Tucson while undergoing chemotherapy, but she gravitated toward the love, sun, and beach in Oceanside. David nicknamed her Princess Fly High because she flew back and forth to visit him for the first year of their romance.

Eventually, she moved to Oceanside with David and sought care at UCLA Medical Center. She and David focused on the present, even if it felt out of order for the young couple to be focused on her chemo treatments, special diets, and MRI appointments. They drank in balmy summer evenings, watched many suns melt into the Pacific Ocean, and sat around the fire pit roasting marshmallows at the beach most evenings. They never watched television. Juanita always wanted to be outside, in conversation with people, living life, not watching it.

Gradually Juanita grew to understand that she probably wouldn't live long or have children. But her sister, Rosaria, gave her such a gift in a devastating sea of impossibility. Juanita's verve rebounded with the news of a baby. She participated in every step of the process, from recording the birth plan to helping Rosaria set up for the new arrival. Rosaria decided on natural childbirth with a midwife in a birthing room at a hospital. Juanita flew up to Rosaria's home in Palo Alto in the last week of January to hunker down and wait. On January 31, about eleven o'clock at night, Rosaria announced, "It's time." Juanita burst with ecstasy. She timed the contractions and coached her sister through the birth. Juanita was awestruck with intense love when Satya emerged from the womb on February 1, 2006. Juanita cut the umbilical cord and washed Satya. She shared a deep connection with her niece, who sustained her as life grew shorter and the cancer grew stronger.

On December 11, ten days before her arrival at San Diego Hospice, Juanita saw her MRI at UCLA Medical Center. A dozen lesions massed at the base of her brain. The shocking image needed no explanations from her oncologists. She immediately started vomiting into a trash can in the examining lab. When she stepped out of the hallway, she turned to David and her mother.

"Wow, I guess I'm going to die," she said. "But then we all are, aren't we?"

Linda turned her eyes outside the hospice window reflecting the moon's glow on the crashing waves below. Soft vibrations reverberated from Juanita's sound-healing CD, which balanced the now midnight ambiance with Tibetan singing bowls mixed with ohms.

Rosaria announced that it wouldn't be long now. The family lay folded within each other's arms and legs cuddling Juanita in the bed. At around two o'clock in the morning, Juanita started to breath heavily, and Linda found herself holding her breath, just waiting, hoping for one more breath. Just one more breath. David placed his hand on her neck, feeling her pulse. Howard, Juanita's father, rested his head on her chest and listened to her heartbeat slowing to a quiet patter.

David could no longer feel the pulse in her neck.

"Her heart stopped," he cried.

Howard said, "It's still going, it's still going, it's still going."

Just before three o'clock in the morning on December 22, she took a few long deep breaths and paused, and then one took more breath. Howard raised his head.

"Her heart stopped."

David kissed her. Everyone embraced Juanita for the rest of the night. They whimpered, "I love you" between sobs. The social worker arrived as dawn broke the darkness outside. The social worker sat huddled in the room with David and Linda.

"Do you know what Juanita wanted?" he asked regarding her funeral plans.

"I just know she wanted to be cremated," Linda said. "But not for three days."

Juanita believed that it took three days for the soul to separate from the body. The caseworker knew of an alternative funeral service that might be able to help Juanita and her family. An hour later, Eric Putt, with his long flowing brown hair, handsome face, and gentlemanly nature, approached the room. He wore jeans and a light blue button-down shirt. He introduced himself and Thresholds, a holistic in-home funeral service. He shared that if they wanted a direct cremation for Juanita, he could help them arrange it, but his main question was what they wished to do with Juanita during the period before the cremation.

"I can take her now and she would have to be placed in refrigeration at the crematorium," he said.

David frowned. Juanita hated the cold. She hated to be alone.

"Or you can take her home."

"Home," Linda said, thinking that was pretty radical, but taking Juanita away at that moment seemed incomprehensible.

"We can take her home?" she and David asked in unison.

Eric explained that they had the right to take her home. She didn't have to go into refrigeration or endure embalming to preserve her body.

"You're allowed to care for her until the cremation," he said.

David remembered his promise to Juanita, that he'd never leave her alone and that he'd stay with her till the end. Now the end took on a whole different meaning. Linda remembered what the hospice worker said: "Take the journey with her." They both felt it would be wrong to store Juanita in the chill of a refrigeration unit in the crematorium.

They decided that Juanita's home with David, which was just an apartment, was too small for a wake, but the house that Rosaria had just bought could be the right place to bring her home. It was a real home, where Satya would grow up. Rosaria and her husband just purchased the home in San Diego to be closer to Juanita. Rosaria agreed Juanita's arrival and wake would christen her home.

Eric called the crematorium and because of Christmas they wouldn't be able to set a date until the morning of December 26. Everyone agreed on holding a wake for four days until the cremation. Eric began filling in the paperwork to get the discharge papers from San Diego Hospice. He'd completed this transaction dozens of times before, but this time he decided to make a request.

"Usually they ask us to take the body out the back door, near the dumpster, and I'd like to see if they'll make an exception for Juanita," Eric said to David. "Wait here, I'll be right back."

The family packed the decorations and went ahead to set up Rosaria's house. Eric met the head nurse in the hall. He returned fifteen minutes later to find David sitting at the bedside holding Juanita's hand.

"All right, someone second-in-command to the man upstairs," Eric said, pointing to the heavens, "approved us to go out the front door. It's the first time anyone has ever gone out the way they came in."

Eric parked his van and pulled the mortuary cot through the entrance of the hospice. A hospice attendant stopped him.

"You can't do that here," he said.

"Yes, I have clearance," Eric said politely. The grumbling man disappeared into the hospice and never returned.

Meanwhile Eric wheeled the empty gurney into the room where David sat with Juanita. The two men carefully lifted her onto the gurney and Eric draped and fastened her in. David stood in front of the gurney, and Eric pushed from the back. He carefully guided the gurney through the halls of the hospice. Each time they passed a patient or family members, the strangers stopped quietly, made way, and paid reverence. David felt tears streaming down his face. He was profoundly moved by their reactions, and he couldn't help but wonder why the deceased were sent out the dumpster door.

As they passed through the double doors and into the sunlight, David and Eric guided the gurney over the bumps so as not to jostle Juanita.

When they buckled Juanita safely into the back of the van, David took a seat up front with Eric. He nodded his head to Eric.

"Hey, I like your vibe, man," David said.

"I like yours, too," Eric said. "Why don't we take the streets so we keep this ride as smooth as possible for Juanita?"

Eric handled David's fiancée with as much care and concern as if she were his own. Meanwhile, Barbara Kernan, Eric's "other half," had arrived at Rosaria's house with the dry ice and three midwifery bags in tow. She had brought a massage table, but it was plain and needed dressing up. Linda dug through Barbara's bag full of beaded throws. Linda and Barbara draped the table with emerald and violet velvet throws and then laid a padded blanket on the surface. They set up Juanita's resting place in the living room across from the fireplace and then arranged the couches and rocking chair near the table.

Eric and David arrived with Juanita. They removed the shroud from her body and face and lifted her onto the cradle. She still wore her hospital gown. Barbara asked if there was something that maybe they wanted to dress her in. David and Linda made a quick journey to pick out an outfit from Juanita's closet. They chose a flowing purple skirt adorned with an embroidered daisy. They also picked up her makeup bag, shower gel, nail polish, and a necklace with a daisy made of mother of pearl.

Barbara suggested bathing Juanita before placing the skirt and white shirt on. She filled up two basins of warm soapy water. David held Juanita's head ever so gently, so Linda could wash off the blood and iodine from the surgery. Rosaria, Linda, and David used baby shampoo in a cup to rinse her head and hair. Rosaria combed her hair with delicate hand. Linda tenderly bathed her daughter one last time. She felt like Juanita was a newborn baby, so vulnerable, unable to do this for herself, but wanting it. Linda felt no change in Juanita between her last breath in hospital and now as she lay here in Rosaria's home. Linda's sister, Sandy, stood by holding the sacred space like a guardian angel.

Linda sensed a responsibility to her daughter to cleanse and honor her body by removing the hospital gown and restoring Juanita. This ritual of sacredly purifying her daughter seemed to wash away all the pain, erase all the traces of cancer, and free her body. As she touched her hands and arms, she cried, and her tears dropped onto Juanita, mixing with the water. With each caress of Juanita's hair and rotation of the sponge on her delicate face and hands, Linda shed the shock and delved deep in her lament. She couldn't have allowed anyone else to do this. She realized as she looked upon Juanita's angelic face that death wasn't scary or ugly. This was Juanita, not just a corpse.

Linda recognized Juanita was in transition, moving out of her body, and it was her responsibility to care and tenderly watch over her. She watched Barbara place dry ice wrapped in paper beneath Juanita's neck, back, and legs.

They opened the vast array of bouquets brought to the house and surrounded Juanita with dozens of red roses, pastel rose buds, lilac orchids, violet irises, multicolored carnations, and yellow sunflowers. Rosaria strung the white aromatic plumerias, traditionally used in Hawaii to make leis, into a crown. They surrounded Juanita with an aurora of flowers and a corona of plumerias.

She looked like the enchanted Princess Aurora, a sleeping beauty on a bed of fresh flowers. The living room glowed with twinkling blue lights, cherub angels, and a garland-adorned fireplace as the sun began to set. The Christmas tree illuminated Juanita's head and an altar lay at her feet. The altar table displayed a magnificent eleven-by-seventeen professional photograph of Juanita in her last year of life and some of her personal effects, including a Yoda doll and a statue of Mary. White votive candles glowed around the Yule logs that reminded everyone of Juanita's love for nature. The nieces used Juanita's new organic purple nail polish to paint her nails to match her skirt.

In the adjacent room, a buffet table began to steam with a large pot of lentil soup, casseroles, and some apple pie. The house buzzed with a constant flow of visiting friends and relatives. As Rosaria arranged the food and beverages in the kitchen, a tsunami of grief enveloped her. Rosaria felt her legs buckle beneath her, and she collapsed, crying hysterically. Linda and others in the kitchen held her up. The sorrow of watching Juanita's physical body stop living and the unimaginable terror of realizing that life from that moment would go on without her sister Juanita set in. At the same time, she felt cloaked in safety to be able to express this raw, primordial grief in the bosom of home and family. Not only was it a time of transition for Juanita, but it was also the time for her survivors to slowly internalize her death.

Simultaneously, opposite emotions were occurring in the backyard where David and all of Juanita's cousins and close friends from the beach toasted her life with her favorite beer, Stone Smoke Porter. She loved to sip just one while sitting around a bonfire on the beach in Oceanside. David reminisced with friends about how Juanita always basked in the warmth of the fire and the company of close friends with the sound of the ocean crashing on the beach.

"She never forgot to bring out the bag of big marshmallows, Hershey bars, and graham crackers," David said.

Before nightfall, David asked everyone to honor his wish of not leaving the living room empty.

"Please don't leave Juanita alone," he said. "If you are in there and no one else is, then please let someone else know or come and get me."

Linda followed Barbara's suggestion to decorate Juanita's cremation casket. It was the standard cardboard box the crematoriums use. Barbara brought the box to the house for the family to blanket it in their love. The next day Linda brought all of Juanita's art supplies. She visited the fabric store to select a velvet shroud and a sheer lace for the casket. Linda set out an art therapy corner for all visitors to decorate Juanita's final cradle in the family room.

The family room turned into an art and memorial gathering to reflect on memories of Juanita and paint her casket similar to the way the Egyptians prepared a casket for a queen. They painted scenes from her life and places they'd visited with Juanita. They wrote long letters, poetry, and prayers. The casket decoration provided a vehicle for expressing the powerful impact Juanita had on their lives and a platform to physically work through their grief by performing one last act of love for her. Similar mourning art was seen in the nineteenth century through elaborate quilts, sewn into designs that celebrated the life of the deceased. It was a festive atmosphere of reminiscing, but sometimes the mood turned to a quiet reverence when someone would break down into tears. Everyone stopped, surrounded, and comforted the person to lift him or her back up.

David encouraged the friends and family to decorate the entire cradle with the exception of the inside of the lid, which they reserved for Rosaria, Linda, and himself. Rosaria painted a giant plumeria that would rest above her heart. She used carbon paper to ink Satya's footprints and handprints in a circle around it. David painted across the top the words "Princess Fly High." The nickname took on a new message. He now wished for his princess, his angel, to fly high, free. Linda drew a heart with a smiling face in the middle, the same one she used to draw on Juanita's lunch bags every day before sending her off to school.

Linda then lined the inside of the casket with emerald velvet and an elegant sheer white mesh drape. The long wake for Juanita allowed an intermingling of generations to come together and unite in their honoring the irreplaceable Juanita while immersing themselves in an intimate, close-knit, safe space to gradually come to terms with Juanita's death. In their own time, they could go in, hold her hand, say their good-byes, read her a poem, paint her a picture, reminisce among her intimates, and prepare the bed where she would lie for the last time. Juanita's long wake defied our society's conventions to abbreviate a viewing to a couple of hours in a funeral home and keep our grief publicly composed. Juanita's wake recognized that avoiding or denying death estranges us and that by bringing our loved ones home and spending time with them in vigil, or as Jews say, *sh'mira*, allows us to be human together, to touch, to cry, to laugh, to share, and to support each other. Rosaria left her doors open twenty-four hours a day.

On Christmas Eve, the family sat in the living room around Juanita. David asked his niece and nephew to sing "Silent Night" in their mother's native language, Hawaiian. The girls, not even in second grade yet, were embarrassed to sing in the room full of more than twenty people. David started the words in English and everyone joined in. As the moon cast a silvery glow through the living room window, the sound of all those mourning voices bound together was like a lullaby. The words "sleep in heavenly peace" suddenly felt poignantly perfect.

Around dawn on Christmas morning, Juanita came to Rosaria in a dream, she poured out love and gratitude. She was saying, "Thank you, thank you, thank you. I've made my transition. Thank you for helping me along my journey. Now it is my turn to help all of you." When Rosaria awoke, she realized it was Satya's first Christmas morning.

The family gathered around Satya in a circle near Juanita and opened presents. Rosaria felt a deep gratitude that Juanita's physical presence was there. She couldn't have imagined celebrating any other way. David's friend sent over a Christmas feast. David felt like all the family and friends were one love bound together by Juanita.

At around eleven o'clock in the morning on December 26, David and his friends gathered around Juanita and tenderly lifted her into the casket. Before they closed the lid, he prayed aloud. They lifted all the Yule logs from the altar and placed them in the casket with bouquets of flowers. Rosaria realized that the cremation fire would become the Yule fire. As the tradition goes, some ashes from the Yule fire must be saved to burn in the fire the next year to represent the continuum of life, and some ashes from that fire saved for the year after that, and so on.

Linda kissed and hugged Juanita and then pulled the sheer white lace like a veil over her daughter. J.T., now at her level, kissed her as well.

Linda gasped at Juanita's intoxicating beauty surrounded by a deep emerald velvet shroud, bouquets of fragrant flowers, and the Yule wreaths. She looked like a fairytale princess. Linda felt as though the invisible hands of angels surrounded them at that moment. She watched David slowly slide the lid and both of them drank in her beauty just one more time.

David and Juanita's cousins carried her out to Eric's van. David sat in the front seat with Eric on the way to the crematorium. A caravan followed. Barbara had warned them the building was industrial and to prepare themselves for a sterile environment as they stepped from their cars into the parking lot and then into the crematorium. She led the group into the witnessing area while David and Eric placed Juanita on the conveyor belt. The casket came around and stopped right in front of all the witnesses. David opened the box one more time to say farewell and clip a little piece of the lace from her veil. The big metal door opened up and she entered into the flames. They never left her alone. They took the journey with her. They went as far as physically possible with Juanita. The finality gripped each one of them, creating an outpouring of mourning. Together they huddled, embraced.

"You know, this is not the place to mourn. We should find a better place to gather and grieve," David said. He felt as though he heard Juanita's voice say, "Go back to where we started."

David looked at Linda through his red, swollen eyes and suggested everyone gather in Oceanside at the beach for a bonfire. David led the group in a caravan to Oceanside where he and Juanita had met. Like a mourning parade rather than a procession, they flooded the beach and encircled a fire pit. David and the cousins threw logs in the pit and struck a match to ignite the fire just near the pier where the waves crashed on the shore.

Linda walked up to the pier and happened to hear her favorite song pouring out of the restaurant speakers, "Somewhere over the Rainbow" sung by Judy Garland. Tears flowed as she watched David and the cousins create a large heart out of flowers on the sand, and they all watched when the rising tide eventually washed them away. Rosaria turned her eyes to the sky, awestruck to see the clouds moving into the formation of a phoenix, the bird that dives into the fire and is resurrected out of the ashes.

They spent the afternoon in quiet mourning around the fire, watching the flames rise and fall in and out of the pit. The flames represented Juanita dancing in her now elemental form. Three hours later, they returned to the crematorium to pick up Juanita's ashes tucked in an urn and brought her home.

TWELVE The Living Unveiling: Technology Innovates Memorializing

Instead of waiting for their monument to be unveiled at their deaths, the healthy Orin Kennedy and Bernardo Puccio chose to invite all of their friends and family to a living unveiling at a cemetery to celebrate their lives and their thirty years spent together. The invitation for this unprecedented event read:

> You are selectively invited to attend a very special event to honor the long-time partnership of Bernardo Puccio and Orin Kennedy at the dedication of their monument and red carpet premiere of the personal documentary *Two Hearts, Two Souls*, Sunday, June 11, 2006, at 5 p.m.
> Cocktails and Hors d'oeuvres,
> Cocktail Attire.
> Lakeside in the Garden of Legends
> Hollywood Forever
> 6000 Santa Monica Boulevard, Hollywood, California.

About a hundred Beverly Hills and Hollywood socialites received an invitation, which purposely omitted the word "cemetery."

The unveiling is a Jewish mourning custom that usually takes place a year or within a year after the death to consecrate the tombstone. Before the ceremony begins, a cloth is placed over the tombstone. The cloth is lifted during the ceremony followed by a eulogy for all to take one last look together at the most salient qualities of the person. Orin and Bernardo's event differed from a living funeral in that Orin and Bernardo were not on death's door. In fact, both are healthy sixty-somethings.

On that bright Sunday morning in June, Bernardo, a high-profile interior designer, and Orin, a former locations manager for such television shows as *L.A. Law, The Practice, Chicago Hope,* and *Ally McBeal,* directed the cemetery crew on veiling their monument for the highly anticipated celebration.

"Well," Orin said, "It's sort of a coming-out party."

Then he motioned to the cemetery ground with a chuckle, "At least it's not a going-in party."

By dusk, Orin and Bernardo were greeting their arriving family and friends on the red carpet for cocktails and hors d'oeuvres served beneath a tent fronting their lakeside monument. The men and women present were a virtual showcase of just about every designer name emblazoned on Rodeo Drive storefronts. The trendsetting crowd was no stranger to dressing up for red carpet occasions, but the combination, or should I say contrast, of sunny apparel complemented by spring hats and black garb conveyed their confusion about what they were in for. Some of the guests, surprised by the cemetery setting, couldn't help but ask if either man might be terminally ill. The men of the hour didn't set a clear example for their perplexed guests. Orin, a slender blond standing well over six feet, looked like a Ralph Lauren model in his white slacks and dazzling turquoise jacket over a multicolored striped shirt. And Bernardo looked like a carbon copy of Tony Curtis, but even more dazzling in a stunning black suit complemented by a rhinestone-studded tie and dark sunglasses. As the cocktail hour moved from the red carpet to a formal setting on the lakeside, Orin, the master of ceremonies, turned on the music with a remote and "The Twelfth of Never" by Johnny Mathias played.

Orin said, "This is a day of celebration, and when we're finished, we're going into the cathedral to see a movie."

A LIVING UNVEILING

Orin and Bernardo stood arm-in-arm in front of their grand monument, which rose like the Parthenon. The gleaming white marble carved in ancient Roman-Grecian architecture looked like a tomb of kings veiled in royal purple and white sheer robes.

They radiated.

Orin announced: "Bernardo and I dedicate this monument so that future generations will know we proudly, proudly walked this earth with a lifetime of love and commitment for each other."

As the veil lifted, an opera performer sang "Unforgettable"; the stunned audience was awed. "Puccio Kennedy" was inscribed at the top of the glorious monument and in the middle an "in memoriam" for their cat Cristal, whom they often called their son and who had blessed their lives for eighteen years. The crowd, mostly older heterosexual married couples, buzzed with excitement.

"Only in L.A., only in L.A.," one lady said.

"I think it's a great idea to celebrate one's life before it's over," said a gentleman in his sixties. The group surrounding him agreed as they raised their wine and martini glasses.

Bernardo and Orin led their guests into the cathedral on a pathway lined with beautiful violet bouquets, which matched those adorning the monument. Inside, the guests took their seats on either side of a white center aisle. Orin stepped up to the podium.

"I wish to thank Tyler Cassity and the staff of Hollywood Forever for their time and understanding in making our dream a reality . . . and Forever Studios under the dedicated direction of Jay Gianukos . . . Hopefully they've created an insightful as well as entertaining look into our lives. Now you are going to see Orin and Bernardo as viewed with independent eyes."

Orin continued, "This film is testament about how—" He choked up, then soldiered on. "About how love and respect transcends prejudice and discrimination."

He introduced Bernardo. As Bernardo walked down the white center aisle, he received a glorious ovation. It was the first and more than likely the last time, he'd walk down the aisle to join Orin for a celebration of their life together. Bernardo welcomed the guests and spoke of how this day was four years in the making.

"I know I'm the first to do this," he said. "But I won't be the last."

Nearly two decades prior, he purchased the lakeside property and then threw the deed in their safe.

"God forbid," he said, "if anything ever happens to either one of us, at least I'll know where we'll go."

In 2003, he began sketching the design of their monument, working with architects and finally carving the Carrara marble he had imported from Italy. He spoke of how Jay, the filmmaker in all of this, had followed him and Orin for a year.

YOUR LIFE ON THE SILVER SCREEN

Bernardo introduced the film and then turned to the 120-inch screen illuminated behind him. The story traveled back to Orin's hometown of Brooklyn, New York, and Bernardo's birthplace in Alabama. The men share their coming out stories. Orin remembers being introduced to a "whole new world, a gay world." They told their stories of coming to Hollywood with aspirations of becoming stars on the silver screen. Lana Turner added the extra "o" to Bernard's name, and Orin changed his last name to Kennedy because, well, in the 1960s everyone wanted to be a Kennedy.

In the film, Orin and Bernardo returned to Hollywood and sat in the restaurant where they first met to tell their tales of young love and the choice to build a life together. The film fast-forwards to their life now as they hold a spectacular dinner party among their friends, all married couples. In intimate interviews, friends and family talk about the rare love Orin and Bernardo share.

At the end of the premiere, Bernardo exhaled. It was exasperating to see himself go from a twenty-year-old to a sixty-year-old in the span of an hour on a 120-inch screen in front of an audience. But then he turned to the crowd and saw a room full of tears.

"I've never accepted an Academy Award, but I think this comes pretty close," he thought to himself as he heard shouts of "magnificent" and "bravo" echo around him.

"At least we know now we won't miss our 'funeral,'" Orin said, smiling as he looked out at the setting sun turning the blue sky to orange backlighting the monument that honored the sunset of their lives.

THE LAST REAL ESTATE

Glitz and glam aside, in the privacy of their home, Orin and Bernardo allowed me to dig deeper into their raison d'être and the evolution of unveiling their monument. It was the AIDS epidemic that incited Orin and Bernardo to make their end-of-life plans. In the 1980s, they lost what Bernardo remembers as dozens of friends to AIDS. They both talked of how their relationship, which had dawned on the cusp of the AIDS epidemic, saved them from the fateful end many of their friends suffered. Death surrounded them and forced the question "What will happen to us when we die?" Most people don't ask these questions until they or their loved ones are at death's door, but when you live in death's neighborhood, it seems inevitable that you would ask the question. Orin and Bernardo began searching for final resting places. They felt it was their responsibility to handle their end-of-life plans and not expect Bernardo's sister, their closest living relative, to have to sort this out from her home in Alabama.

Two decades later, Bernardo began drafting the blueprints for their monument with an architect. Although Orin is Jewish and Bernardo is Roman Catholic, they made the decision to be cremated. Neither one wished "to decompose," as they put it, beneath the ground. Since the unveiling of the monument, Orin and Bernardo spend weekend afternoons at the cemetery. Bernardo gardens and landscapes his lakeside property. It's a quiet, serene place in the middle of their busy Los Angeles lives. They've decided that their dates of death will not be written on the monument because they want their love for one another to be carried on into eternity.

Orin and Bernardo are now living legends at Hollywood Forever, the Cemetery of Immortals. Their monument resides in the company of such Hollywood legends as Fay Wray, Tyrone Power, Marion Davies, Agnes Ayres, and Douglas Fairbank. Hattie McDaniel, who was the first African American woman to receive an Academy Award, for her role in *Gone with the Wind*, has a cenotaph at the cemetery. In 2004, an eight-foot bronze cenotaph of Johnny Ramone, born John William Cummings, playing his electric guitar was erected near the lake. Hollywood Forever Cemetery is on the list of U.S. National Register of Historic Places. Many future occupants believe that choosing to be interred in this cemetery recognizes they're making Hollywood history. As for making their own history in Hollywood, Orin and Bernardo will play on at the cemetery, www.forevernetwork.com, and www.orinbernardomovie.com.

THE MAKING OF HOLLYWOOD FOREVER AND THE A&E-STYLE DOCUMENTARY

In ancient times, the Greeks and Romans believed that people achieved immortality through eulogy at the funeral. The priest only eulogized influential people of the culture. Now eulogies are the centerpiece of modern funerals. Today the culture selects those who will be immortalized by writing a biography or producing a video biography. Tyler Cassity, the owner of Hollywood Forever Cemetery, believes every life should be remembered in the twenty-first century. This philosophy is an easy sell in our memoirist culture. He figured the best time for people to be thinking about producing a biography would be around the time they mapped out their death plan and purchased their final piece of real estate, a resting place on Earth.

At Hollywood Forever, in the heart of Hollywood, ordinary people can collaborate with professional biographers, historians, and filmmakers to produce biographies of their loved ones or themselves. Visitors can view the biographies on silver screens in the mausoleum and kiosks embedded in monuments throughout the grounds. Through these videos, grandparents pass on their life stories in their own voices to future generations. Children can see grandma kissing grandpa at their wedding, sharing the story of how they met, telling tales of coming to America, going to war, protesting war, embarking on parenthood. Some of the videos played grandmother and grandfather singing "Happy Birthday" to their next generations.

Here in the cemetery, a virtual relationship between the living and the dead is formed. There was a time when ancestors' stories passed from generation to generation like myths and folklore, through repeating life stories around the village fire. The dinner table eventually became the modern-day village fire, but even that has disappeared from many busy, modern homes. This ancient oral tradition is now reborn with more efficient technology.

In fifty to a hundred years, the occupants of this cemetery will still be sharing their stories in their own voices with crystal clear transmission—at least that's Tyler's dream. He birthed the idea after discovering an audiotape of his grandmother's voice in 1986, a few years after she died. The tape captured the key and cadence of her voice and suddenly became the most valuable personal effect she left behind. Listening to the tape left Tyler and his family with a combination of bittersweet emotions. They reveled in hearing her voice again, but mourned the fact that they only had just this one tape.

At Forever Studios, film crews interview family and friends for a personal documentary. These A&E-style biographies are family investments. Film producers suggest filming a reminiscing party where family and friends gather in one place. This, of course, cuts down on the travel and filming costs. A slideshow with music costs from $300 to $400, but with a live-action video and film crew another zero is added to the bottom line. And when film crews are traveling to a person's birthplace and multiple locations for interviews, then the overall cost of the video can reach upwards of $10,000. The video premieres at the funeral, the wake, or a memorial gathering planned on the birthday of the departed, an anniversary of death, or an unveiling ceremony, when the headstone is placed on the grave. The family keeps a copy for home and Tyler stores the other one in the digital video archive at the cemetery "forever." All of the Forever Network cemeteries throughout California and the Midwest are wired with touch-screen video kiosks and theaters connected to the reels of digital archives.

Tyler came from a family in the funeral industry, yet he never considered the family business until death hunted him after he left home in St. Louis, Missouri, to go to Columbia University in New York. He reached New York City at the height of the AIDS epidemic. He came out as a gay man when every young man in New York was asking himself, "Am I dying? Will I die?" For a young gay man living in New York City in the early 1990s, he remembered reading that he had a 50 percent chance of surviving AIDS. His idea for reinventing the twentieth-century funeral arose from the unconventional ways gay men memorialized their loved ones after death. Some of his friends supplanted the outdated funeral with a last request from the departed for friends to go out and celebrate his life at his favorite nightclub or Broadway show. Just as he embraced the gay life, he was immersed in the gay way of death. Ultimately his experiences led to his rethinking the modern-day cemetery practices. Hollywood Forever Cemetery became the incubation lab for his ideas.

In Hollywood, people are eager to weave their faces and footprints into the luster of Tinsel Town. Young aspiring stars from every small town across America come to Hollywood to make it big, walk the red carpet, and receive a standing ovation at the Academy Awards. Those wishing to remain in Hollywood forever even after their deaths, search for the same impression on the surface of the earth with their headstones and monuments. Tyler encourages his future occupants to integrate their individuality and personality when designing their monuments because one day in the not-too-distant future the cemetery will no longer be able to accept new occupants and the grounds will become a historical art museum.

Hollywood Forever is certainly not the only way to preserve your personal history and funerary directives. In Hollywood, a funeral planner is helping healthy people touch the untouchable.

PLANNING YOUR PERSONAL TRIBUTE

Lynn Isenberg, a.k.a. the Funeral Planner, helps the healthy envision their own death with three questions:

"How do you want to be remembered?"

"What do you want to happen at your end-of-life celebration?"

"If you have the option, do want to participate in the celebration of your life?"

The questions spark introspective wonderment, says the forty-something Hollywood scriptwriter. She designs personalized tributes and produces movies that portray a person's biography to premiere on the silver screen at these events. In the twenty-first century, when *Time* magazine chooses to name the Person of the Year "YOU," lionizing your life like we immortalize Hollywood's glitterati and heads of state is not a hard sell. There are a growing number of people starting this process of producing their life tributes before they reach death's doorstep, and a new kind of funeral planner leads the way. Many of Lynn's clients are healthy baby boomers whose search for a way to create an end-of-life plan that preserves their life is sparked by the loss of their parents.

As a funeral planner, Lynn doesn't supplant the funeral director, but instead enhances the process of planning your own funeral. A funeral director handles the body disposal and the delicate rituals of grief surrounding your death—but what about the after-party, the celebration? Lynn had never heard of a funeral planner when she spoke at her father's funeral in 1998 and her brother's funeral in 1999.

The flash of genius came when Lynn sat in the audience of her brother's funeral. A professional singer performing a cappella, planned by her brother before his death to be given as a gift to all those who came to honor his life, surprised her. The stark difference between her father's traditional funeral and this performance left a searing impression. The song exemplified her brother's soaring spirit far better than the canned eulogy given by a clergyperson. A cousin at the funeral confirmed her thoughts when she said, "I wish I'd brought my son. He would have enjoyed this."

Lynn imagined people actually planning their funerals as personalized celebrations their loved ones would enjoy and remember rather than just endure.

The performance inspired her novel *The Funeral Planner* about a young woman, Madison Banks, attending business school and designing Lights Out, a company that coordinates end-of-life celebrations. In researching the book, Lynn audited business classes at Michigan University and learned that Lights Out would capitalize on two upward trends in the multibillion-dollar funeral business—personalization and pre-need services. Lynn realized, as does her protagonist, that there is no one person or company that offers this service. In the book, she fills the void. For the generous real estate developer and golf enthusiast, she suggests a nine-hole golf game at midnight for a hundred of his closest friends and family, including a ninth-hole tee-off that encourages everyone to launch glow-in-the dark balls to light up the night sky followed by a live orchestra playing his most beloved symphonies and his bio-video projected on a wall at the golf course. For the animal rights activist, she suggested a life celebration at the zoo and memories of him shared at every exhibit. For the disco lover, she planned a disco party on her favorite mountaintop, where her ashes would be scattered and all the guests would come dressed in their dazzling dancing threads.

As Lynn began discussing her novel at cocktail and dinner parties with friends, she noticed an unusually high curiosity in the subject. After her book launched, she followed the footsteps of her protagonist, Maddy, and opened Lights Out Enterprises in 2006. One afternoon, shortly following the launch, she was walking her dog, Tao, at the dog park in Venice Beach when she met up with her real estate agent, Jack Susser. She told him about Lights Out.

PRODUCING A TRIBUTE MOVIE

The idea of producing a tribute movie instantly intrigued him. Jack is a youthful fifty-seven-year-old and former theater teacher for the Los Angeles School District. He studied acting with some of the famous coaches in Hollywood. Although many of the heavyweights in Hollywood gave him the green light, encouraging him to pursue a career in acting, he put on the brakes to start a family. At first glance, one can tell his naturally rosy cheeks, aqua eyes, and magnetic personality belong on the screen.

Lynn asked him, "How do you want to be remembered?"

He'd never really contemplated his own death, but spent nearly half his life worried about his father's demise. Moses Susser, Jack's father, fell victim to a heart attack in Jack's first year studying theater at Cal State Northridge. Despite grim diagnoses and warnings from the doctors to slow down, Moses refused to taper his lifestyle, often saying, "If I can't dance, I can't live." He never let the aftermath heart attacks dampen his busy life in real estate. For thirty years, each time a heart attack hit, Jack dropped everything to go to Moses' bedside, prepare for the worse, and say his good-byes. Every time, his father left the deathbed and returned home to resume his active life. In 2000, at eighty-three years old, another heart attack put Moses in hospital. Assuming it was just a minor tremor and his father would be home in a couple of days, Jack set sail for a weekend on Catalina Island. On that Sunday, a relapse swept the life out of Moses.

Two years later, Jack started seeing a psychologist because he couldn't shake his father's passing. The countless times Moses beat death had fabricated a Peter Pan–like syndrome in Jack. His father's last breath awakened Jack to the loud ticking clock on his life. As he started to grow old, lose his hair, grow thick around his waist and other places, he felt uncomfortable in his aging shell. His mother's progressing Alzheimer's disease didn't help. She eventually moved in with him. Death suddenly felt closer and too familiar.

Contemplating a tribute film felt wildly refreshing, and enlightening. When Jack told his wife about possibly working on a "based on truth" movie about his life, she dissuaded him, feeling as though they might be preempting his death. Eventually her fears dissipated with his enthusiasm. Lynn wrote a comedy screenplay that included some Hollywood talent, animation, and, most important, Jack in the leading role. Together, Jack and his wife collaborated with Lynn to produce and act in his movie, entitled *Jack the Mench*.

At the beginning of the second half of his life, Jack lived a dream he'd left behind in the first. He studied his lines and prepared to act in his own live-action Hollywood film, written for and about him. During the filming, his wife, seeing his spirit grow brighter, suggested he leave the family business to his daughter and take up a second career in acting. All of those years of acting classes and having majored in theater suddenly didn't feel in vain. *Jack the Mench* would be his legacy to leave to his children, grandchildren, and great-grandchildren.

The short film starred Jack, a guy who meets God, and is sent on a mission to elevate the morals and values of people on Earth, similar to a modern-day Moses, a cross between *It's a Wonderful Life* and *A Fish Called Wanda*. *Mensch* (as it is properly spelled) is a Yiddish word that describes an upright, decent, admirable human being. *Jack the Mench* is a comedy. God is a talking fish that Jack meets when scuba diving in the ocean. There's a moment in the movie when Jack questions why God chose him for this mission, and there are beautifully illustrated reflections of Jack and his wife scuba diving together and exchanging their vows beneath the sea, followed by reflections from his daughter complemented by eight-millimeter footage and pictures of him as a young, doting father. The film seamlessly blends real photos, video, and interviews into a comedic short.

When they completed the short, Jack sees and realizes another dream of viewing himself on the silver screen and acting in front of audiences when they travel to film festivals. He loves watching people laugh and enjoy a film about his life. He knows one day they'll be watching this movie when he's gone, but for now he plans to play it at his next milestone birthday celebration the big six-oh. The budget for the film, the trailer, and the priceless credit "starring Jack Susser" rounded off to just over $75,000, a small budget by Hollywood standards. Jack's final wishes for an end-of-life celebration include the film being played on a cruise ship carrying his closest friends and family to his favorite dive spots in the world. The memorial gift will be a scuba mask or snorkel inscribed with his name.

Lynn is the first to admit her custom end-of-life services are still a novelty, and she has yet to carry out the final plans of any of her clients, but she has a file cabinet storing these special plans for when the time comes. People in need of inspiration when it comes to designing an end-of-life plan and party have drawn on her expertise and her collection of grief wellness and grief tributes books. She was even an invited guest speaker at the annual National Funeral Directors Convention. That invitation alone speaks volumes about the real shift in consciousness in the funeral industry toward accepting the personalization of the rote funeral ritual, technological innovations, and the movement toward celebrating life.

PROTECTING YOUR END-OF-LIFE PLAN

After spending time with Lynn in "introspective wonderment," I wondered how people could transmit last wishes without spending thousands on a funeral planner and a tribute movie. The Funeral Consumers Alliance, a national organization "dedicated to protecting the consumer's right to chose a meaningful, dignified, and affordable funeral," advocates that every person should pre-plan, but not pre-pay. From the Funeral Consumers Alliance website, I ordered a do-it-yourself funeral planning kit. The kit, Before I Go, You Should Know—Funeral Planning, has a twenty-page booklet to help you make final plans, covering a range of topics, from a living will and an advanced medical directive to wishes on body care and mode of interment to choosing songs to play and poems to recite at the memorial service or funeral. The booklet has dozens of questions that guide an individual on an in-depth tour of funeral planning, which ultimately means the family is relieved of the burdens of guesswork. There's a section for writing down details regarding matters of life insurance, a will and living trust, bank account numbers, location of safe deposit box and key, online/email passwords, "When I'm Gone" instructions, and last words for family and friends. The FCA recommends storing the kit in the freezer with the supplied magnet on the front indicating the contents inside. This is a concrete way to ensure your beloveds receive your final plans.

In the twenty-first century digital age, how we envision our final plans and for that matter how we store and transmit these last wishes is constantly shifting with new technological platforms. Today, our important documents regarding a will, estate, and funerary plans could also be stored in an online safe deposit box. The documents are encrypted when uploaded to the website for security. You're able to write last emails, with photos and videos attached, to be posthumously sent to family and friends. You pay an annual subscription. You're given an encrypted key that your family member must provide with a death certificate to activate the account. I had already written a last email to my family members that detailed my final plans for my death, then after talking to Lynn, I added the details about my life celebration.

MEMORIALIZING IN THE DIGITAL AGE

The Internet has also birthed new mourning and memorializing rituals that dissolve geographical boundaries that once limited us. Digital memorialization is the process of preserving and paying tribute to a life using biographical digital images and video to transmit a life story. Lynn directed me to the social networking website called Ourstory.com that offers a free online tool to organize your life stories complemented by pictures and video into an animated timeline and published in a book that can be displayed on the memorial table at funeral. I intended to create a timeline of my mother's life, but realized I had few digitized photos. Instead I started a timeline of my trip around the world. I typed in some travel journal entries with pictures, then presto! Like magic I watched a timeline of my life events float across the screen.

To design a timeline of my mother, I started scanning in the pictures of the biographical memorial collage that we displayed at her memorial service. While digitizing the photos, I came across a perfectly timed article in *The New Yorker* entitled "Remember This?" that profiled Gordon Bell, a seventy-two-year-old researcher at Microsoft and early architect of networking supercomputers, now called the Internet, engaged in a life-logging experiment. For nearly three years, he's recorded every interaction, transaction, conversation, thought, and emotion while tracking the location, date, and time using a SenseCam, a small camera worn around his neck that passively takes pictures without user intervention. He clicks on a digital recorder to collect his thoughts and conversations. In 1998, he created a digital archive of his life by scanning every piece of paper and artifact collected, including the papers in his file cabinets, memos, books in his library, books he's authored, his collection of family photo albums, and home movies. In an article titled "A Digital Life," written by Bell and his partner, Jim Gemmel said, "Perhaps most important, digital memories can enable all people to tell their life stories to their descendants in a compelling, detailed fashion that until now has been reserved solely for the rich and famous."

Life logging, the act of digitizing the human memory, is a radical solution to losing a life story like my father's. Yet the tedious task of digitizing our family photo albums to produce an honorable timeline for my parents at Ourstory.com seemed too time consuming. I sought out other legacy and memorial social networking sites. I found several destinations with thousands of pages specifically dedicated to the dead. Survivors design tributes for their loved ones by uploading pictures in a slideshow to music, video, and/or a written biography with added features such as timelines and family trees. Each page connected entire communities of mourners.

We've become accustomed to stay in touch with people over the Web, so it's not a far leap to memorialize and connect to the departed online. When someone dies in the social networking community, his or her personal page on such websites as Myspace.com and Facebook.com is eerily frozen in time and becomes an online memorial where friends leave messages to the recently deceased, such as "How's it going in heaven? We really miss you down here." The sites are also places where intimates can leave heartfelt condolences to the family.

At some online memorial sites, you can erect a virtual headstone, light a candle, or leave virtual flowers for the deceased. These meditative places allow users to commune with the dead and other mourners from the comfort of a home computer. Some messages I saw said, "I'm thinking about you today, every day, every second . . . stay close so I can feel you." There were many heartfelt messages from a mom to her child saying, "I love you . . . I can't wait to see you again! xoxo" and "Happy

Birthday" and so on. The operators of these websites note that traffic is highest in the morning and the evening when survivors start and finish their day with thoughts and reflections of their departed. Some sites are free; others require a membership fee.

I erected two online memorials for my parents that required a photo and written biography. I found myself returning to their memorial sites to leave memories in the following days and weeks. After a month, the sites felt ephemeral, which fueled a deeper desire to produce a true biography documenting their lives to pass on to their next generations.

I visited Hollywood Forever Cemetery to get some professional advice. I met biographer and film director Jay Gianukos at Forever Studios to discuss the process of producing a personal history documentary post-death instead of pre-death, like he did for Orin and Bernardo. I wanted to synthesize the home videos, volumes of photo albums, and audio recordings of my mother. The process of digitizing an entire library of home videos and photo albums to carve out a movie would cost upward of $3,000 if a professional filmmaker did the work. If you add live-action film shoots, like interviews with family members, the price increases. I began to rethink investing the money in a professional like Jay to produce a documentary over the course of four to six weeks. I was beginning to think that I might instead invest my time in a do-it-yourself biography.

Jay sealed my fate during our meeting when he turned from his usual jovial nature to a more serious tone.

"Denise," he said to me, "making the documentary will lead us to the truth about your mother's life."

His words resonated with me. Although I wasn't a professional documentary filmmaker like Jay, I felt compelled to take the solo journey of biographer that would lead me to the "truth" about my parents' lives.

THIRTEEN Her Truth: Finding Life
after Death

In the spring of 2006, I instinctively returned to the place where my grief began to start a new life, like a sea turtle returning to her birthplace, the very same beach, to give birth. Nineteen years ago, a wooden cross washed up on this beach in Hanalei Bay, Kauai, the day my father died. I was twelve years old then. Now I'm thirty. I asked Simon to return to this paradise with me. Just as I remembered, majestic mountains covered in rain forest and cliffs gushing with waterfalls surrounded the pristine crescent-moon sandy beach. Gray rain clouds brimmed in the bay all weekend. I silently asked a special request of my mother to pull some weather strings; the sunshine would let me know she and my father shone with me in spirit.

Since adolescence I had dreaded instead of dreamed of my wedding day. Who would walk me down the aisle? I'd resigned myself to never experiencing this rite of passage because I belonged to no man. The ceremony wasn't the typical dream wedding you read about in *Bride*, but for me the ritual honored a vow to renew. I skipped the white gown because on my first shopping trip, I found myself eavesdropping on and missing mother/daughter conversations in the dressing rooms. Instead, I picked out a simple sundress online.

In that white strapless dress, barefoot, I walked along the beach without an aisle. I learned from my sources in researching this book that a rite of passage could be reinvented and personalized while preserving the magic of crossing a threshold to something new. I found the perfect spot to get married as the sun came out from the gray clouds and rays of light danced across the ocean surface crowning the spot in a ring of sunlight. We stood beneath a tree in a lei of fragrant plumerias, my favorite flowers. I placed a lei around Simon's neck and whispered in his ear.

"Now onto the better in 'For better or worse.'"

The minister initiated the ceremony by asking, "Who gives this woman away?"

A man's voice cleared his throat behind us.

"I do," said my twenty-four-year-old brother, Ryan.

At that moment, I turned to my brother and the warm sun's rays hugged me. I knew we'd be okay without my parents. We remained a close family, the three of us, just as we promised Mom. The minister recalled the story of Simon bending down at Mom's bedside to ask for my hand in marriage. Ryan pulled the rings from his pocket and placed them in Simon's hand. Simon and I turned to face each other. I placed the ring on Simon's finger and said the traditional vows. Then he placed the ring on my finger and promised "to love me in sickness and in health, till death do us part."

Just as we stepped beneath the awning of the hotel, the gray clouds released the rain. Not one raindrop fell on my head. I looked at my hand folded in Simon's and smiled. "It was perfect," he said, then he looked up at the sky and gave thanks to "the invisible hands." It's not so bad having your parents bless your wedding in spirit. It made the day heavenly.

After the wedding, Simon and I moved to the west side of Los Angeles. We felt a cyclical pull to return to Marina del Rey, where we nurtured the first bonds that held us together to start our life as husband and wife.

As my mother's personal effects disappeared from my life, a growing urge to preserve her consumed me. I began shuffling through a folder entitled Mom Movies on my computer. She never seemed too far with her smile, voice, and laugh just a click of a mouse away. I watched a clip of Mom and me laughing until tears streamed down our cheeks on a road trip to Carmel. I particularly loved the interview clips of her talking candidly about her life in England and recalling our weekend trips to the tide pools.

The clips on my hard drive were strikingly similar to my mind full of memories—no organization or story line. I wanted the whole story, not just clips, family photo albums, or a life review interview, but instead a biography that integrated all of these pieces that I could pass on to my children, her grandchildren. I clicked through the interviews searching for the interview about my father's life.

Deflated, I knew Mom's memories alone couldn't produce a solid biography of him. I had less than a skeleton of his life. The day we buried my father's body, we also buried his life stories. I don't even know where in the Philippines he was born. I have a photo album of his life before America, but the images are void of a story. I know he put the album together, but you know how they say a picture is worth a thousand words. In this case, I just wanted a few words that would describe his early life growing up in the Philippines and what inspired him to move to America. Maybe some of my father's cousins or his brother could answer these questions, but I hadn't seen them since his funeral.

I paused the video on my computer and clicked on a desktop folder entitled Wedding. I sent out a note to friends and family with pictures announcing the wedding. My father's widow, Brenda, returned an email of congratulations. I asked her to meet with me for an interview. A few weeks later, I visited her home in Upland, about thirty miles east of Los Angeles. We sipped lemonade in the June sun and talked about my father's last year. She wiped away tears from her eyes and tried to turn the mood of our conversation, asking if I recalled any of the weekends by the pool swimming and barbecuing with Dad. I laughed nervously, realizing my memories of his death story overshadowed his life story. She disappeared into her garage and returned with a box full of pictures of Dad. It was a treasure chest.

"Take anything you wish," she said.

I pored over photos and a few memories trickled in, but my well of memories felt dry. I found a VHS tape entitled "Richard and Brenda's Wedding." I ended up taking the box home. Before I left, Brenda hugged me.

"I know you lost so much, Denise," she said. "Do you ever think about having a child?"

"No, I'm not planning on it," I said.

"I believe a child will make you whole again and give you all the love and affection you've desperately missed since your dad died," she said.

"Thank you for your honesty and all of these treasures," I said as I lifted up the box.

I was one step closer to rediscovering my father's life. I knew producing a biography about Mom would be challenging—adding Dad's life was nearly impossible. I heard Jay's voice in my head reminding me that producing this biography would lead me to the "truth" about my parents' lives. I found encouragement as my weary eyes slid down stacks of videotapes and photo albums that I would have to review, digitize, and then shape into a story. Admittedly the task was intimidating enough to prevent me from starting a formal journalistic search of my father's family. I taught myself how to use iMovie, a software program on my Mac computer that helps me turn my home videos and photos into professionally polished documentaries. It's software for amateurs along the lines of Final Cut Pro, which Hollywood professionals use. I was instantly attracted to how technology gave me a tool, a platform to sift through the scrambled memories.

I spent days, weeks, and months importing VHS tapes, Super-eight millimeter videotapes, and flipping through photo albums picking out pictures to complement the stories Mom shared in our interviews.

One idle afternoon in the summer of 2007, I was immersed in some interview video clips on my laptop in my home office when I received an email from my father's cousin, Tim Cuellar, sent via OurStory.com.

Dear Denise,
I don't know how to start so here goes . . . I searched your name and
found your OurStory. I hope this doesn't come as too much of a shock
for you. I feel compelled to reach out to you and being in Pasadena, CA
working may give me an opportunity to visit with you if you like. You
may recognize my name. I am your father's first cousin . . . Your grandmother, Mae, and my mom, Peggy (Auntie Peggy, remember?) are
sisters. Your dad lived with us in Des Moines, IA when he emigrated . . . .
I would like the opportunity to talk to you if you want. Send me an
email or call . . . —Tim

Without hesitation, I dialed his digits. After a few phone calls, we arranged to meet at my home and then visit my father's resting place in
San Bernardino. He gave me a Beatles CD because he remembered that
Dad loved the Beatles and listened to their albums repeatedly in Tim's
basement in Des Moines. He reflected on how Dad strove to emulate
everything American. We looked at old pictures. Tim drew a family tree
for my paternal grandmother's side of the family. After lunch, we started
the hundred-mile road trip to the cemetery, but failed to make it before
the gates closed at sundown. We agreed to meet again on July 22, the anniversary of my father's death.

July 13, the weekend before, I visited my childhood friend, Gina Betancourt, now Calderone. She'd become a physical therapist. In her practice, she witnessed a link between physical ailments and emotional
wounds. That afternoon at her home in Long Beach, we discussed how
grief, an emotional wound, harbored in the body could manifest into
unexpected problems such as cancer later on in life. Grief has traditionally been viewed through a prism of psychological coping mechanisms
without much attention or research on how to deal with the physical
manifestation of grief.

She knew I'd traveled a long road to redemption and recovery, but
sensed I still held on to my father physically in a way that I'd already
released my mother. As we talked, an epiphany dawned. Since Dad's
death, I felt like my body laid in a coma, completely shut off. She asked
me to get comfortable on the couch and then close my eyes. Gina guided
me through an internal body scan. She asked me to describe how I felt in

my head, between my ears, in my chest, and so on, all the way down to my feet. It was like going through the tunnel of a CAT scan machine, but instead of a computer scanning my body, I reported levels of pain, and pressure. For the first time, I clocked my breathing and noticed places of discomfort that I'd previously ignored. My knees hurt and I could feel tension in my female organs. At the end, she asked me to open my eyes. I could *feel* my body talking to my mind and the over-stimulation gave me a headache.

She asked me why I felt cut off from my body for so many years. I remembered the instance when I shut down. On the first anniversary of Dad's death, I fell to my bedroom floor writhing and silently sobbing in the fetal position. Until that moment, I'd erased the memory. I looked up at her and said the words I felt that day: "I miss his hug." I've searched and never found the unconditional hug of my father in any man, not even my husband. As a survival mechanism, I suppressed the pain stemming from the physical detachment. She turned from an empathic friend into a straight-talking physical therapist.

"You will never find this hug or that love again," she said. "You have to let him go because he is blocking you from having your own family." She suggested that I'd been stubborn and inflexible in holding onto the old, the past. "You need to release the old and welcome the new."

I arose the following Sunday, July 22, 2007. I met Tim for breakfast in Pasadena and then we picked up Ryan, my brother, and drove out to San Bernardino. Tim entertained us with the Beatles CDs and silly Richard Carson stories on the two-hour drive. He talked about how my father loved to cook and always dreamed of one day opening his own restaurant. Ryan found many similarities to himself in the details and stories shared about his father. As we approached the cemetery, Tim pointed out St. Bernardine's Hospital, where my father worked for most of his adult life before opening his own business. I remembered being a little girl holding my father's hand walking into the automatic doors of the hospital, him in his suit and me so proud to be with a celebrity. Everyone in the hospital knew him. I was five or six. He took me to work on my days off from school. And a flood of memories that I'd closed off for so many years filled me. I turned to Tim.

"I didn't realize the hospital was across the street from the cemetery," I said.

We drove through the iron gates and serendipitously the song "Yesterday" filled the car and our minds, plagued with memories of our last visit. We all remembered he rested beneath an oak tree toward the back of the cemetery. I switched on the video camera remembering that the camera will turn an otherwise introspective moment into a shared experience. We failed to find the Richard Carson plot, but as we racked our memories, other reflections from his funeral rose. Tim remembered carrying the heavy mahogany casket on the sweltering day. Ryan remembered Mom yelling at him not to step on the graves. Then Ryan turned to me, remembering the day we came to grave after the headstone etched with a picture of my father and Brenda was set.

"Do you remember placing the grass on Brenda's face?" Ryan asked.

"Wow, for a five-year-old that must have really left an impression on you," I said.

We drove back to the cemetery office. Tim asked the lady at the counter for "Richard Carson's plot." She pulled out a map of the cemetery and marked the spot. We took it as if it were a treasure map and started across the cemetery. As I approached the oak tree that shaded us at his funeral, my eyes fell on his headstone. I read the inscribed word "Carson" above an open book with one page dedicated to Richard, August 18, 1949 – July 22, 1987. I collapsed. Crumpled on the ground, I caressed the picture of my father and a rush of tears burst like a hot geyser from deep in my core. I couldn't see any more. My sobs turned to snot-filled clogged-up wails. I felt like a twelve-year-old crying uncontrollably missing my daddy. I wanted to claw the manicured grass, dig into the soil, and lift out my father. For the first time in my life, I wailed loudly for the loss of my father and our family.

I'd spent most of my life despising Dad, stuck underground so far from my home, but now I understood it was a part of a triangle of places that housed his spirit for many living years. He spent hours working in the hospital across the street and at his business, Carson Medical Management, around the corner, and now for twenty years, his final remains lay right here beneath this ground. It no longer felt like a wasteland, but instead like sacred ground. As the wailing turned to soft sobs, I let go of my daddy, not intellectually, not emotionally, but physically. I could feel the heavy lead lifting from my body as I rubbed my snotty nose on my sleeve, an action my father would have yelled at me for if he could. I could even hear in my mind his voice say, "Denise, use tissue." I answered him in my mind, "There's no tissue, Dad. Cut me some slack."

It took me twenty years to finally terminate my fear of forgetting him and allow him to become a spiritual part of my life. I intuitively under-stood the importance of the cemetery visits in the first few years after a loved one dies. I needed to have a physical place for him in my life. In those cemetery visits, I would have allowed my father's physical pres-ence to transcend to a spiritual one. Instead, he remained a physical defi-cit. These rituals oftentimes seem unnecessary in our modern thinking, where we believe the spirit is no longer a part of the body, but it takes time to physically assimilate.

I asked Tim to start us in prayer. I lifted myself up so that we could hold hands and encircle the grave. Tim held me tight in a fatherly hug. After the prayer, my brother knelt down and placed grass over Brenda's face on the headstone portrait. I hugged my brother, and we laughed.

"Ryan has a similar portrait of my dad on his back," I said to Tim. Ryan lifted up his shirt to reveal a permanent memorial to my parents on his back. Shortly after my mother died, Ryan started to memorialize our parents in ink like me—except instead of on paper, his was on his skin.

"I never needed to visit my dad here or my mom in the cemetery be-cause they're always with me," he said.

Tim was awed. He stared at the black and gray fine-line and intri-cately shaded portrait of Dad with that captivating smile inked onto Ryan's back behind his left shoulder and a beautiful ethereal portrait of Mom smiling behind his right.

"They're watching over me," Ryan said.

"Yes, they sure are, Ryan," Tim said.

Scrawled above Dad is the prayer "Give me Strength" and above Mom is another prayer, "Teach me Love."

"I put them on my skin so I could let go, but never forget them," he said.

On his chest was a portrait of the Madonna holding the baby Jesus with the words above "A Mother's Love." Ryan wrote a poem called "Fallen" that he also intends to ink on his back. I asked him to share some of the lines.

> Born to this world I suffer alive
> The more I suffer I learn to survive
> A knife in my back from the first of June
> The ones you love always leave here too soon
> Two souls in my heart, two loves that were slain
> I'd give anything to see them again . . .

Ryan lifted up his arms and turned 180 degrees. He showed us his right arm permanently marked with two black armbands wrapped around his lower bicep. I commented on how in the Victorian era mourners wore black cloth armbands while observing their grief.

"It's a display of pain," Ryan said of all the tattoos. He shrugged. "It's kind of my life story."

Although his shirt was off, his back, arms, and chest looked like walls of a museum in the midday sun. All of his eighteen tattoos were designed by the famous tattooist Kat Von D, a clever young woman with her own hit reality television show called *LA Ink*. They're the same age. In 2002, he sought out the best local artist to ink Mom and Dad. She had a reputation for her black and gray memorial portraits, which shortly after catapulted her to television when she appeared as a featured artist on the hit reality show *Miami Ink*. Although tattoos have been around since time immemorial, memorial tattoos have been on an upward trend since the turn of the twentieth-first century in America, most notably among my brother's generation. Yet tattoo artists today are finding people of all ages using ink to honor their departed. It's another way people are reinventing mourning rituals to publicly and privately memorialize. Even I had a symbolic memorial tattoo inked on my back.

It's of two dolphins making a circle on my lower back. The purple dolphin represents my mother and the aqua dolphin represents my father in the endless circle of life. I think my brother, like me, suffers from the same visceral need to protect and preserve our family's memory.

The pain welling inside him eventually excreted on his skin. When people ask him about his tattoos, he's able to tell our parents' stories, express his grief, which as a young man he finds difficult. As I gazed upon his back, I realized that he sought a sense of permanence in what felt like an impermanent existence. The three of us walked arm and arm back to the car. Tim drove us to Dad's former office around the corner.

"First he started in that corner office," Tim said. "Then he moved to that one next to it, then the business expanded to the whole upstairs. We took over the whole building. His business exploded in a year. Wow, he was really at the top of his game."

I piped in. "I remember my dad would sit me in his big black executive leather chair and say, 'One day, Denise will be president of this company, so you all better treat her well now.'"

I remembered him taking me into a room packed from floor to ceiling with a machine whirring and blinking with red lights. He said it was a computer.

"He warned me that the computer ran his entire business. He pointed to a button. 'If you ever hit this button, you will shut down my whole business. So never touch this button.'"

We laughed. It was great to touch happy memories of Dad. I no longer felt tormented by the past, but rather enchanted. As we drove out of the parking lot, I was no longer listening to Tim's stories to try and remember my father. I could finally tell my own.

Still there were many gaps that left Dad's whole life a blur. Tim volunteered to contact some of my father's first cousins. The following week, I received an email invitation to sign up for Myfamily.com, a social networking website that united the entire family from Canada to Hong Kong. He set up the site with a view to getting everyone together for a family reunion in July 2009. On the site was every number and email address I needed, but before I could reach out, I received an email from my father's cousin Mattias San Andres.

Hi Denise Grace,
Hello and how are you? . . . I am your uncle Matt from Canada . . . I believe, the last time I saw you was in 1986 when I visited your late dad Richard in La Verne, California and again in July 1987. How is your

mom Linda and brother Ryan? Are you still living in California? May I ask how old are your children? . . .

God bless you and take care,
Uncle Matt

Our emails turned more emotional as we traded pictures and memories of my father. He expressed such happiness for finally finding me and reconnecting. Matt sent a tattered sepia photograph of my father at three years old sitting among his cousins and his brother. Matt was six months older than my father, and they were like inseparable twins growing up in the Philippines. I shared the news of losing Mom and the blessing of saving her life story. Matt said that since our reunion, he'd been engulfed with memories of his childhood and young adulthood spent with my father. I returned an email saying I'd be a captive audience.

On an idle afternoon on the last Saturday in July, I rattled on about my progress of rediscovering my father and my parents' documentary, while Simon and I dined on the back of our sailboat. Simon looked pensive.

"I think we should have a baby," he said.

"Wow, okay," I said. A bit shocked, but happy. He'd seen a transformation in me. I'd lowered the physical barriers erected after Dad's death. As a result, the intimacy between us deepened.

I visited the doctor for my yearly examine, which differs from most women my age. I have an ultrasound on my ovaries.

This time I asked the ultrasound tech, "What are you looking for?"

"Any changes in the ovaries," she said.

"Well, the cancer you're looking for, the cancer my mom had, was like fine grains of sand. Could you see sand on your ultrasound?"

"No," she said.

I told my doctor about a recent discussion with my husband about getting pregnant. She understood my concerns and ordered a CA-125, a more advanced cancer-screening test that counts the cancer cell activity in my body. A nurse took my blood. I'd receive the results in a week.

A couple days later, I clicked open an email from my father's cousin Matt and inside was an attachment entitled "Memoirs of Richard."

I gasped as eight pages of single-spaced text sharing my father's early history unfolded. I drank in every word, detail, and memory like they were gulps of water after walking through the desert. The story began with my grandfather James Leo Carson landing in the southern part of the Philippines with the American troops commanded by General Douglas MacArthur during the last stages of World War II to liberate the Filipino people from the Japanese regime. After the war, he married Naomi Basconcillo and gave birth to my father in a small town called Villasis, near Rosalas, the town my father grew up in. Thrilled to have finally learned the name of my father's birthplace, I plugged the towns into Google and found a map with the name of the river Agno my mother spoke about. Mom and Matt shared the same story of Dad jumping into the river to save a drowning piglet during a storm. Matt's memoirs were reminiscent of the Kite Runner, a story of two boys growing up together in Kabul—except these two boys' adventures happened to be in the Philippines. I imagined my father as a boy using a slingshot to shoot down mangoes from the fruit tree by the stem with such accuracy that he never bruised a fruit and courageously climbing toward the clouds up a palm tree to pick coconuts. I laughed out loud reading of how they caught spiders, kept them for days in boxes, and then let them out to have spider fights. Dad and Matt made wooden sabers to play Zorro the Masked Avenger. They also carved wooden guns and switched off playing the Lone Ranger and Tonto.

At ten years old, Dad left the province to reside in Manila, where my grandfather could be treated for tuberculosis at Veteran's Memorial Hospital. At a young age, he exhibited early entrepreneurial skill. His first business was collecting golf balls on the military base golf course and then selling the balls to golfers.

Two years after their move to Manila, his father died. His mother stayed in the city, connected to the military base, rather than return to her family in the province. Her decision enabled Dad to get a high school education. He spoke three languages, English, Tagalog, and Ilacano, a dialect of the province he grew up in.

As the boyhood stories turned to teenager tales, I recognized the man who became my father. He and Matt used to go to the movie theater on the American military base because Dad could get them in for free. His charisma and light skin attracted the girls, who called him Americano. He won dance contests and stood out in the crowd. Dad changed girls like he changed his clothes. Ringo Starr, Richard Starkey, of the Beatles was Dad's hero, inspiring him to change his middle name to Starkey. My father left the Philippines with the help of an American missionary, who sorted out a visa for him to move to America. His dual citizenship fast-tracked his American visa.

I flipped through the photo album of Dad in the Philippines. Sensory-rich stories filled the once silent void. I pulled out a small walnut box where I saved Dad's personal effects. I shuffled through the photos he shot on his last trip to the Philippines, six months before he died. I found a picture of a boy climbing a coconut tree and a picture of his father's sarcophagus that I now knew lay in Villasis. I discovered Dad made a pilgrimage to his birthplace. In Matt's memoirs, he spoke about his last conversation by telephone to his cousin Richard. He quoted him as saying, "Your health is your wealth; material things mean nothing if you cannot share and enjoy it with someone." I found comfort in discovering Dad might have taken some time for reflection on his deathbed.

My wish for birthing a biography of my parents now felt possible. I sat down and sketched out the scenes of the documentary. I would use mostly Beatles music as the soundtrack. I planned to open the biography with some eight-millimeter video footage my mother transferred to VHS as a gift to me on my eighteenth birthday. I found it among the collection VHS tapes I'd been digitizing in iMovie. It was titled "Denise." I played the tape of my parents' bringing me home from the hospital and cuddling me in my first weeks of life. For the first time, I witnessed the illuminating love between my parents that created me.

A week later the cancer-screening test came back. I'd lived in the shadow of cancer for years. The cancer-free news gave me a new lease on life.

On the eve of Thanksgiving, I took a pregnancy test. A big bold blue + appeared in the window. I rubbed my eyes as if it couldn't be and checked the directions to make sure the plus sign meant positive. I could hear Simon in the bedroom.

"What's the result?"

"It's positive."

We met at the doorway.

"We're having a baby!" he cried.

"Yes, we're having a baby!" I squealed.

I threw myself into his arms and received the best unconditional love hug on record. He lifted me off the bathroom floor and squeezed me tight.

"We're going to have a family of our own!" I cried with utter joy.

The biography now turned from a visceral to a familial mission. I had a real audience, their grandchild, who would watch and learn about his or her maternal grandparents. Illuminated in the quiet of my home office, I walked back in time, transported to my parents' first home and the blissful days of my babyhood. I watched videos of our first Christmases, my first crawl, steps, and laugh. I saw pure joy on my parents' faces, and their body language toward each other exuded love. As their biographer, I heard a conversation rise out of the video. It wasn't a conversation that we're accustomed to, but instead communication delivered to me through their body language depicted in the videos and photos. They raised me to be an individual, a survivor. Even at a young age, I saw an air of independence and confidence in me nurtured through their unconditional love.

I felt the first flutters of my baby moving inside while incubating this biography. Strangely, as I physically created the baby, I felt a deeper connection to my parents. In their own way, my parents prepared me for motherhood. I heard their parental advice that the best home I could give to my child was not made out of bricks and mortar, but instead out of the parents' love for each other. I don't think my parents could have told me this if they were alive because they would have been at a different point in their lives—divorced.

I joined my parents through the videos and pictures on their first landings in America's Midwest and sat in the back seat of their cars on Route 66 as they drove separately but within a year of one another across America to chase their California dreams. I selected an evocative track for this journey, "California Dreaming," by the Mamas and the

Papas. My unborn child eavesdropped on the recorded conversations between Grandma and me. An overwhelming sense of abundance replaced the once burning void. I played my father's wedding video over and over to hear his laugh, see him dance, but found few recordings of his voice. I also had a VHS entitled "Richard" given to me by my father's friends at his funeral. It captured the funny faces that he often made at the dinner table or across a crowded room or behind my mother's back to make me laugh, but no voice. As I edited the eight-millimeter silent film in iMovie and watched him kissing me and talking to me, I could suddenly hear his voice with a slight broken accent in my mind. The video allowed me to access memories tucked away in the farthest recesses of my brain.

In spring 2008, Jane Herges, my childhood friend, and her mother, Buffy Daignault, threw me a baby shower in Buffy's home, where I had spent many weekends as a child. Buffy suggested that I contact my mother's friends. In the invitation, she wrote "In Honor of Linda Carson." The shower turned into a reunion with all of the women my mother loved in her life. I hadn't seen many of these women since my mother's memorial service. It was the perfect ritual to gather in her name. The shower was an extension of my mother's life because now we celebrated the birth of my child, her grandbaby. Their presence evoked my mother at my initiation into motherhood.

We all stood in a circle and held hands. Buffy led us in a beautiful prayer that invoked my mother's heavenly spirit and God to uplift me and my baby through the pregnancy, birth, and motherhood. Although my baby wouldn't have a maternal grandmother, all of these women intended to unite to give my child grandmotherly love. Each one planned to come to my home and spend a day when the baby was born. Beverly, my mother's best friend, planned to fly in from Colorado, where she now cared for her two grandchildren, and stay for three days. I wouldn't be alone.

Admittedly, the absence of my mother led me to seek out a birth doula. I felt like I needed a surrogate. My research on death doulas helped me to understand that a birth doula coaches the woman mentally, physically, and spiritually through the pregnancy, labor, and birth. In my prenatal yoga class, I received a referral for Anna Verwaal, a birth doula and former labor and delivery nurse in the University of California at Los Angeles Santa Monica Hospital. As part of my homework before our meeting, she asked me to watch the documentary *The Business of Being Born*, by Ricki Lake. I noted that in the documentary Ricki compared the differences between her institutionalized hospital birth with her first baby and the intimate, communal home birth with her second baby much in the same way that I contrasted my father's death in a hospital and mother's death at home. Ricki interviewed Anna in the documentary. Simon commented that the labor, the period of waiting when the family hunkers down, is reminiscent of the last week with my mother. He even commented on the documentary that all those present at the births reflected a look of profound awe mirrored in our eyes during my mother's last week.

"It's not much different in terms of that period of time when everyone is focused on bringing that life into the world, just the same we focused on guiding your mom out of this world," he said. "If you look at it on a spiritual level it's like this world is aligning with the next and for a short period a doorway is open and the dimensions become one as a soul enters or exits."

This moment is often compared among death doulas and death midwives. Just as I guided my mother out of this life, my labor would likewise bring my baby into this life.

Anna made her first house call three months later, on Labor Day weekend. She radiated a force to be reckoned with. I needed a strong woman at my side during labor. She reflected a vast knowledge for the science, spirituality, and communality of birth. Her techniques of conscious birthing paralleled the conscious dying rituals that I unwittingly practiced with my mother and later learned that Megory, the death doula, practices at the bedside. Anna was nearly ten years my senior and a wise woman with an intrinsic nature to empower and guide the body on its natural course.

She asked my expectations of her. I wished for her to help me labor at home as long as I could before going into hospital. She agreed to come when I entered active labor and would support me until the baby latched on to the breast. In her postnatal visit, we would all share our stories of the labor and birth and then marry them together to make one birth story. She asked us to try and remember anything from our births and write down our fears about the upcoming birth and our birth plan. Anna creates the most optimal condition for the baby to enter this world, which meant preparing me and weeding out the problems that might arise emotionally, spiritually, and physically during labor.

In the final weeks of the pregnancy, I placed the finishing touches on my documentary. I wrote the introduction and voiceover parts. My best friend, Denise, came over and filmed me introducing the biography of my parents to their grandbaby. We used my video camera propped on a tri-pod. I sat in the nursery rocking chair and rubbed my belly while talking about creating this video for my children to meet their grandparents.

As the narrator/biographer, I anchored the video with the introduction followed by a short video of Mom, Dad, and me as a baby set to a narration of life wisdom and lessons I believed they wished to impart to their grandchildren. The last lesson, to live life like an adventure, dove-tailed into their intrepid tales of coming to America, their great love affair, my father's leaving for Vietnam, and their wedding. I reflected on their heritages in foreign countries that inspired dreams of building a life in America. The final half of the film focused on their separate lives. I used the track "Staying Alive," by the Bee Gees, to complement Dad soaring as an entrepreneur in the 1980s, weekend parties, and his second wedding. For his final days, I chose the track "Yesterday," by the Beatles, played over video of his first and only pilgrimage to the Philippines and the last photographs I took of him before I left for Kauai. I completed his life with shots of him making goofy faces on video.

My mother also made one and only pilgrimage to England, with Ryan and me the summer after his death. This chapter of the video, en-titled "Just the Three of Us," shared the story of a strong, single mother raising us. She looked absolutely radiant in her wedding video with Gil. I played the Beatles song "Here Comes the Sun" as she walked down the aisle. The final segment of Mom's life closed with her birthday interview, when she says, "I'm leaving behind a smile for you and Ryan to carry on." It's followed by a photo montage of Mom's brilliant smile to the

Beatles song "There Are Places I Remember" illuminated by video of me twirling around in her clothes. I fall out of the twirl into her arms and we're laughing and hugging. The video freezes on her smiling in our embrace while the song continues and the credits roll.

When I entered the process, I didn't know that it would lead me to so many revelations about my parents, but most important, they taught me that it's okay to love and be loved. Sometimes in the midst of divorce, death, and grief, you forget because you're in survival mode. The video was an extraordinary exercise in allowing me to get to know my parents as I meditated on becoming a parent myself, but I must admit the process was tedious and time-consuming. I now understand why it might be better to invest in someone like Jay to produce a biography. Nevertheless, my mind finally felt freed from holding onto the archives of their lives.

On month nine, Anna made another house call to prepare us for the big day. Anna delicately brought up her concern of a possible struggle for me to let go of the pregnancy. Women like me without a mother apparently battle the unexpected onslaught of grief with the absence of the mother and in my case the parents. I suffered no feelings of void or lack. In fact, in the pregnancy I felt closer to my parents than I had since they died. She countered me saying, "Well, labor will make you be honest, setting all illusions aside, if there are any." She could have replaced labor with death. Anna believed in helping couples get in touch with their fears consciously so they will not manifest into unconscious pain in labor. I assured her I'd come to the end of my grief journey, but admitted loving the solace of my pregnancy and the quiet time to produce the biography of my parents. She suggested taking time before the labor to release this period of wellness.

We reviewed my birth plan, a written document to my doctor and nurses telling my wishes for handling my labor and birth. It reeked of my labor fears and need to control the unknown. The birth plan wasn't too different than an end-of-life plan. Together, we wrote a list of items for laboring at home and packing for the hospital. Anna suggested assembling a playlist of music. I have to thank the home birth/natural birth movement for my doula and the "menu of options" to create the birth experience I envisioned.

On Monday night, August 4, my contractions trumpeted the coming birth. Tuesday night, day two of labor, Anna arrived and checked my cervix. I had to open ten centimeters to give birth. After the check, she sat me down to explain that the cervix had dilated zero centimeters. I felt like I'd run half a marathon, but I hadn't even placed one foot over the starting line. Anna told me to stop fighting the contractions, by pushing back, I gridlocked the progression of the birth.

At four o'clock on Wednesday morning, a roaring thunderstorm pounded my lower abdomen and back as I silently released my pregnancy and the magical period of being enmeshed in the lives of my parents. Dawn lit my bedroom. The last time I'd seen these early hours of the morning was my mother's last week of life. Birth and death have no consideration for our clocks. I felt physically taxed, pushed beyond my mortal limits. Thunder struck.

"Get me to the hospital—I'm ready to have this baby," I yelled at Simon and Anna.

A half hour later, I emerged from the car into the brilliant morning sunshine at the double glass doors of Saint John's Hospital in Santa Monica. We checked into the bright, airy, and spacious birthing room with large windows overlooking the city. The nurse judged by the level of sheer pain I exhibited that I suffered from back labor. I was dilated to four centimeters. The doctor checked the baby's position and confirmed the baby's back was on top of my back.

Anna coached me to get into a Maori warrior position. I had spent time with Maori natives in the north island of New Zealand so I knew exactly what she meant. I crouched down into a war stance—knees bent, arms out in front of me, fists tightened, and feet pounding the ground. I thrust my rump to and fro.

"Match the intensity of contraction!" Anna shouted. "Breathe deep in your abdomen and push it out!"

I growled and grunted, like a she warrior thrusting power from my inner core. My cheeks filled with air and I blew out. I roared like a lioness and felt my primal side take over. I now knew what midwives and doulas meant by empowering the woman.

Dusk fell. The doctor came in at seven o'clock. I was stuck at seven centimeters. He suggested we give it another hour because the baby showed signs of distress with the heart rate swinging high and low below the safe level.

The doctor returned at eight o'clock. I was rolled into the OR.

There are few moments in our life when we are completely present. When you're wholly focused on the breath of life. I recalled feeling a similar awe, grandness of the present, suspension of time, when one breath connects us to something greater than what we can see and touch in our physical world. I could feel the walls thinning. For a split second, one breath, that wall disappears. A peaceful, familiar stillness descended over the room. I could hear almost as if in the distance, muffled by a calm wind, the doctor say, "I see a head."

My ear zeroed in on the purist sound ever to blow through its canal. A soft gasp, followed by my baby's first breath of life, and then a cry. "She's a girl," I heard a voice say. I cradled my baby girl on my chest. I looked into her bright, alert eyes.

"I'm your mommy," I said to my daughter.

Her wide eyes blinked as if recognizing my voice, and we both sighed simultaneously as if still physically connected. We stared at one another in awe. I felt a cloud of bliss showering us as we reached the end of a long journey to come face to face. My eyes traced her sweet nose and tiny tulip-shaped lips, and my hands brushed her velvety brown hair. I'd never seen such beauty in my life. I could feel my heart pounding, growing exponentially with true unconditional love. I listened to the purity of her first breaths of life. She looked at me in silent wonderment.

"You're name is Verity Linda," I said to my daughter.

Verity means truth. I'd survived the loss of my most precious mother/daughter relationship to birth a new mother/daughter relationship and continue the cycle of life. I'm no longer a daughter looking back at a season of lasts, but instead a mother on a new journey of truth toward many of life's firsts.

Notes

INTRODUCTION

1. National Hospice and Palliative Care Organization, "NHPCO Fact and Figures" Report (2006), http://www.nhpco.org/files/public/2005-facts-and -figures.pdf/ and http://www.nhpco.org/i4a/pages/index.cfm?pageid=3303.

2. Baohui Zhang, Areej El-Jawahri, Holly G. Prigerson. "Update on Bereavement Research: Evidence-Base Guidelines for Diagnosis and Treatment of Complicated Bereavement," *Journal of Palliative Medicine* 9, no. 5. Also, Deaths Preliminary Data 2003. Centers for Disease Control's National Vital Statistic Reports 53, no. 15 (February 28, 2005), cdc.gov/nchs/data/nvsr/nvsr/nvsr53/nvsr53_15.pdf.

3. *Associated Press*, "World's Population to Triple by 2050," reported and released by the U.S. Census in a report entitled "Census Bureau Reports World's Population Projected to Triple by 2050" (June 23, 2009).

4. Michael Rybarski, "Boomers After All Is Said and Done," *American Demographics Magazine*, June 2004, page 34.

5. *Associated Press*, "World's Population to Triple by 2050," reported and released by the U.S. Census in a report entitled "Census Bureau Reports World's Population Projected to Triple by 2050" (June 23, 2009).

6. Interview on May 5, 2005 with Gary Laderman, Emory University (Atlanta) professor of American religious history and culture specializing in death rituals and author of *Rest in Peace: A Cultural History of Death and the Funeral Home in the Twentieth Century* (New York: Oxford University Press, 2003), and *The Sacred Remains: American Attitudes Toward Death, 1799–1883* (New Haven: Yale University Press, 1996).

7. David Wendall Moller, *Confronting Death: Values, Institutions, and Human Mortality* (New York: Oxford University Press, 1996), 77.

8. Catherine Bell, *Ritual Theory, Ritual Practice* (New York: Oxford University Press, 1992), 3.

9. Philippe Ariès, *The Hour of Our Death*, trans. Helen Weaver (New York: Alfred A. Knopf, 1981), 579.

10. Lynne A. DeSpelder and Albert L. Strickland, *The Last Dance: Encountering Death and Dying*, 6th ed. (McGraw-Hill Higher Education, 2002), 37.

11. Interview on March 21, 2007, with Markella Rutherford, Wellesley College professor studying the sacralization of the individual in American culture.

12. Interview on August 18, 2006, with Diane Meier, director of the Center to Advance Palliative Care and the Hertzberg Palliative Care Institute, Mount Sinai School of Medicine, and professor, Geriatrics and Internal Medicine, Mount Sinai School of Medicine.

13. Roslyn Lindheim, "Birthing Centers and Hospices: Reclaiming Birth and Death," *Annual Review of Public Health* 2 (May 1981): 21.

14. Philippe Ariès, *Western Attitudes Toward Death: From the Middle Ages to the Present* (Baltimore: Johns Hopkins University Press, 1975), 12.

15. Ibid.

16. Interview on September 19, 2006, with David Rothman, Columbia University medical historian and on the board of Project on Death in America.

17. Ibid.

18. Philippe Ariès, *The Hour of Our Death*, trans. Helen Weaver (New York: Alfred A. Knopf, 1981), 579.

19. National Hospice and Palliative Care Organization, "NHPCO Facts and Figures: Hospice Care in America," Reports (2004, 2006, 2010).

20. National Hospice and Palliative Care Organization, "NHPCO Facts and Figures: Hospice Care in America," Report (2010).

CHAPTER ONE

1. Interview on July 24, 2006 with Robert Burt, Yale University historian and scholar, member of the Project on Death in America, and author of *Death Is That Man Taking Names: Intersections of American Law, Medicine, and Culture* (Berkeley: University of California Press, 2002).

2. National Hospice and Palliative Care Organization "NHPCO Facts and Figures" Report (2004).

3. Interview on August 18, 2006, with Diane Meier, director of both the Center to Advance Palliative Care Director and the Hertzberg Palliative Care Institute, Mount Sinai School of Medicine, and professor, Geriatrics and Internal Medicine, Mount Sinai School of Medicine.

4. Philippe Ariès, *Western Attitudes Toward Death: From the Middle Ages to the Present* (Baltimore: Johns Hopkins University Press, 1975), 86.

5. Interview on July 24, 2006, with Robert Burt, Yale University historian and scholar, member of the Project on Death in America, and author of *Death Is That Man Taking Names: Intersections of American Law, Medicine, and Culture* (Berkeley: University of California Press, 2002).

6. Joanne Lynn and William Knaus, Study to Understand Prognoses and Preferences for Outcomes and Risks of Treatment (Princeton, N.J.: Robert Wood Foundation, 1989–1994), Introduction.

7. Interview on July 19, 2007, with Sharon Kaufman, medical anthropologist at University of California, San Francisco.

8. Interview on June 12, 2006, with Dr. Robert Butler, gerontologist, psychiatrist, and Pulitzer Prize–winning author.

9. Interview on August 18, 2006, with Diane Meier, M.D., director, of both the Center to Advance Palliative Care and the Hertzberg Palliative Care Institute, Mount Sinai School of Medicine, and professor, Geriatrics and Internal Medicine, Mount Sinai School of Medicine.

CHAPTER TWO

1. Interview on May 5, 2005, with Gary Laderman, Emory University (Atlanta) professor of American religious history and culture, specializing in death rituals, and author of *Rest in Peace: A Cultural History of Death and the Funeral Home in Twentieth-Century America* and *The Sacred Remains: American Attitudes Toward Death, 1799–1883*.

2. David Moller, *Confronting Death: Values, Institutions, and Human Mortality* (New York: Oxford University Press, 1996), 89–90.

3. Ibid.

4. Mitch Albom, *Tuesdays with Morrie: An Old Man, a Young Man, and Life's Greatest Lesson* (New York: Doubleday, 1997), 12.

5. Interview in February 2005 with Megory Anderson, theologian specializing in death rites at the University of San Francisco and founder of the Sacred Dying Foundation

6. Philippe Ariès, *Western Attitudes Toward Death: From the Middle Ages to the Present* (Baltimore: Johns Hopkins University Press, 1975), 63.

7. Interview on July 26, 2007, with John Hogan, former president of the National Funeral Directors' Association (2006–2007) and funeral director of Fogarty Funeral Home, in Queens, New York.

8. Jeffrey Zaslow, "And He Was a Terrible Gambler: When Eulogists Get Carried Away," *Wall Street Journal*, July 10, 2003.

9. Interview on May 3, 2005, with John Melloh, a Catholic priest and theologian at the University of Notre Dame (Indiana) who specializes in death rituals.

10. Interview on February 10, 2007, with Justin Holcomb, Episcopalian priest and sociologist in the field of death and dying at the University of Virginia.

11. Interview on May 5, 2005, with Gary Laderman, Emory University (Atlanta) professor of American religious history and culture, specializing in death rituals, and author of *Rest in Peace: A Cultural History of Death and the Funeral Home in Twentieth-Century America* and *The Sacred Remains: American Attitudes Toward Death, 1799–1883*.

CHAPTER THREE

1. Interview on June 12, 2006, with Dr. Robert Butler, gerontologist, psychiatrist, and Pulitzer Prize–winning author.

2. Robert Butler, "The Life Review: An Interpretation of Reminiscence in the Aged," *Psychiatry* 26 (1963): 66.

3. Barbara K. Haight, Appendix G, in *The Past in the Present: Using Reminiscence in Health and Social Care* (Baltimore: Health Professions Press, 2004).

4. Robert Butler, "The Life Review: An Interpretation of Reminiscence in the Aged," *Psychiatry* 26 (1963): 68.

5. Robert Butler and Myrna Lewis, "Life Review Therapy: Putting Memories to Work in Individual and Group Psychotherapy," *Geriatrics* 29 (1974): 165–73.

6. Ibid.

7. Ibid.

8. Interview on July 13, 2007, with Holly Prigerson, Ph.D., director for Psycho-oncology and Palliative Care Research focused on loss, bereavement, and complicated grief and associate professor of psychiatry, Harvard Medical School.

CHAPTER FOUR

1. Loraine Kee, "An Indelible Memory," *St. Louis Post Dispatch,* July 10, 2003.

2. Lynette Alvarez "Farewell, With Love and Instructions," *New York Times,* October 6, 2005.

3. Interview on August 7, 2007 with Susan Block, M.D., Chair of Psychosocial Oncology and Palliative Care at the Dana Farber Cancer Institute and Co-Director of Harvard Medical School Center for Palliative Care

4. Interview on July 25, 2007, with Dr. Harvey Chochinov, director of the Manitoba (Canada) Palliative Care Research Unit, Winnipeg, and University of Manitoba psychiatry professor.

5. Chochinov, Harvey Max, Thomas Hack, Thomas Hassard, Linda J. Kristjanson, Susan McClement, and Mike Harlos. "Dignity Therapy: A Novel Psychotherapeutic Intervention for Patients Near the End of Life." *Journal of Clinical Oncology* 23, no. 24 (August 20, 2005): 5520–5525.

6. Ibid.

7. Faith Gibson *The Past in the Present: Using Reminiscence in Health and Social Care* (Baltimore: Health Professional Press, 2004), 101, 115

CHAPTER FIVE

1. Arnold Van Gannep, *The Rites of Passage: A Classic Study of Cultural Celebrations* (Chicago: University of Chicago Press, 1960).

2. David Moller, *Confronting Death: Values, Institutions, and Human Mortality* (New York: Oxford University Press, 1996), 24.

3. Ibid.

4. Thomas Driver, *The Magic of Ritual: Our Need for Liberating Rites That Transform Our Lives and Our Communities* (San Francisco: Harper 1991), 156.

CHAPTER SIX

1. Jack Riemer and Nathaniel Stampfer, eds., *So That Your Values Live On: Ethical Wills and How to Prepare Them* (Woodstock, VT: Jewish Lights Publishing, 1991), Preface.

2. Ibid.

3. Ibid.

4. Philippe Ariès, *Western Attitudes Toward Death: From the Middle Ages to the Present* (Baltimore: Johns Hopkins University Press, 1975), 63.

5. Harvey Max Chochinov, Susan McClement,Thomas Hack, Thomas Hassard, Linda Joan Kristjanson, Mike Harlos, "Dignity Therapy: Family Member Perspectives," *Journal of Palliative Medicine* 10, no. 5 (October 2007): 1076–1082.

CHAPTER EIGHT

1. *Hamlet,* The Oxford Shakespeare Works ed. 1843–1906 (London: Oxford University Press: 1914.), Act III, Scene I, 1350 p.
2. San Francisco Department of Public Health AIDS Office (March, 1997). AIDS Surveillance Report.
3. Anne T. Richards, Judith Wrubel, Susan Folkman, Death Rites in the San Francisco Gay Community: Cultural Developments of the AIDS Epidemic, *Omega* 40, no. 2 1999–2000, 338.
4. Ibid., 339.
5. Ibid., 339.
6. Sheila Rothman, *Living in the Shadow of Death: Tuberculosis and the Social Experience of Illness in American History* (Baltimore: Johns Hopkins University Press, 1995), 70–71.
7. Ibid., 124–125.
8. Sharon Kaufman, . . . *And a Time to Die: How American Hospitals Shape the End of Life* (New York: Scribner, 2005), 93.
9. Don Campbell, *The Mozart Effect for Children: Awakening Your Child's Mind, Health, and Creativity with Music* (New York: William Morrow, 2000).
10. Megory Anderson, *Sacred Dying: Creating Rituals for Embracing the End of Life* (New York: Marlow & Company, 2003), 91.
11. Kenneth Kramer, *The Sacred Art of Dying: How World Religions Understand Death* (Mahwah, NJ: Paulist Press, 1998), 163.
12. Ibid., 164.

CHAPTER NINE

1. Stephen Prothero, *Purified by the Fire: A History of Cremation in America* (Berkeley and Los Angeles: University of California Press, 2001), 133.
2. Gary Laderman, *The Sacred Remains: American Attitudes Toward Death, 1799–1883* (New Haven: Yale University Press, 1996), 167.
3. Gary Laderman, *Rest in Peace: A Cultural History of Death and the Funeral Home in Twentieth-Century America* (New York: Oxford University Press, 2003), 8.
4. Ibid., 8.
5. Ibid.

6. Peter Metcalf and Richard Huntington, *Celebrations of Death: The Anthropology of Mortuary Ritual*, 2nd ed. (Cambridge, UK: Cambridge University Press, 1991), 192.

7. Gary Laderman, *Rest in Peace: A Cultural History of Death and the Funeral Home in Twentieth-Century America* (New York: Oxford University Press, 2003), 4.

8. Ibid., 22.

9. Stephen Prothero, *Purified by Fire: A History of Cremation in America* (Berkeley and Los Angeles: University of California Press, 2001), 17.

10. Ibid.

11. Ibid., 148.

12. Ibid.

13. Gary Laderman, *Rest in Peace: A Cultural History of Death and the Funeral Home in Twentieth-Century America* (New York: Oxford University Press, 2003), 22.

14. Stephen Prothero, *Purified by Fire: A History of Cremation in America* (Berkeley and Los Angeles: University of California Press, 2001), 182.

15. Ibid.

16. Gary Laderman, *Rest in Peace: A Cultural History of Death and the Funeral Home in Twentieth-Century America* (New York: Oxford University Press, 2003), 144.

17. Interview with on February 10, 2007 with Justin Holcomb, sociologist of death and dying at University of Virginia and Episcopalian Priest

18. Kathleen Garces-Foley and Justin Holcomb, "Contemporary American Funerals: Personalizing Tradition," in *Death and Religion in a Changing World*, ed. Kathleen Garces-Foley (Armonk, NY: M.E. Sharp, 2006), 224–225.

19. Gary Laderman, *Rest in Peace: A Cultural History of Death and the Funeral Home in Twentieth-Century America* (New York: Oxford University Press, 2003), 167.

CHAPTER TEN

1. Interview on March 21, 2007 with Markella Rutherford Sociology Professor studying the sacralization of the individual in American culture at Wellesley College. At the time of the interview she was researching the study and book chapter "Selling the ideal birth: Rationalization and re-enchantment in the marketing of maternity care, with her co-author Selina Gallo-Cruz and editor Barbara Katz Rothman for the book entitled *Patients, Consumers and Civil Society: Advances in Medical Sociology, Volume 10* (Bingley, U.K.: Emerald Group Publishing Limited, 2008), 75–98

2. Gary Laderman, *Rest in Peace: A Cultural History of Death and the Funeral Home in Twentieth Century America* (New York: Oxford University Press, 2003), 147.

3. Stephen Prothero, *Purified by Fire: A History of Cremation in America* (Berkeley and Los Angeles: University of California Press, 2001), 15.

4. Ibid., 17.

5. Gary Laderman, *Rest in Peace: A Cultural History of Death and the Funeral Home in Twentieth-Century America* (New York: Oxford University Press, 2003), 146.

6. Ibid.

7. Ibid., 144.

8. Funeral Consumer Alliance reports seven states still have legal obstacles to caring for your dead: Connecticut, Indiana, Louisiana, Mississippi, Nebraska, New York, Utah. www.funerals.org

9. Lisa Carlson, *Caring for the Dead: Your Final Act of Love* (Hinesberg, VT: Upper Access, 1998), Introduction.

10. Nancy Rommelmann, "Crying and Digging: Reclaiming the Rituals and Realities of Death," *Los Angeles Times*, February 6, 2005.

11. Gary Laderman, *The Sacred Remains: American Attitudes Toward Death, 1799–1883* (New Haven: Yale University Press, 1996), 30.

12. Ibid., 29.

13. Ibid.

14. Ibid., 31.

15. Ibid.

16. Ibid., 35.

17. Ibid.

18. Rochel Berman, *Dignity Beyond Death: The Jewish Preparation for Burial* (New York: Urim Publications, 2005), 31.

19. Interview on May 6, 2005, with Rochel Berman, author of *Dignity Beyond Death: The Jewish Preparation for Burial* and a member of the Westchester, New York, *hevra kadisha*, the Jewish burial society.

20. Rochel Berman, *Dignity Beyond Death: The Jewish Preparation for Burial* (New York: Urim Publications, 2005), 30.

21. Ibid.

22. Marco R. Della Cava, "Moving on from Life Naturally," *USA Today*, February 3, 2004.

23. Kenneth V. Iserson, *Death to Dust: What Happens to Dead Bodies?* 2nd ed. (Tucson: Galen Press, 2001), 183.

24. Interview on March 21, 2007 with Markella Rutherford Sociology Professor studying the sacralization of the individual in American culture at Wellesley College. At the time of the interview she was researching the study and book chapter "Selling the ideal birth: Rationalization and re-enchantment in the marketing of maternity care, with her co-author Selina Gallo-Cruz and editor Barbara Katz Rothman for the book entitled *Patients, Consumers and Civil Society:*

Advances in Medical Sociology, Volume 10 (Bingley, U.K.: Emerald Group Publishing Limited, 2008), 75–98

25. Ibid.

26. Interview on March 21, 2007, with Joe Sehee, director of the Green Burial Council.

27. Interview on March17, 2007, with John Hogan, former president of the National Funeral Directors Association.

28. Interview on March 21, 2007 with Markella Rutherford Sociology Professor studying the sacralization of the individual in American culture at Wellesley College. At the time of the interview she was researching the study and book chapter "Selling the ideal birth: Rationalization and re-enchantment in the marketing of maternity care, with her co-author Selina Gallo-Cruz and editor Barbara Katz Rothman for the book entitled *Patients, Consumers and Civil Society: Advances in Medical Sociology, Volume 10* (Bingley, U.K.: Emerald Group Publishing Limited, 2008), 75–98

CHAPTER ELEVEN

1. Stephen R. Prothero, *Purified by Fire: A History of Cremation in America* (Berkeley: University of California Press 2001), 121.

2. Ibid.

3. Ibid., 122.

4. Ibid., 121 and 122.

5. Edward Wong, "Coffins, Urns and Webcast Funerals." *New York Times.* Published: October 5, 2000.

6. Interview on July 16, 2007 with Rabbi Regina Sandler-Phillips, founder of the Hevra Kaddisha at Park Slope Jewish Center in Brooklyn, New York.

7. Interview on July 24, 2004 with Kurt L. Soffe, CFSP, National Funeral Director's Association and co-owner of Jenkins-Soffe Funeral Homes and Cremation Center located in the Salt Lake City, Utah.

Bibliography

Albom, Mitch. *Tuesdays with Morrie: An Old Man, a Young Man, and Life's Greatest Lesson.* New York: Doubleday, 1997.

Alvarez, Lizette. "Farewell, with Love and Instructions." *New York Times,* October 6, 2005.

Anderson, Megory. *Sacred Dying: Creating Rituals for Embracing the End of Life.* New York: Marlow & Company, 2003.

Ariès, Philippe. *The Hour of Our Death: The Classic History of Western Attitudes Toward Death over the Last Thousand Years.* New York: Knopf, 1981.

———. *Western Attitudes Toward Death: From the Middle Ages to the Present.* Baltimore: Johns Hopkins University Press, 1975.

Ashenburg, Katherine. *The Mourner's Dance.* New York: North Point Press, 2002.

Baines, Barry K. *Ethical Wills: Putting Your Values on Paper,* 2nd ed. Cambridge, MA: Da Capo Press, 2006.

Bell, Catherine. *Ritual Theory, Ritual Practice.* New York: Oxford University Press, 1992.

Bellah, Robert. *Habits of the Heart: Individualism and Commitment in American Life.* Berkeley and Los Angeles: University of California Press, 1995.

Berman, Rochel. *Dignity Beyond Death: The Jewish Preparation for Burial.* New York: Urim Publications, 2005.

Birren, James, and Linda Feldman. *Where Do We Go From Here: Discovering Your Own Life's Wisdom in the Second Half of Your Life.* New York: Simon & Schuster, 1997.

Bregman, Lucy. *Death and Dying, Spirituality and Religions: A Study of the Death Awareness Movement.* New York: Peter Lang Publishing, 2003.

Brooks, David. "View; The Valley of Death, Another Boomer Test." *New York Times,* June 25, 2000.

Brownlee, Shannon. "Better Final Days: the end of life need not be filled with medical costs and intensive care." *Los Angeles Times,* November 26, 2005.

Burt, Robert. *Death Is That Man Taking Names: Intersections of American Law, Medicine, and Culture.* Berkeley and Los Angeles: University of California Press, 2002.

Butler, Robert. "The Life Review: An Interpretation of Reminiscence in the Aged." *Psychiatry* 26 (1963): 65–76.

———. *Why Survive? Being Old in America.* New York: Harper & Row, 1975.

Robert Butler and Myrna Lewis. "Life Review Therapy: Putting Memories to Work in Individual and Group Psychotherapy." *Geriatrics* 29 (1974): 165–73.

Byock, Ira. *Dying Well: Peace and Possibilities at the End of Life.* New York: Riverhead Books Press, 1997.

Callanan, Maggie, and Patricia Kelley. *Final Gifts: Understanding the Special Awareness, Needs, and Communications of the Dying.* New York: Bantam Trade Back Paperbacks, 1997.

Campbell, Don. *The Mozart Effect for Children: Awakening Your Child's Mind, Health, and Creativity with Music.* New York: William Morrow, 2000.

Carlson, Lisa. *Caring for the Dead: Your Final Act of Love.* Hinesberg: Upper Access, 1998.

Centers for Disease Control's National Vital Statistic Reports 53, no. 15 (February 28, 2005), cdc.gov/nchs/data/nvsr/nvsr/nvsr53/nvsr53_15.pdf.

Chochinov, Harvey Max, Thomas Hack, Thomas Hassard, Linda J. Kristjanson, Susan McClement, and Mike Harlos. "Dignity Therapy: A Novel Psychotherapeutic Intervention for Patients Near the End of Life." *Journal of Clinical Oncology* 23, no. 24 (August 20, 2005): 5520–5525.

———. "Dignity Therapy: Family Member Perspectives." *Journal of Palliative Medicine* 10, no. 5 (October 2007): 1076–1082.

Davis-Floyd, Robbie. *Birth As An American Rite of Passage.* Berkeley: UC Press, 1992.

Della Cava, Marco R. "Moving on from Life Naturally." *USA Today*, February 3, 2004.

DeSpelder, Lynne Ann, and Albert Lee Strickland. *The Last Dance: Encountering Death and Dying*. Boston: McGraw Hill Higher Education, 2002.

Driver, Thomas. *The Magic of Ritual: Our Need for Liberating Rites That Transform Our Lives and Our Communities*. San Francisco: Harper, 1991.

Garces-Foley, Kathleen, and Justin Holcomb. "Contemporary American Funerals: Personalizing Tradition." In *Death and Religion in a Changing World*, edited by Kathleen Garces-Foley, 224–225. Armonk, NY: M.E. Sharp, 2006.

Gibbs, Nancy. "Rx For Death." *Time Magazine*, May 31, 1993.

Gibson, Faith. *The Past in the Present: Using Reminiscence in Health and Social Care*. Baltimore: Health Professions Press, 2004.

Gilbert, Susan. "For Cancer Patients, Hope Can Add to Pain." *New York Times*, June 9, 1998.

Goldman, Ari. *Living a World of Kaddish*. New York: Schocken Books, 2003.

———. "The World: Dealing With Death; Confronting Grief, Not Burying It." *New York Times*, September 7, 2003.

Grimes, Ronald L. *Deeply into the Bone: Reinventing Rites of Passage*. Berkeley and Los Angeles: University of California Press, 2000.

Gross, Jane. "For Families of the Dying, Coaching as the Hours Wane." *New York Times*, May 20, 2006.

———. "Scientist at Work/Diane Meier; Providing Care, When the Cure Is Out of Reach." *New York Times*, November 18, 2003.

Haight, Barbara K. Appendix G, in *The Past in the Present: Using Reminiscence in Health and Social Care*. Baltimore: Health Professions Press, 2004.

Isenberg, Lynn. *The Funeral Planner*. Ontario, Canada: Red Dress Ink, 2005.

Iserson, Kenneth V. *Death to Dust: What Happens to Dead Bodies?* 2nd ed. Tucson: Galen Press, 2001.

Kaufman, R. Sharon. *. . . And a Time to Die: How American Hospitals Shape the End of Life*. New York: Scribner, 2005.

Kee, Loraine. "An Indelible Memory." *St. Louis Post Dispatch*, July 10, 2003.

Kleinfield, N.R. "In Death Watch for Stranger, Becoming a Friend to the End." *New York Times*, January 25, 2004.

Kramer, Kenneth. *The Sacred Art of Dying: How World Religions Understand Death*. Mahwah, NJ: Paulist Press, 1998.

Kübler-Ross, Elisabeth. *On Death and Dying: What the Dying Have to Teach Doctors, Nurses, Clergy, and Their Own Families*. New York: Simon & Schuster, 1969.

———. *Death: The Final Stage of Growth*. Upper Saddle River, NJ: Prentice Hall, 1975.

Laderman, Gary. *The Sacred Remains: American Attitudes Toward Death, 1799–1883*. New Haven, CT: Yale University Press, 1996.

————. *Rest in Peace: A Cultural History of Death and the Funeral Home in Twentieth-Century America.* New York: Oxford University Press, 2003.

Leland, John. "It's My Funeral and I'll Serve Ice Cream If I Want To." *New York Times,* July 20, 2006.

Lindheim, Roslyn. "Birthing Centers and Hospices: Reclaiming Birth and Death." *Annual Review of Public Health* (May 1981): 21.

Lynch, Thomas. "Our Near Death Experience." *New York Times,* April 9, 2005.

Lynn, Joanne, and William Knaus. Study to Understand Prognoses and Preferences for Outcomes and Risks of Treatment. Princeton, NJ: Robert Wood Foundation, 1989–1994.

Marantz Henig, Robin. "Will We Ever Arrive at the Good Death?" *New York Times,* August 7, 2005

Metcalf, Peter, and Richard Huntington. *Celebrations of Death: The Anthropology of Mortuary Ritual,* 2nd ed. Cambridge, UK: Cambridge University Press, 1991.

Mitford, Jessica. *The American Way of Death.* New York: Simon & Schuster, 1963.

————. *The American Way of Death Revisited.* New York: First Vintage Books, 2000.

Moller, David Wendell. *Confronting Death: Values, Institutions, and Human Mortality.* New York: Oxford University Press, 1996.

Morrison, Sean, Catherine Maroney-Galin, Peter Kralovec, and Diane Meier. "The Growth of Palliative Care Programs in United States Hospitals." *Journal of Palliative Care Medicine,* Volume 5 (November 6, 2005), 1127–1134.

National Hospice and Palliative Care Organization. "NHPCO Facts and Figures," Report (2004).

————. "NHPCO Facts and Figures: Hospice Care in America," Report (2006).

————. "NHPCO Facts and Figures: Hospice Care in America," Report (2010).

Ó Súilleabháin, Seán. *Irish Wake Amusements.* Dublin: Mercier Press, 1967.

Pelaez, Martha and Paul Rothman, for the Hospice Foundation of America, *A Guide for Recalling and Telling Your Life Story.*

Prothero, Stephen. *Purified by Fire: A History of Cremation in America.* Berkeley and Los Angeles: University of California Press, 2001.

Rando, Therese. *Loss and Anticipatory Grief.* Massachusetts: Lexington Books, 1986.

Ray, H. Paul, and Ruth Anderson. *Cultural Creatives: How 50 Million People Are Changing the World.* New York: Harmony Books, 2000.

Richards, Anne, Judith Wrubel, and Susan Folkman. Death Rites in the San Francisco Gay Community: Cultural Developments of the AIDS Epidemic. *Omega* 40, no. 2, 1999–2000.

Riemer, Jack, and Nathaniel Stampfer. *Ethical Wills: A Modern Jewish Treasury.* New York: Schocken Books, 1983.

————. *So That Your Values Live On: Ethical Wills and How to Prepare Them.* Woodstock, VT: Jewish Lights Publishing, 1991.

Rommelmann, Nancy. "Crying and Digging: Reclaiming the Rituals and Realities of Death." *Los Angeles Times,* February 6, 2005.

Rosenthal, Elisabeth. "To a Drumbeat of Losses to AIDS, a Rethinking of Traditional Grief." *New York Times,* December 6, 1992.

Rothman, Sheila. *Living in the Shadow of Death: Tuberculosis and the Social Experience of Illness in American History.* Baltimore: Johns Hopkins University Press, 1995.

Rutherford, Markella, Selina Gallo-Cruz, and Barbara Katz Rothman, eds. "Selling the ideal birth: Rationalization and re-enchantment in the marketing of maternity care." In *Patients, Consumers and Civil Society: Advances in Medical Sociology, Volume 10.* Bingley, U.K.: Emerald Group Publishing Limited, 2008, 75–98.

Rybarski, Michael. "Boomers After All Is Said and Done." *American Demographics Magazine,* June 2004, 32–34

San Francisco Department of Public Health AIDS Office (March, 1997). AIDS Surveillance Report.

U.S. Census, in a report entitled "Census Bureau Reports World's Population Projected to Triple by 2050." Printed as an article entitled "World's Population to Triple by 2050." *Associated Press* (June 23, 2009).

Van Gannep, Arnold. *The Rites of Passage: A Classic Study of Cultural Celebrations.* Chicago: University of Chicago Press, 1960.

Webb, Marilyn. *The Good Death: The New American Search to Reshape the End of Life.* New York: Bantam Books, 1997.

Witoszek, Nina, and Pat Sheeran. *Talking to the Dead: A Study of Irish Funerary Traditions.* Amsterdam: Rodopi, 1998.

Zhang, Baohui, Areej El-Jawahri, and Holly Prigerson. "Update on Bereavement Research: Evidence-Based Guidelines for Diagnosis and Treatment of Complicated Bereavement." *Journal of Palliative Medicine* 9, no. 5 (2006): 1188–1203 .

Text: 10/14 Palatino
Display: Univers Condensed Light 47 and Bauer Bodoni
Compositor: Westchester Book Group
Printer and binder: Sheridan Books, Inc.